Praise for *Loving the Hell Out of Ourselves*

As wounded healers, Elaine and Jeanine offer us their unique interwoven strands of a shared journey through deep poverty, unspeakable abuse, violence, loss and complicated grief. That any of this could result in faith, hope and abiding love reveals a resilience that could only come from an indomitable desire and commitment to be whole. It was difficult to put this book down. When I wasn't reading it, I was thinking about it. At times, I found myself cringing, crying, laughing, cursing and grieving alongside them. Elaine and Jeanine create much needed space for us to reflect upon own journeys and embrace the unique opportunities we might have to love the hell out of ourselves and others.

—Rev. Gary Alan Shockley, MDIV, MA, CGC
Author, *The Meandering Way* and *My Heart Sings a Sad Song*
Author, Artist, Spiritual Director and Grief Counselor

Once I began reading, I could barely put the Heath sisters' book down and at times, could not hold back tears. It is like taking a walk with two friends on their lifelong journeys from systemic abuse and abandonment to healing and changing the story. As a priest, I found myself ashamed and furious as they walked me through the ways in which the Church mistreated each of them. I wanted to kneel down and beg forgiveness on behalf of the Church. As a father and grandfather, I cried and wanted to apologize on behalf of mothers and fathers everywhere for the many ways that they were abused, neglected and abandoned. This book is absolutely engaging, heartfelt, searching, personal, and deeply reflective. I am so proud of the courage the Heath sisters—truly faithful old souls—have shown.

—Rev. Dr. Robert W. Nelson

This is a story that needs to be shared and wisdom that needs to be heard. Two sisters who experience severe abuse throughout their childhood and teens and yet emerge with a deepened faith in life and an amazing capacity to love. Their unique perspectives offer two windows into the dysfunction they suffered and the coping skills they developed to not only survive but to excel in life. Riveting and profound, their story will provoke awe in the capability of the human spirit to heal from a devastating start in life and respond by helping others on their journey.

—Marcia Wakeland, Spiritual Director, Pastor,
Writer and founder of the Listening Post of Anchorage, Alaska.

"Heartbreaking, raw, darkness and light, above all permeating mercy and grace"

—Martha Hutchison LCSW

Loving the Hell Out of Ourselves transports the reader into the vagabond life style of one family through the eyes of two sisters who grew up seven years apart. Each sister tells her story of childhood abuse, toxic church patriarchy, and the overarching trauma of poverty. While they lead divergent lives, they both find a path of healing through education, a deeply personal relationship with Spirit, and occupations that give back to their communities. Their stories are a testament to grace and atonement outside of dogma. A must read for those seeking to explore the power of resilience in the face of modern-day hells.

—Candace Lewis, PhD
Neurogenomist, Turman and Fulbright Scholar

Whether you have suffered abuse in your life or work with those who have, this book is a refreshing approach to a difficult topic, written by two sisters who are both professionals in their own right. Through them we experience two insightful perspectives (theological and psychological) on the same family upbringing. It is not a self-help book; rather it is a narrative of the journey from trauma to survival to healing, and joyful, productive living.

—Jack N. Lawson, Ph.D.
Retired Prison Chaplain

When a piece of pottery is broken in Japan, it is not always discarded but, instead, mended by using gold in a technique called "Kintsugi," which is derived from the worlds "Kin" (golden) and "tsugi" (joinery), which translate to mean "golden repair." I have had the privilege of knowing both Elaine and Jeanine for many years, and have watched their journeys of healing come through the painful "fire" of redemption. This form of "Kintsugi" describes well how their shattered lives have been transformed into something quite beautiful through therapy, enormous courage, tenacity and the love of one another.

Having spent over three decades in private practice counseling survivors of sexual abuse, I've heard too many tragic stories, only a few of which compare to the experiences of these sisters. Having been victims of many traumas, both Elaine and Jeanine, who radiate warmth and tender compassion as soon as you meet them, have chosen to do the hard work to come through to the other side. Now they minister to others. This is a book I am delighted to recommend.

—Morven Baker, D.Min., LPCC

In this piercing and deeply affecting book, two sisters tell the truth of their experience of abuse and abandonment and of their spiritual journey through trauma towards healing and reconciliation. Weaving together personal story and insights from both theology and depth psychology, they point to the wisdom that spiritual transformation depends in part on deep self-knowledge and the capacity for painful, bracing honesty. As they share the discoveries of their lives and their encounters with God—because they can't keep all this healing to themselves—what unfolds is a profound and poignant treasure.

—Trey Hall, Director of Evangelism and Growth, Methodist Church in Britain

Painful stories from the experience and language of a child invite your empathy and compassion immediately, as these sister-healers turn what they went through into a way for us all to heal. The surprise is when the reader in us who does not want to see suffering head on, finds a way into the wholeness beneath all brokenness. Follow these two brave sisters as they take us through hell and into the True Home we all seek.

—William Thiele, Ph.D., author of *Monks in the World*
Founding Director of The School for Contemplative Living

As we begin to discover the impact of trauma, we will need courageous examples from survivors to give us hope. This book provides hard earned wisdom rooted in deep faith. It is an incarnation of the accountability and grace needed to confront the destruction created by trauma. We rarely are able to see such a full picture of those who are in the middle of the chaos. These stories can provide insight for pastors, caretakers, and others who support survivors of violence and abuse. It is a gift to all who desire justice, healing, and reconciliation.

—Rev. Adam Barlow-Thompson
Co-Founder and Executive Director of the Neighboring Movement

The Heath sisters, with unflinching honesty and vulnerability, share their experiences of growing up in a home marked by violence, neglect, and poverty and tell of the trauma that they carried into adulthood. Ultimately, this is a story of hope, of the power of God's grace to enter our lives through unexpected people, and the way the healing journey can turn our deep wounds into the wellsprings that provide us with wisdom, compassion, and insight. This book is a precious gift to all of us seeking to heal from the past and claim the fullness of our humanity as a beloved child of God.

—Bishop Karen Oliveto, Bishop in Residence
Mountain Sky Conference of The United Methodist Church

Follow Elaine and Jeanine as they chronicle their lives of abuse, and their experiences of spiritual awakening to facing their pain, forgiving themselves and others, and becoming with God's help and direction, the gifted wounded healers that they are to many, including myself, and anyone who reads this book. These two women are warriors!

—Nick Swirski, M.Div.
Retired Prison Chaplain

This book continues to permeate my life in profound ways, giving me an opportunity to revisit my own stories of abuse and how that trauma continues to shape me today. Elaine and Jeanine invite us to witness the marvelous and mysterious ways that people come into our lives as pure grace meeting us where we are and offering us the space to heal, little by little. The authors give us eyes to see how the Beloved seeks to be with us even in the depths of despair. In the telling of their own story, they gently invite us to redeem our own. They offer no easy answers; simply a lifetime of deep listening and growing trust in the power of Love to heal through the messes, pain and uncertainties of life. If you need a word of hope to accompany you on your own healing journey, read this book. It certainly has been a balm of grace for me.

—Beth Ann Estock
Integral Master Coach
Author, *Weird Church,* and *Discernment*
www.bethestock.org

These two sisters have given us a gift in sharing the story of their lives with such vulnerability. Their narratives reveal—especially to parents, spouses of survivors, and religious leaders—the devastating impact of abuse and trauma upon survivors. At the same time, these stories bear witness to hope and the power of God—that healing and transformation are possible, this side of heaven, and that survivors can be God's mightiest agents of blessing in the world.

—Rev. Dr. Charles Kiser, Storyline Christian Community, Dallas, Texas

LOVING THE HELL OUT OF OURSELVES

(and others)

ELAINE A. HEATH AND

JEANINE B. HEATH-MCGLINN

BIRCH & ALDER

Loving the Hell Out of Ourselves (and others) © copyright 2021 by Elaine Heath and Jeanine Heath-McGlinn. All rights reserved. No part of this book may be reproduced in any form whatsoever, by photography or xerography or by any other means, by broadcast or transmission, by translation into any kind of language, nor by recording electronically or otherwise, without permission in writing from the author, except by a reviewer, who may quote brief passages in critical articles or reviews.

ISBNs: 978-1-7368455-0-9 (pbk); 978-1-7368455-1-6 (ebook)

Cover and book design by Mayfly Design

Library of Congress Control Number: 2021904872
First Printing: 2021
Printed in the United States of America

Birch & Alder Press
Anchorage, AK

*With deepest love and gratitude for
our brothers and sister, Mike, Jeff, and Julie*

CONTENTS

Acknowledgements xi
Introduction xiii

Part One: The Adventures of Toughest Jim Schwartz

Chapter One: Babies 3
Chapter Two: Sunflowers 9
Chapter Three: Skating 25
Chapter Four: Bride 33
Chapter Five: Mothers and Daughters 41
Chapter Six: The Dentist 51
Chapter Seven: The Principal 57
Chapter Eight: O Canada 61
Chapter Nine: Mother Bumblebee 69
Chapter Ten: Seminary 75
Chapter Eleven: A New Beginning 83
Chapter Twelve: Us and Them 87
Chapter Thirteen: How Old Are You? 93
Chapter Fourteen: Salvation 103
Chapter Fifteen: Deep in the Heart of Texas 109

Part Two: Showing Up to Love

Chapter Sixteen: Old Hands 129
Chapter Seventeen: Chaos Breeds Chaos 145
Chapter Eighteen: Good Enough 153

Chapter Nineteen: Expanding Horizons 173
Chapter Twenty: Birch Trees 185
Chapter Twenty-One: Sacred Love 195
Chapter Twenty-Two: Warrior 207
Chapter Twenty-Three: Table of Plenty 217

Epilogue: A New Day 225
About the Authors 235

ACKNOWLEDGEMENTS

I, Elaine, am grateful in ways that words can never fully tell, for the love and support of my spouse Randall, daughters Anna and Kat, and son-in-law Mark. My heartfelt gratitude extends to my beloved, healing friends, congregants, professors, mentors, teachers, students, colleagues, health professionals, spiritual directors, and so many more who have been with me along the way. I would not be well and possibly not even be alive, were it not for all of you.

I, Jeanine, marvel at the abundance of love and encouragement from my beautiful wife, Jackie, and our children, Stephanie, Elizabeth, Kirk, and Katy, their spouses and all of our grandchildren. My cup of gratitude overflows as I consider the many people who have loved me well and offered sacred communion in our relationships. Whether friends, teachers, healers, colleagues, students, or clients, each one of you made all the difference.

Both of us are deeply grateful for the dozen or so readers who read our manuscript and provided helpful feedback throughout the writing process.

INTRODUCTION

WHAT YOU HAVE IN YOUR hands is the story of how two sisters—a theologian and a therapist—survived a childhood and young adulthood riddled with abuse, violence, neglect, and abandonment. We experienced all of that in our family of origin and from the churches and clergy to whom we turned for help. Our two narratives, though presented as separate stories are bound together because we pulled each other out of hell, and like Andy Dufresne in *Shawshank's Redemption*, crawled together through the sewer of shame and fear to find freedom, find our voices again, get an education, become the selves that had been suffocated by all that violence and neglect from our family of origin and from toxic religion.

Our adult vocations are as healers. I, Elaine, am a healer through my work as a theologian and as an ordained Elder in the United Methodist Church. I, Jeanine, am a healer through my work as a therapist and decades as a high school counselor. The compassion and wisdom needed for our professions, indeed our experiences of being called to do the work we do, originated in our own healing journeys.

We want you, our readers to know what it means to love the hell out of yourself after experiencing years of devastating trauma that put the hell *into* you in the first place. We invite you into our stories, to journey with us through the remarkable process of healing and coming home to ourselves. Along the way we hope you will see how it is that in loving the hell out of ourselves we also found capacity to love the hell out of others including, eventually, even those who harmed us. That means in addition to coming to a place of forgiveness and reconciliation with our parents, we also found ourselves on a path of loving the hell out of the church.

We did not tell our siblings' stories, other than in brief references to events in which our lives were bound together. We love and honor our brothers and sister, who are also survivors, who are each resilient in their own way and whose lives have made such a positive impact in this world. They read our manuscript and blessed our endeavor.

We have changed the names and identifying details of some individuals and events, to protect the privacy of vulnerable people.

If you are a survivor of violence, our story may trigger your personal memories of abuse and trauma. We encourage you to seek professional support as needed, just as we learned to do.

It will come as no surprise, we think, that our "voices" in telling and reflecting on our stories, are as individual and unique as we are. We begin with Elaine's story. Jeanine's story comes next. We included a selection of photos from our childhood between our stories so that you can see us in the context of some of the events we describe. More photos from our adult lives are at the back of the book.

Writing this book has been one of the best things we ever did together. We started it as a planning retreat on the Outer Banks of North Carolina one wintry week in 2019. We completed the first draft around Easter, 2020, then began revisions until we completed our final draft during Advent, 2020. We hope to write more books together that we can use in the healing retreats we lead. Most of all, we hope that this book helps you to know that love—not shame, not fear, not hate, not damnation—love is God's meaning. Healing is possible for even the deepest of wounds. Forgiveness for appalling harm, can happen.

Elaine A. Heath
Jeanine B. Heath-McGlinn
Christmas, 2020

Part One

THE ADVENTURES OF TOUGHEST JIM SCHWARTZ

(Elaine's Story)

CHAPTER ONE

Babies

I POKED OUR MOTHER'S BELLY and said she was getting fat, but she said it was not fat, she had a baby in there. After Jeff and I recovered from our surprise, having retreated to the yard in order to discuss this development privately, we went back into the house where she was smoking and staring off into space. We wanted to know if she would eat the afterbirth like the cat did when the kittens were born. No, she said, she would not, and to get our asses back outside and give her some goddamn peace and quiet. She had on her white nurse's uniform and white cap, but she had taken her white stockings off and tossed them in the corner with her white shoes because her ankles were swollen. She had just come home from the night shift.

We lived in a sorry shack at the top of a hill that offered glorious views. We could watch Piper Cubs land at the little airport below, any time we wanted. There was a sawmill down there, too, which was no longer in operation, which was a good thing because it had become a playground for Jeff and me. The buildings had been vandalized and smelled of old diesel and lumber and bitter things I could not name. We loved climbing on rusty equipment as big and extinct as dinosaurs. There were still logs in the millpond which our mother said was dangerous, stay away or we could drown. But we found the pond impossible to resist. Our father was mad all the time and mostly stayed in the house. We mostly stayed gone because of that.

Our house was heated by a woodburning stove. We had no refrigerator because the jackass who rented the place before us took it, but we were lucky to have running water, our mother said. Jeff got to go to Riverside Elementary School. He was almost two years older than me and could read books, which made me wildly jealous. I would start first grade in the fall and then I planned to read a hundred books, more books than you could count. But now it was early Spring, cold and wet with rain that never seemed to stop. The rain came through our roof but don't worry, our father found old jars and bowls to catch the inside rain so it didn't matter. I stood outside with Jeff, holding my doll, Zeezee, whose eyes opened and shut if you tipped her up and down. I wondered what it would be like to hold our mother's baby.

When Mom's belly was so round she looked like a big old garden spider we got in the truck and left the house, the sawmill, and the mother cat. We were going to Montana, Dad said, where a man could piss off his porch without the fucking cops showing up.

We moved into an old house in the back country, whose previous owner was said to be a communist. He was holed up out there to escape notice. He up and died suddenly, leaving his house and horse behind. I have no idea how these two items ended up in our father's possession, but they did. There was no running water nor was there a toilet in the house. Our mother cooked on a black wood burning stove.

I was in heaven what with the mountains, the pine trees that went up to the clouds, Rocky the horse, and all that space to run and play with Jeff. I loved the sweet smell of Rocky's hay, and the huckleberries that grew in bushes by the road. Mom said the bears would eat me up if I picked berries by myself but sometimes I did it anyway. My brothers, Jeff and Mike slept in a cabin in the yard. I slept in the attic on one side and my father on the other side. There was a blanket pinned up so that we each had our own room. He had a lot of pictures of women with no clothes, pinned to the slanted ceiling of his room. I thought they might get cold being naked and all. He said I had to stay the hell out of there. Our mother slept downstairs on the couch because she said her belly was too big to go up those narrow stairs.

One day I was under the pine trees in the moss with Zeezee, looking for fairies. The lady from across the road drove into our driveway in her car, as if she was too tired to walk across the road. But she was lively enough when she jumped out and ran to me and hugged me so hard it hurt. "I have come from the hospital," she cried. "Your mama had the babies!" she said. "You have two sisters, two precious little twin sisters. You're a lucky girl!" Then she handed me a white crocheted doll dress with a matching hat for Zeezee. It was the prettiest thing I ever saw, with red edging and fancy lace. She said I ought to have a present because I was a big sister now.

A few days later Dad brought Mom home in the truck. She had two babies, one for each arm. We all went in the house and sat down. She put one baby in my arms and one baby in Jeff's arms. We stared at their wrinkled little faces with no teeth, and arms waving around as if they had lost their minds. "Say howdy to your new sisters," Mom said. "Jeff, thatn's Julie. Elaine, you've got Jeanine." We had no idea there would be two babies, nor did we realize how our lives were about to change. What I knew was that I was head over heels in love.

Two weeks later I started first grade. Jeff and I walked a long way to get to the two-room schoolhouse. I sat in the first grader's row and he sat with the second graders. Everyone's mothers except ours took turns cooking our lunches and we ate every bite. Jeff asked one of the mothers for her recipe for meat loaf. It was that good. The teacher was always in a hurry what with having to teach kids in eight different grades. She had wrinkles between her thick, gray eyebrows from trying to keep track of all us kids. Sometimes I didn't know what she wanted, like standing up straight and facing forward in line, and saying "yes, ma'am," and other things I never heard of. One day she clobbered me with the chalkboard eraser for asking without raising my hand, why we had to put our heads down on our desks when we weren't sleepy. But it didn't hurt much.

All my dreams came true when I figured out how to read. The book was about Dick, Jane, Sally, and their dog, Spot. They had a cat, too, named Puff but it didn't have kittens or eat the afterbirth. Their mother wasn't a nurse like ours. Their father read the paper and drove a car. He wore a suit and hat. He was nothing like our father. Everyone in the book was happy all the time. They ate supper together and smiled a lot. It made me happy to read it.

When the twins were six weeks old our mother said she wasn't taking Dad's shit any more, that she was going back to Oregon to work in the goddamn Veteran's hospital and taking me and the twins with her. She put on a dress and hat, not the white ones she wore to work but the kind that Dick and Jane's mother wore. The next thing you know we were back in Roseburg and she was back in the hospital where she worked before her belly got so big. I stayed home with the babies when I wasn't at school. The woman next door watched after them when I was gone. Her house smelled like moth balls and she had lines on the sides of her mouth from being a grouch. My belly hurt when I thought about Jeff. I cried every day because we left him behind and there wasn't a single thing that I could do about it. By then I learned how to change the babies' diapers and fix their bottles. I held them the way our mother said, so their heads would not bob around and break their necks.

Jeff appeared one day, right out of the blue. I could not believe my eyes. My heart broke with joy. Now my world was right again. Soon we were back in the dirt playing with the little cars and trucks. We learned to ride an old bicycle one of the nurses gave our mother. We were cowboys who went on expeditions in which we defeated our enemies. My cowboy name was Toughest Jim Schwartz. Jeff was Toughest Jim Jones. Zeezee kept her name because I couldn't think of anything more exotic than that.

I have lost track of how many times we moved over the next year but one of the places we lived had a basement where the Jehovah's Witnesses met for church. We found a bunch of Watch Towers piled up in a corner, which they must have forgotten because they left in a hurry. The Watch Towers had pictures of people that looked like Dick and Jane's mother and father, only they were running for their lives because the world was on fire. I threw them in the trash but we liked pretending to tap dance on the little stage in the basement.

By this time I was in second grade. We often went with Mom to see her friend, Jolly, who worked with her at the goddamn hospital. Jolly's husband Abe drank whiskey and smoked cigars all night long, so he smelled worse than a wet dog and looked exhausted all the time. I called him Ape, which made him laugh but I could tell Jolly did not approve. Mom left Jeff and me with Jolly and Ape for a few days so she could visit our father. I don't know where she left the twins.

Jolly said I had to sleep in a baby crib because she didn't have any more beds, which made me mad because I was a big girl with baby sisters who slept in cribs. I knew how to read. I was that big. Jeff got to sleep on the couch. Jolly said we had to say "may I be excused" before we could leave the supper table, but I wouldn't say it because we didn't talk like that at our house and I had never eaten at a supper table with everyone there like that, saying things I never heard of. So I sat there with my empty plate until bedtime and then Jolly gave up and told me I was excused so I went and climbed into the crib.

Not long afterward our father showed up with no warning. He had his truck and a bunch of stuff. He said he sent our brother Mike to live with Grandma and Grandpa in Michigan. We moved out of the Jehovah's Witnesses house and went to a strange little house out in the country by some hills. I say it was strange because there were two kitchens, two living rooms, two bathrooms, and two porches. It was as if the house had magicked itself into twins. My father said it was called a duplex. He set about tearing down some walls and taking out one of the kitchens.

The hills weren't anything like the mountains in Montana, but they were better than being in town. The Umpqua River was close by. You could fish and swim there and have a good time although people drowned every year so we had to watch out. There were farms up and down our road. Our mother enrolled us in the new school. It was our third school that year, but I liked it best because the playground had rings hanging from chains on a big wheel and at recess you could swing and go around as if you were in the circus. School let out not long after that, which meant there was plenty of time for us two Toughest Jims to go on adventures and along with Zeezee, get the lay of the land. And that was the beginning of the trouble.

CHAPTER TWO

Sunflowers

WE MET OLD MAN DODSON while trespassing. Fences never stopped us when we needed to get somewhere. We were on our way back from poaching trout in some guy's pond a mile away. We called him Fatty, and if you saw him you would know why. Fatty came after us once with his shotgun, cussing as effectively as our father. We were in Fatty's boat on Fatty's pond and really couldn't do a thing but row back to his dock and try to high tail it out of there without getting shot. Jeff rowed, his little back bent to his work, the dingy zig zagging with his efforts. I white knuckled the sides hoping we would not tip over because I did not know how to swim and the water was deep. We got to the dock, climbed out, tied up the boat, and to our great disappointment were unable to hide the trout. "Get the fuck off my property!" Fatty shouted, jowls flapping, pig eyes squeezed tight against the sun. "Read the goddamn sign!" he shouted, pointing.

It was a huge sign, at least three feet in each direction, white, with block letters that said KEEP OUT! PRIVATE PROPERTY! Jeff and I shrugged. "We can't read," I lied, shifting from one foot to the other, speaking into middle space. Jeff, who had been tested by the school psychologist because he wasn't doing well and had an attitude, actually had a genius IQ. He joined right in with my charade. We could have done improv, we were that good. "Yeah," Jeff said stupidly, staring in confusion at the sign. "I dunno. What's it say?"

"Bullshit!" the man spat, grabbing the trout. It was close to 20 inches, big enough for supper. Cripes, Fatty had a whole pond full of fish. Why'd he need this one? "I'm calling your parents!" he yelled, waving the gun, "They're gonna whup your ass." But we were already in the woods, laughing our heads off, knowing he would not call our parents because our house did not have a phone.

We were on the way home from Fatty's pond on another occasion when old man Dodson materialized in front of us. We froze and stared like feral cats. "Hello, children," he said in a sweet voice that made us instantly suspicious. "I'm Mr. Dodson. What are your names?" He had a garden rake and wore coveralls and a plaid shirt. A straw farmer's hat covered his head, leaving his narrow face in shadow. He reminded me of Mr. McGregor in the Beatrix Potter books. "Don't be afraid, I won't bite you," he said. We slowly walked toward him, ready to bolt. Old men, as a rule, wanted nothing to do with kids. We were royal pains in the ass.

Minutes later we were under a big old willow tree in his yard, gorging on cookies and milk. Mr. Dodson sat on an upturned bucket beside us, smiling, wiping sweat from his horsey face. He was scrawny with long yellow teeth and a dusty, old man smell. His wife appeared briefly at the kitchen door, a scowling, pinch-mouthed woman in a fancy apron. I wondered how our mother would look in an apron like that with ruffles and lace, only on top her nurse's uniform. There were pink flowers embroidered on the pockets. Nurses did not wear anything but white so she could not have an apron like this for her uniform. The woman's angry eyes bored through me until she slammed the door shut. She gave me a weird, scared feeling. But the old man seemed to like us for some reason. He had treats. We were all in.

Mr. Dodson's garden was our go-to hangout as summer wore on. Unlike Fatty, he was always glad to see us. He let us each plant sunflowers in his garden so that we could have a race to see whose flower would bloom first, and which plant would get the tallest. Jeff had a red ribbon on his. Mine was blue. Sometimes I snuck over and switched the ribbons if I thought he was gaining on me. I'm pretty sure he did the same thing. We basked in the attention, reveled in it. Mrs. Dodson never came outside or spoke to us, and we never went in their house, but I sometimes saw her angry eyes at the window.

One day we were there lounging under the tree like a bunch of lizards. The old man asked me to sit on his lap. I shook my head but he grabbed me and made me sit on his lap anyway. "Come here, Honey," he said with chewing tobacco breath hot on my neck. I jumped off like a pumphouse frog. "You're a quick little thing," he said. "Let's go check the garden, shall we?" I dashed off with Jeff, glad to escape his foul breath and vice grip hands.

The next time I went to the garden I was by myself. Jeff was tired of the sunflowers and said he knew I cheated. It was like an oven outside, so after walking through the field to the garden I went under the big tree. I was surprised to see the old man, deep in shadow. His face had a weird look, as if he was excited because it was Christmas and there were presents under the tree. After that my memories get jumbled into bits and pieces. Breath knocked out. Something hard, sharp. Burning, burning. Mrs. Dodson's eyes. The old man throws me. I bounce when I land. My head hits the ground. I see stars. Running away. Running. Falling down. Throwing up. I shake and sweat. I feel cold but it is hot. The sky.

I've heard preachers say that in the Garden of Eden the woman took the fruit and seduced Adam, and that he couldn't resist her feminine wiles and didn't stand a chance, the poor sap. I've heard sin was all her fault and you can't trust women because of Eve. I stopped agreeing with that pack of lies a long time ago. What I think is that snake was grooming children in the garden. Christ have mercy. The Lord never said "Keep away from the snake!" So they listened to it. And it talked and talked and talked to them, showing them the fruit all the time, maybe taking a bite itself now and then to show them how good it was. The snake kept at it, relentless, persistent, waiting for an opportune time.

I wonder if Eve ran through a field until the pain was too much. Did she fall down and vomit? Did she try to disappear? Did the shock of it all make her need the sky to help her thoughts go somewhere else until she fell asleep in Eden's field?

That night Mrs. Dodson came to our house, knocking on the door quick, loud, without stopping until my mother opened it a crack. No one ever came to see us. Jesus Christ who was coming in the dark, pounding the goddamn door off the frame?

"Your daughter seduced my husband!" the old woman shrieked, throwing the door wide and rushing in. "She is an evil, nasty girl!" Her bony finger pointed at me like the Wicked Witch of the West. She was hunched and terrible to behold. I shrank back into the shadows, away from her rage. Dad came with his gun. Shoved it into her chest, screamed, "Get out of my house, you sick, fucking bitch! Jesus Christ what is wrong with you? She is eight goddamn years old. Get out!" The witch woman ran out, incoherent.

They turned to me then, enraged. "What the hell is she talking about?" Mom shouted. Dad and the gun trembled with fury, threats of violence in his eyes. He teetered and steadied himself.

"I don't know," I whispered. "I don't know what seduce means." Nor did I know the word "rape," but I knew its meaning. I ran and hid, curled in upon myself, late into the night. They never spoke of it again. Nor did I. Due to their state of intoxication they likely had no memory of Mrs. Dodson by the next morning. My flesh slowly healed but the nightmares began. In most of them my mother left me in the road and walked away. I ran after her, crying, calling her name but she never saw me. She looked past me. I had dreams that I was drowning and no one came.

Mrs. Lyons was my salvation that year. She was my third-grade teacher, young and pretty with black hair and red lipstick. I thought she looked just like Snow White. Mrs. Lyons always smelled nice. My favorite part of the day was when she passed out graham crackers and milk, pulled out whatever book she was reading to us, and with her melodic voice took us to distant lands. We were out on the prairie in a sod house with Ma and Pa Ingalls when the Indians paid a visit. Next we traveled with Carcajou into the wilds. Off we went with Wilbur the Pig to have a word with Charlotte. And on it went. On weekends I could not wait for Monday to come so I could find out what happened next in the story. Mrs. Lyons had kind eyes. I could feel her love for me. I think she must have made everyone feel that way.

One day when the bell rang for recess Mrs. Lyons asked me to stay back for a minute because she had a thing to say to me. I began to tremble. What had I done? My belly hurt because I did not know what I would do if Mrs. Lyons got mad at me. After the other kids were out on the monkey bars Mrs. Lyons beckoned me to her desk where she opened a side drawer. I looked down, scared. She pulled out a white and blue tube of Avon skin cream. Removing the cap she took my little arm and held it in her warm, soft hand. Her nails were neatly trimmed, and clean. She had on a Timex watch and a polka dot dress. She wore glasses.

"Elaine, I noticed your skin is dry. I thought you might like to have some lotion for it," she said, squeezing a half inch strip of cream onto my arm. Still holding my arm in one hand she placed the tube on her desk and used her other hand to gently rub the cream into the skin of my arm. I knew that my dry, rough skin was different from other kids, but there was not a thing I could do about it. If anyone said anything mean about my skin, I punched them. As far as hygiene and such went, we got a bath once a week if someone remembered to tell us, which was not a sure thing. At times the houses where we lived did not have indoor plumbing so when we did have a bath our mother would fill a washtub from the kettle and we would take turns using the water. We did not brush our teeth unless we happened to be in the mood and there happened to be toothpaste in the house, nor did we know about daily ablutions that were routine for most people, until we were older and saw how other people lived.

Mrs. Lyons replaced the cap on the tube of skin cream, the sweet fragrance wafting up into my face. I gazed up at her, slack jawed with wonder, until she said, "You may go outdoors now, after you put this in your desk. This is for you to keep." She handed me the tube of cream. It was as if the wise men had arrived with their bizarre baby gifts of gold, frankincense, and myrrh and laid them all at my sorry ass feet. I put the cream in my desk, went out, and for the rest of the day kept my arm to my nose, sniffing with all my might.

Between Mrs. Lyons, adventures with Jeff, the bookmobile and candy, I more or less made it through third grade. I still have my report card for the end of the year, although how I managed to keep it through everything else that happened in my life is beyond knowing. In the small "comments" section at the bottom of the card, Mrs. Lyons wrote with a tidy hand: "Elaine has unusual insight for a child her age."

When summer came and school let out, all hell broke loose. We had our own personal apocalypse. For some reason I cannot recall, I was in the truck with Mom and Dad, wedged in between them in the cab, going down the road. I have no idea where everybody else was. My parents were discussing how to rid themselves of us.

"Get rid of the bastards!" Dad shouted. His hands were tight on the wheel so the knuckles stuck out like the bone hands of a skeleton. He wanted Mom to give all us young'uns to somebody else. He said he'd had enough of our goddamn assholes, elbows, and knees climbing into the bed at night. Bad dreams his ass, we were spoiled rotten and it was Mom's fault. If he had the guts he'd shoot all of us right now and escape the hell hole of his life.

Mom took the pleading tone that I knew would go nowhere.

"What? But what about the twins?" She was from Kentucky, a coal miner's daughter and had a wonderful, soft accent that I loved. None of the kids at school had mothers who sounded like mine or called their kids "young-uns" because we lived in Oregon and none of them were from Kentucky. None of their mothers were nurses, either. They all stayed home and cooked dinner and sewed, and came to class with cookies because they were Room Mothers. Mom got really mad when I talked about Room Mothers and wanting her to be one, so I learned to keep my trap shut about that.

"They're still babies."

"Give the little shits to Rosie," he shouted. Rosie was the babysitter who took care of the twins when Jeff and I were at school and Mom went to work. Mom said Rosie was unable to have babies of her own so she took good care of everyone else's. Rosie spoiled them, had toys, put them in cribs with clean sheets. She never ran out of milk. "Maybe Rosie would take them," Mom said. "They'd be better off." She stared ahead with the tired, blank face she had when she gave in.

My belly hurt, thinking about the twins going to Rosie and never coming home.

"But what about the other young'uns?" she asked. "Jeff and Elaine?"

"Get rid of the fuckers!" When he shouted his breath blew the hair off my forehead. I leaned into Mom but could not stop my left arm from touching Dad's right arm. I began to shake. There was not room in the truck to move or get out. We were not allowed to touch Dad because he said we were dirty. He never ate with us, either. It's as if we were a goddamn child leper colony.

Where would I go? Would Jeff be with me? The twins needed me. I could not go to Rosie's house by myself to see them unless I hitch-hiked. She lived too far away. You had to go in a car. Rosie would not want Jeff and me because we were kids. She only liked babies. Mom said Jeff and I were not allowed to hitch-hike because bad people might do things to us. But we did it anyway. I did not know if I could hitch-hike without Jeff. I felt so much braver when I was with him.

"We might keep Elaine," Dad said. I stared. Maybe I would not have to go. "As long as she don't cause trouble. Anyway, she's the easy one." Mom looked at him, her face crowded with unsaid words. A tiny flicker of hope sprang up inside of me. Maybe I could stay. But what about Jeff? What about the twins? Mike had come back from Grandpa and Grandma's house earlier that year because Grandma was sick and couldn't take care of him anymore. What would happen to Mike? I thought of the fist holes Dad made in the wall by Mike's room, close to the door. The next time his fists broke Mike's jaw. Now Mike slept with the axe under his bed, just in case. I saw it.

When we pulled into the driveway Mom jerked me hard by my shoulders, like she was mad at me. My head snapped back. "Don't you tell the other young'uns what you heard." Her voice was loud, harsh, cold like Dad's. I said I wouldn't. My teeth chattered, I was that scared.

Mike left soon after. His clothes were gone along with the axe. I know because I looked. Mom said he went off to live with neighbors down the road who had the dairy farm. They were rich, she said. They'd give him a hell of a good home, his own room, plenty of chow. He could work for his keep. He'd be happy now and that's all she ever wanted, she said. She just wanted some goddamn peace and quiet. I wondered if Mike's new room had blue wallpaper. I wondered if there were sheets for his bed. Rich people had such things.

The night after Mike and his clothes and the axe disappeared there were fists, things thrown, breaking, bodies heaved up against the wall. Mom ran out into the night. She said she was going to drive the car over the cliff into the Umpqua River, and off she went. The door slammed. I crawled out from under the bed and ran after her but it was too late. The old car was gone and there wasn't a thing I could do. The next day the car came back, and Mom with it. She had to sleep for a long time. I ate crackers and played with the twins. They could walk by then but that was about it.

After Mike left things simmered down a little.

Jeff and I befriended some kids who lived up the road whose last name was Hogg. I thought it was wildly funny because their family had a small farm with hogs, chickens, cattle, dogs, and a whole lot of old junk in the front yard. Their father walked around in his underpants inside the house, which made my stomach hurt, but other than that he seemed all right. Their kitchen always smelled like burnt roast beef and their dishes were never done. They had a lot of flies. I loved playing with Betsy, who was my age. We pretended we were horses and galloped all over the place neighing our heads off. When we weren't horses we ate cheap sandwich cookies and colored in her coloring books.

One day Mr. Hogg up and gave me one of his chickens. I thought I had died and gone to heaven, I was so happy. I brought the poor thing home. In hindsight she was probably of an age to go in Mrs. Hogg's stewpot, but Mr. Hogg knew I was in love with his chickens so he gave it to me. I put it in the shed that night. The next day I went out and found the chicken and one egg, and could hardly believe my good fortune. I talked to that chicken all day and wanted to put clothes on it and give it one of the twins' bottles, but the chicken had other ideas. The next day I went out and she was gone. I saw no trace of her, not even one feather, nor did I find an egg. I suspect Jeff felt sorry for her and set her free. What with coyotes, owls, and who knows what else she probably went to her immediate demise. But maybe she flew back to Mr. Hogg. When I saw that she was gone I made up my mind that when I grew up I would have a dozen chickens and live by myself. We would have a little house in the woods with a clean white fence like Dick and Jane and there would be no junk in the yard, or flies in the kitchen. Those chickens and I would have ourselves some goddamn peace and quiet.

Our mother had found cheap bread, a nickel a loaf at the day-old Wonder Bread store in town. We called it the used bread store and gloried in our newfound largesse, purchased at a fraction of the usual price. I was in the kitchen one Saturday morning making used bread toast. The twins fussed in their cribs in the little nook by the kitchen. It used to be a porch before we moved there, but now had become an official room. They were hungry, maybe had wet diapers. Then they started to scream, all mad and outraged the way babies get when they have needs. Dad appeared from nowhere, roaring, "Shut the hell up!" He began to beat them with a rolled up paper. He beat the shit out of them in his plaid bathrobe, ordering the little bastards to shut their goddamn mouths. They screamed, gagged, couldn't breathe. I dropped the toast and ran fast, out of my mind with fear and rage. I grabbed his terrible arms, hung on, yelled. The babies wailed, bodies stiff with screaming and fear. The three of us would die now. He stopped and stared at me, eyes bulging, face flushed as purple as grape jelly. I saw the whites of his eyes all around the brown part, bloodshot and crazy.

Mom told us all the time how good-looking Dad was, and it was true. He was a dead ringer for a young Robert de Niro. All the women wanted him, Mom said. He dropped the paper and shook me off, turned, left. I took the twins out of their cribs, one at a time. We sat there on the floor, my legs stuck out straight like Pinocchio before he turned into a boy, Julie on one leg, Jeanine on the other, little blond heads tucked up against my bony chest trying to get over all that crying. We rock, rock, rocked everything away.

The next day Dad left. Mom threw him out. Jeff and I couldn't believe it, but there he went, down the road. He had on a suit and hat. All the women would want him. Mom said she was getting a divorce, that she still loved him but Jesus Christ she couldn't put up with his shit any more, not after Mike's jaw and the axe. With the coast clear, Mike came back from the rich people's house. He had a job now at the high school cleaning the floors at night. So he brought home a record player from the high school when no one was looking and said we had to keep our trap shut. He brought some 45's, too. He played records and we all listened. We felt like we were somebody.

One day around that time after Dad left Mom came home from working the day shift. She had gotten a ride home from one of the other nurses because our old car was broke down. Jeff had taken the keys when Mom was asleep after the night shift and he had gone off down the road to see somebody. He had trouble seeing over the dashboard and soon went off the road. Somebody called a wrecker and the next thing you know he and the rumpled car were back home, with Mom still asleep. So for awhile Mom had to bum rides from people.

I was out in the yard holding a piece of rope when she came home, trying to figure out how to jump criss cross like the big girls at school. Mom waved and smiled, walked over, asked if she could jump, too. Flabbergasted, I handed her the rope. Right there in the gravel driveway with weeds coming up and the whole of creation watching, she jumped. There in her white uniform, white stockings, white shoes, and white cap, our mother executed a flawless criss cross over and over, singing a little rhyme as she jumped. She then jumped forward, backward, double step, and skip. Up and down the driveway she went. She handed me the rope, laughing hard, and trotted into the house. I gaped after her, mute with surprise. Decades later, pondering this event, I thought she would have played with us every day if her life had been different. Things were hard for her, too. And yet, she kept choosing not to play, not to hear us, not to see what we endured.

Toward the end of summer after I passed from third grade to fourth grade Jeanine got sick, so sick she had to go to the hospital. She had quit eating and no one knew why. Mom said Neanie might die but she wouldn't let us kids go see her. Children couldn't visit in the hospital, Mom said, and she knew because she was a Registered Nurse.

My belly hurt every day. Mom said the goddamn doctor couldn't find a thing wrong with Neanie. One day she came home and said that when she went to see Neanie in her little hospital crib, she turned her face away so she wouldn't have to look at Mom. When Mom said this, she cried for a long time. I cried too. I thought if they would just let me go to the hospital Neanie would not turn her face away from me. I could hold her and she would get better.

But our girl did not die. One day she came back to us, just like that. Mom got out of the car with her. Neanie reached her stick arms out so I could take her. My heart burst with jubilation. She smiled at me with the same dimples, but now she had old people eyes, sunk back into her head, full of wordless thoughts I did not understand. I buried my face against her neck, breathing in the bitter hospital smells that lingered on hair and skin. Mom said the goddamn doctors said Neanie's sickness was Failure to Thrive. For some reason she was mad about it. She said it was my fault, Jeff's fault, Mike's fault. It was Julie's fault for being so damn chubby and cute. Everybody wanted to hold Julie instead of Jeanine. Julie was too cute. We had to pay more attention to Jeanine, now, put Julie down, pick Jeanine up. We didn't pick her up enough. It was our fault.

Pretty soon school started again. I was in Mrs. Maxwell's fourth grade class. I realized at once that she was going to be nothing like Mrs. Lyons. She was what the other kids called "strict," and when she fixed her watery pale blue eyes upon my bedraggled self I wanted to hide. We learned how to do long division and play some new games in the gym. Halloween came and went. One day when it was getting close to Thanksgiving and we had traced our hands onto construction paper and made some nice turkeys to hang on the wall, Mrs. Maxwell came into the class looking crazy. "Boys and girls, boys and girls," she said, repeating herself as if she wasn't sure she could believe her own mouth. "Something terrible has happened. President Kennedy has been assassinated. Someone shot him. He is dead." With that she burst into wild sobs as if she had lost her mind. I wondered what assassinated meant. I knew what shot meant because I saw Dad shoot plenty of things including the time he shot a hole in the roof of the truck with Mom and the twins and himself inside. Jeff and I were down in the stream catching frogs. We were in the woods camped out on the side of some logging road, campfire smoking, rain spitting but not enough to make you go in the tent. We heard the gun go off and the first thing

Jeff said was "He killed her." We ran back and saw them standing out in the rain staring at the hole in the roof wondering how the hell that happened, as if they didn't know.

What shocked me that day with Mrs. Maxwell, was not the death of our president, but that she could cry. I didn't think she had it in her.

Three weeks after President Kennedy died, Dad reappeared without warning. A taxi brought him to the house, which thinking back, must have cost a fortune. We lived far out in the country. He got out, looking like Dick and Jane's father, dressed in a suit and hat, smelling of Old Spice. But there was tension. He ruffled my hair and called me Sweetheart, which confused me because of all we had been through. It made me happy and afraid at the same time. He and Mom went in the house. Jeff and I looked at each other and wondered what the hell was up. We kept playing with our little cars in the dirt, watching the door from the corner of our eyes, ready to bolt as needed.

The next morning while it was still dark, Mom woke Jeff and me up, told us to hurry up and get dressed because Jeff and I had to go to the train station with our father. Her eyes were red and swollen. She said she wasn't coming with us and handed us each a paper bag with some peanut butter and crackers and an apple. A yellow taxi came and picked us up. It smelled faintly of old cigars and puke. Jeff and I fell asleep leaning on each other in the back seat. When we woke up we were in the biggest city I ever saw, a place called Portland. The train station was a seething mass of rails, people, trains, and fumes. Like Jonah's whale it swallowed us alive as the taxi driver took us deep into its body and set us free. We hopped out of the cab and followed Dad, who acted like he owned the joint. It didn't surprise us that everyone jumped to do what he said. The young women seemed to like him a lot. They smiled up at him through their lashes and called him Mr. Heath. With his jaunty fedora tipped to one side and his white shirt and tie he looked every bit as fancy as the preacher at the Baptist church.

But he was no preacher. Soon we were on our way on a long train that had plush seats and a double decker car so we could watch the Rocky Mountains and the villages and farms go by. It was the week before Christmas. The pretty ladies who worked on the train could hardly keep away from our father, bringing him snacks and drinks, sitting on the armrest of his seat and watching him play cards. I saw him pull a wad of dough out of his pocket, held in place with a rubber band. It was the size of a softball, all that cash. I couldn't believe my eyes that he had so much money. Dad tossed bills on the card table as if they were scrap paper and tucked a few more into the hand of the woman at his side. He had a different way of talking than at home, smooth and confident like he was somebody. People laughed and smoked and had a good time.

Because we were his kids, the pretty ladies were very good to us. We had cocoa and sandwiches, potato chips, and candy canes, all we could eat, whenever we wanted. We didn't even have to ask, or swipe anything. They just kept offering loot, and we just kept saying yes. We stuffed our pockets with whatever we didn't eat, just in case. One night we all sang Christmas carols, the whole train full of us. I didn't know most of the words but faked my way along. Nobody cared. It seemed like a dream world. Mom, the twins, the grown-ups' obsession with the president's assassination all moved to the back of my mind as Jeff and I absorbed every moment.

After what felt like a month later but was really just a few days, we pulled into the station in Cleveland, Ohio. The degree of industrial filth made the Portland station seem like a garden. What amazed me the most was my first glimpse of African American people, their beautiful dark skin and the melodic accent of their voices. We changed trains there, taking the last leg of our journey to Toledo, Ohio. Grandpa met us and drove us to his tidy little house in the village of Lambertville, Michigan, just across the border from Toledo.

We had come to a new world where for the better part of a year and the only time during our childhood, we would experience a stable home. Our father would go to work every day and come home for our supper prepared by his father, recently widowed. We ate that simple meal together at the kitchen table, like other people did. In the evenings Dad watched TV, we all drank Pepsi, and Gramps taught Jeff and me to play Pinochle. Every morning Gramps fixed breakfast—burnt toast and Tang—and packed school lunches for us with Wonder bread and thick, indigestible slices of sharp cheddar cheese and mustard. It was the best food we ever ate.

One day soon after we arrived, Dad took me to Sears and Roebuck, corralled a young clerk, told her I needed 5 dresses, 5 sets of underwear, 2 pair of pajamas, and shoes. He stared at her from beneath his brows while she hastened to assemble my new wardrobe. Nothing like this had ever happened before, nor has it since. He even bought me some hair ribbons. He took me to a salon so I could have the first proper haircut of my life. The beautician told me my daddy was awfully nice.

Weekends held more delights as we went to the village library to check out arm loads of books and avail ourselves of hundreds of View-master slide wheels, while Dad paid the bills and grocery shopped. Impy, the old cat, survived Gramps' attempt to euthanize him after Jeff and I rescued him from the box and set him loose. I have no idea why Gramps thought it was Impy's time to go to heaven and his job to get him there, but we made sure Impy got away. I suppose he's still alive out there, yowling for Grandma. I stopped missing Mom and began feeling joy over our unrecognizable father, which made me feel guilty and confused. I worried about the twins, which sometimes made me cry.

Our teachers were very fond of our father and felt sorry for him because he was a struggling single parent. It didn't hurt that he was easy on the eye. They were clueless about everything. But we took advantage of their sympathy and reveled in all the special treatment. The other kids thought we were exotic, not having a mother. Of course, by then we had regular baths, clean clothes, and Gramps made sure my hair was combed before I got on the school bus. We had friends.

A couple of months after school let out, a big black car pulled into the driveway. The door to the back seat opened and our mother stepped out. Her face was swollen from crying. She was wearing a beautiful green print dress and hat with a matching pocket book, and looked thinner than I recalled. As I registered that fact, two little girls hopped out in matching red dresses and stood behind her, peering around her legs. They stared at me shyly and I realized with a shock that they were the twins. They asked our mother a question, and she answered. They could talk now, and use the toilet, I soon learned. They were kids now, no longer babies.

Everyone went in the house. The moment I saw our mother I longed for her again. She wrapped me in her arms and held me tight. I did not know how much I still missed her until she was there. I laughed and cried at the same time, like a crazy girl. Her mother died, she said, just a couple of weeks back. She had to leave Arizona where she had gone off with some man, to go to the funeral, and she decided to go get the twins and bring them with her. She did not say where they were, that she had to go get them, but I hoped they had been with Rosie. Now that her Mama was gone, she needed to see us, she said. All this time that she explained everything, tears ran down her cheeks as if there were an open faucet inside of her and she couldn't figure out how to turn it off.

By supper time she and Dad were roaring drunk. A fight broke out. Jeff and I took the twins and went outside. We were mesmerized by their newfound ability to talk. Our fairy tale life came to a screeching halt. The fight escalated. Mom called the cops on Gramps' phone, because Dad had the .45 threatening to shoot all us little bastards and then himself. Dad had so completely lost his mind that I became convinced he was now going to poison us, so I refused to eat the boiled wieners Mom prepared for our supper. When I told her I thought he poisoned them, she told him what I said, which in hindsight was probably not the best thing to do.

About that time the police cruiser rolled in, lights flashing. Out jumped two uniformed men with badges, guns, clubs, cuffs, and other implements hanging from their belts. I had never seen a police officer up close. Jeff and I kept a sharp watch from our vantage point in the shrubs, not wanting to miss a thing. Dad, who must have seen the flashing lights, graciously came to the door to let them in. He used his Mr. Heath on the train voice to explain to the officers that we were on the verge of leaving town the next day, after spending an extended time helping his recently widowed father with overwhelming grief. He also apologized for acting like a reckless sonofabitch. His disorderly conduct was understandable, the officer said, given all his grief and responsibilities as head of the house. A man can only take so much. It was too bad there weren't more good men like him willing to help his old man at such a time, they said. I expected any minute Dad would pour a fraternal round of drinks for the officers and himself, maybe pull out a deck of cards.

Mom stood defeated and mute, her previously coiffed hair in disarray. The next day we packed up what few things could fit into Dad's truck and Gramps' car, and hit the road, all except Gramps, leaving him carless, staring after us and trying to figure out what the hell just happened. Dad stopped on the way out of town and got his gun back from the cops, who continued to be his best friends. We were on our way back to Montana, goddammit, where a man could piss off his back porch without the fucking cops showing up.

CHAPTER THREE

Skating

HE LOOKED EXACTLY LIKE THE CROONER, Andy Williams. Dark blue eyes fringed with long, dark lashes. Chiseled face. A fine physique. He wore a white turtle neck sweater and brown woolen slacks, the kind our teachers wore, with cuffed hems. My best friend Laurie and I noticed at once when he began showing up at the skating rink. All the other boys wore flannels and jeans. This was, after all, Alaska. We moved there in 1969 in the summer before I started ninth grade. The man with nice clothes had to be from the lower 48, and clearly he was a man, not a boy.

The rink was what sociologists would call our "third space," our high school version of the Beacon Hill pub in *Cheers* where everyone knew everyone's name. At the skating rink I felt like Somebody. I spent every spare moment there, working the skate room in exchange for free admission. I also dated boys, off and on, who worked at the rink. I danced, I raced, I spun, and showed off. Skaters were my people, and the rink was my escape from the chaos at home. Whenever Dad would go into a rage and kick me out, I went to Laurie's house. I dreamed of living there permanently. Her family was what I thought of as normal, which meant her parents seemed to like their kids, and they all ate dinner together at the table. I worshipped them.

For several weeks Laurie and I watched Mystery Man spin, weave, and dance his gorgeous way around our rink, wondering where he came from. He was in a different league than our fifteen-year old selves. So confident.

It happened on a Saturday night. The lights dimmed, the disco ball glittered, and the voice over the loudspeaker said "Couples only." Nat King Cole was barely into the third Mona Lisa when the dark eyed stranger glided to a graceful halt in front of me, extended his hand, smiled with perfectly straight, white teeth and asked if I would like to skate with him.

Laurie's jaw dropped in astonishment as I moved onto the floor. His name was Alex, I learned. He was very, very smart, majoring in chemical engineering, and had finished his third year at New Mexico State University. I knew nothing about universities. Those were places for rich people, not people like me. Also, I thought engineers were the guys who drove trains. Alex was in Alaska on a work-study program that had something to do with the pipeline. He was practically a genius. He would be in town for a few more months and then return to New Mexico to complete his final year of studies.

I was the envy of every girl in the rink as I skated the rest of the night with Alex. He was from a different universe than the usual goofballs I dated. He did not seem to mind that I was fifteen years old and a sophomore in high school. At the end of the evening when he asked for my phone number, I gladly gave it to him.

I was very surprised, though, when Alex called and asked me to go to *church* with him the following week. Somehow religion, geniuses with sexy eyes, and dancing on skates didn't go together in my mind. I had sworn off church two years earlier after narrowly escaping the clutches of a deacon. The police later arrested him for making and selling kiddie porn and there was a terrible scandal. It was in the papers and everything but with a slap on the wrist, promises to turn from sin and a few months in the slammer he was soon back out on the street, ready to resume his habits.

We lived in the Lower 48 at the time, outside of Spokane, Washington, where Mom worked the night shift at the hospital. Right after that ugliness went down we jumped in our old truck and hit the road for Alaska. Church was not on my radar. Church had come to mean men in suits and women with beehive hair acting all fancy and righteous when underneath the surface there were groping hands and secrets and wives who looked the other way. But I was so intoxicated by the thought of dating a college man who could skate backwards, had a car and lived in his own apartment, that I was willing to go just about anywhere with him, even church. So off we went, him in a suit, me in a miniskirt, the twins in the back seat.

We often brought Julie and Jeanine with us, both to church and to the roller rink. I needed to keep them away from Dad. His rage simmered constantly beneath the surface, exploding unpredictably. They were in danger. By then they were eight years old with snaggle teeth and a powerful appetite for candy. When the parent teacher conferences happened at the elementary school that year, I stood in as the parent, telling the teacher our mother had to work so I was helping out. I pushed my cat-eye glasses up on my nose, patted my bouffant hair into place and asked about my sisters' progress.

As the summer progressed Alex took me on many outings on his days off. We ate hamburgers, hiked to Thunderbird Falls, and watched movies. He was a complete gentleman most of the time, but strangely harsh with the twins.

I began to notice that when Julie or Jeanine didn't behave the way he wanted them to, his rebuke was sharp. His expectations were rigid when it came to children and he thought they should be punished at every infraction. This was my first red flag, as they say, about how his own painful childhood formed him, but I had not heard of red flags in relationships and I was used to a violent and capricious father. I found myself saying things to him like, "Hey, they're just eight years old. Let them have the cookies." I used the tone of voice my mother did sometimes when she tried to smooth things over with Dad. I made little jokes and tried to cheer him up when Alex seemed depressed. I started to feel responsible for his moods.

In time we began to talk about getting married someday after he graduated when he had a job and I was an adult, years down the road. It was the sweetly romantic talk of a child who always had to function as an adult, and a gifted, complex young man with undiagnosed mental illness and a history of trauma about which I knew nothing. When I turned sixteen Alex insisted that we talk to my parents about our relationship hopes for someday, and "get their blessing." I was mortified. But I had learned from infancy from our mother that the man's wishes are what matter in a relationship. So on my birthday we ate cake and Alex "asked for their blessing," whatever the hell that meant.

How do you "ask for a blessing" when your parents don't provide you with the blessings of basic medical care, nutrition, or safety, much less that they themselves are the biggest threat to your life? What is a blessing when your father brutalizes the oldest child until he leaves to save his life, and then it is the next child's turn to repeat the process? They seemed befuddled and I blushed furiously. Watching Alex drive away from our trailer in his sedan, Dad breathed hard through his nose. "Goddamn clown," he finally said. "Faggot."

Shortly after Christmas, Alex returned to his studies and family in New Mexico. I missed him terribly. Laurie was my pal, faithfully asking about Alex every time we talked. The church had become by then a refuge for my sisters and me, despite my cynicism and philosophical objections to their evangelical religion. In the youth Sunday School class I told the teacher week by week that I did not believe any of it, especially the doctrine of a flaming hell, because hell is here and now, I said, "the existential condition of the oppressed," a term I learned in school.

I don't remember her name. She was somebody's Mom, round and soft, fragrant with cake mix and Ivory soap. She said in a southern drawl, "Honey, I just don't know what to say about that. But Jesus loves you and we do too. We're so glad you came to Sunday School today." Then she hugged me and tears sprang into my eyes so I had to turn away and high tail it out of there.

After Sunday School I went into the sanctuary with its muted light, stained glass windows, and a sense of peace that was palpable. The pastor and his wife were utterly kind to me, hospitable, gentle, unflinching in the face of the anger and fear that were just beneath my mask of intellectual objections. Week after week I sat in the sanctuary after Sunday School, trying not to weep because of the beauty, warmth, and welcome. I hungered for the God who seemed so real to these people, but between the porn deacon and old man Dodson and a lifetime of chaos and violence, I no longer believed that God was real.

Every smile, every conversation, every relationship there pierced me with longing.

Alex had been gone for several weeks when three things happened, a domino fall that entirely changed the course of my life. The first thing was Jesus. I had been reading one of the gospels in the New English Study Bible with the Apocrypha, a Christmas gift from Mom who knew I wanted a Bible in a modern translation since I was going to church and all. It was dark red, and so big and heavy that it took both hands to carry. It was hilarious that she went to the Book Cache and bought a Bible for me. She had a love/hate relationship with me going to church. On the one hand, it got the twins and me out of the house so she could smoke and stare off into space and collect her thoughts. But on the other hand all that religious stuff made her nervous. By then she'd had her fill of being judged by stuffed shirts. It only took a couple of beers to get her worked up and then I was a self-righteous bitch trying to judge her and by God she would not be judged by my fifteen year old ass.

My relationship with that Bible was as conflicted as Mom's ambivalence toward me. I loved that it was huge and heavy and academic looking, no leather cover, and that it was in a modern translation. There were no thee's and thou's like the flimsy Bibles in the pews. I wanted to dive into it, swim underwater, find meaning in its bookish glory.

I loved books above all else. The Bible pages were thin, but surprisingly sturdy. And the fragrance was intoxicating. I frequently opened to the middle, somewhere around 1-2 Esdras and lowered my face so that I could inhale its delicate scent. This one had its own fragrance, unlike paper or hardback novels, textbooks, or the library as a whole, although I inhaled those, too. But despite its charms it was still a Bible, the book of the Church, the favorite book of men who hurt little girls.

I had also been reading the Lloyd C. Douglas novel, *The Robe* that I found in a rack of approved novels for Mrs. Hamilton's fourth period English class. We got rewards based on how much we read, so I wasted no time but dug right in. Written in 1942, the book presented a very human Jesus in the final weeks of his life. I kept the book longer than I was supposed to. I finally swiped it because I kept wanting to read about the novel Jesus who was unrecognizable compared to the church Jesus. The book made me cry. I found myself wishing the story of Jesus was true and grieving that it wasn't. The novel Jesus was swarthy and had callouses. He spent most of his time outdoors with working folk, unlike the pasty pictures of Jesus with the baby lamb and blonde hair in the Sunday school room. He was nothing like any of the suited men in the church, including the pastor. He definitely was not like my father.

"I could follow the novel Jesus anywhere," I thought over and over, quickly followed by, "but it's a myth. Marx is right. Religion is the opiate of the people." I moved on from *The Robe* to Buddhist mysticism, Tolkien, New Age and cowboy stories but in my heart I kept hankering for Jesus. There were books in my room about astral travel, crystals, and reincarnation, and the Dalai Llama. I asked Mrs. Hamilton if I could count those in my overall tally. She said I had unusual tastes for a junior in high school.

There was music, too, filling my heart—Marvin Gaye, Joan Baez, and Janice Joplin wailing that her love was a ball and chain. I sewed myself a pair of paisley bellbottom pants in Home Economics and felt spectacular each time I wore them. A tenth grader at the roller rink started to take an interest in me, and I kind of liked him, too. He was one of those slapstick kids who make farty noises with their hands in their armpits. We laughed non-stop when we were together. He seemed like an infant compared to Alex, who had gone home to New Mexico, and was too young to drive a car, but all of that was a relief in so many ways. I knew it was unlikely I would ever see Alex again, even though we hadn't "broken up." I tried not to think about my changing feelings. I felt confused.

Dad's binges escalated followed by violent DT's, fueled by the claustrophobia of living in a small trailer in a crappy trailer park with all of us, the dog, and Dad's father who had dementia and had come to reside with us. Mom expected Dad to help Gramps with his bath and such, but Dad couldn't bear it. He would drink himself into a stupor and talk about the tragedy of Gramps's life. Then he would lean over in his chair, put his head in both hands, sway back and forth and sing *The Old Rugged Cross* and *In the Garden*, the two hymns they sang at

Grandma's funeral. He had a sweet tenor and sang on pitch, and he knew every verse by heart.

Dad's rage exploded at the slightest things. We were all at risk all the time. The minute Jeff turned sixteen and could legally do so he had quit high school, taken the GED test with flying colors so he could get the hell away from the violence, and joined the Coast Guard. Now he was down in Virginia living near our mother's people. Dad said they were all hillbillies, which infuriated Mom. I envied Jeff's freedom, imagining him on a boat somewhere doing something important. He'd been gone two years by then, which seemed like a lifetime to me.

Somehow despite his binges Dad hung onto his sheet metal job at Ft. Richardson, the Army base outside of Anchorage. Mom would call in sick for him. But he was spiraling down the way he always had when he began to feel hemmed in by people and their needs.

Dad especially felt trapped by the needs of his own family. It was as if he were allergic to us. We were not to touch anything he owned or God forbid, himself. Not that we wanted to. He was our personal terrorist. But when he wasn't at home, sometimes I snuck into his top dresser drawer and took out the expensive Sees chocolates that Mom stocked for him. I took the box over and sat on his side of the bed like I owned the joint, half wild with fear that any minute the door would burst open and all hell would break lose. I bit into the chocolates and slowly ate them, sweet bits of resistance melting in my mouth one by one. I only took one or two at a time so he wouldn't know. But I knew.

About that time Dad also began to grow a small stash of weed for himself in a hidden corner behind the trailer. He smoked it in secret, he thought, in his little tool shed with all the girly pinup pics inside. It was illegal, of course. But obeying the law had never been a priority for Dad.

With Jeff and Mike long gone I had by then become the target for Dad's incomprehensible pain and mental illness. He hated that I now went to church. He hated everything about "organized religion," as he called it. The mantra in our house was a whispered, "Don't! You'll make Dad mad." Mom coped with Dad through work, sleep, alcohol, country music, and tuning us out. I coped with both of them by going to school, cleaning the house, doing the laundry, cooking, taking care of the twins, and going to the rink whenever possible. Then church got into the mix, and the New English Bible with the Apocrypha, and pining for Jesus. We all walked around on eggshells, trying to avoid the next blow-up. Like every other house we lived in, our trailer had fist holes in the walls.

It happened one morning a few weeks after Alex left, while I was pulling on the leopard print miniskirt I made on the old treadle sewing machine Mom got for me at the Goodwill. It looked great with the green sweater from the yard sale. Longing for Jesus to be real flooded my emotions and I sat down on the bed, stunned with wanting. Then suddenly it was as if liquid light poured into me. I experienced overwhelming love enfold me. My very body knew that despite what happened with the porn deacon and old man Dodson, despite the heinous doctrine of a flaming hell, despite the beehive hair women with secrets and their controlling husbands and the ridiculous, blonde church Jesus, the real Jesus became alive in my heart. I was awash in love beyond words or anything I had ever experienced. I cried and cried with joy. I finally knew why the youth Sunday school teacher was so happy. I'd found Jesus, or more accurately, Jesus found me, and not a moment too soon.

CHAPTER FOUR

Bride

SOME DAYS AFTER FINDING JESUS I came home from school and found Dad morose, head in hands, his normally immaculate hair falling across his forehead. He was deep into a fifth of bourbon. We spoke briefly about Gramps, who was now in the nursing home because of advancing dementia. Mom had Gramps admitted once he started dropping lit matches on the rug. Dad hated that she did this. He wanted her to take care of Gramps at home with dignity because she was a goddamn nurse, but she worked full-time and it wasn't going to happen.

I truly loved Gramps, who was part of that magical year when our father took Jeff and me to Michigan and we lived like normal people. I savored every memory of that year with Gramps. He was the only relative of ours that I actually knew. Under his grief-stricken care Jeff and I thrived and made good grades at school. Other kids wanted to play with us. It was a new day. Dad went to his sheet metal job every day, came home in time for supper, and worked the program with AA. He became a different man. As I child I credited Gramps with the miraculous transformation although looking back the biggest source for Dad's newfound sanity and fatherliness was that he was not with our mother. Somehow our parents could not be together without alcohol induced chaos, violence, and terrible consequences for their children.

But now it was six years later and Gramps was unable to talk with us coherently or play cards, or recognize me. When a second marriage from a money grubbing spinster according to my parents, didn't work out for him, Gramps came to live with us. Now with late stage dementia he was in his final years.

Dad rambled on into his booze about the shame of having his father in a fucking institution, repeatedly wiping hair out of his bloodshot eyes. I said in what I thought was a comforting tone that the old geezer needed care that we couldn't provide but that he was in a good place where they took good care of him. In the next moment Dad body slammed me to the floor, straddled my belly, pinned my arms with his knees and began to strangle me. His eyes were wild, somewhere else, in some other time. He bared his teeth, grimaced like a mad dog. Unable to breathe, I struggled but could not break free. I was certain that I would die. Jeanine stood by, petrified, watching.

Abruptly, he let go, punched a hole in the wall by my bedroom door, and disappeared. In that moment I knew I had to get away. Permanently, not just for a week or two at Laurie's house. I would not survive the fist that would surely find my face if I stayed put. Just as Mike and Jeff had to flee for their lives when I was younger, I now had to find my way out. Mom would not protect me. No one ever had, and no one would.

In all of this I saw Mom as a victim, like us kids, so I always gave her a pass when she let us down. It took decades before I realized the terrible truth, that she was even more culpable than Dad, because she had the ability to say no to his violence and take us away to safety, or kick him out once and for all, yet again and again she chose him, enabling his violent ways and addictions.

It never occurred to me or my siblings to call the police or report Dad to the authorities. We were well trained in keeping family secrets. In those days there were no posters, teachers, or school officials, much less church leaders who spoke of domestic violence, sexual assault, or any of the other traumatizing experiences that were common in our family. There were no messages about where to turn for help. Waves of guilt overwhelmed me at the thought of leaving my sisters behind. How would they survive? But how would I if I didn't? I could not figure out how to leave, or where to go, or what to do about the twins. But I thought about it constantly.

A couple of weeks later a fight broke out at my school in the girls' restroom. Racial tensions had been escalating nationally, and East Anchorage High School began to feel the pain. Someone pulled a knife. A girl was stabbed. Another girl was arrested. It was all over the news. That evening Mom told me that I had to drop out of school, that I had to leave town because it was too dangerous for me. Dad sat beside her, nodding his head in agreement. They offered no ideas about where I was supposed to go. I stared in disbelief. This was the father who strangled me and broke my brother's jaw and brutalized Jeff and beat the twins when they were babies. This was the mother who enabled him, "to keep the peace," always at the expense of her children. These were the parents whose neglect and abuse of every one of us children was criminal in so many ways. What was happening now, I realized, was that they were giving me the boot just as they had done to Mike and Jeff. To make it even more outrageous they were couching it in terms of concern for my safety.

"Why don't you call Alex's parents and see if they will let me live at their house until I graduate?" I blurted. I was a straight A student. I couldn't just quit school. Memories of Alex's adult confidence, church going ways and our many outings filled my mind. I wondered if his parents would take me in like Laurie's family had, because if they would there would be thousands of miles of safety between Dad and me. Moments later Mom called Alex's parents, told them I needed a place to live because of the violence in my school and across the city, asked if they would take me in. The next day I was on a plane to New Mexico.

And just like that I found myself caught in the second set of developments that turned my life upside down. Alex met me at the airport, livid. Once he returned to New Mexico, he said, he realized our talk about getting married someday years into the future was unrealistic. We lived too far apart for one thing. Sure he had loved me and we had some good times, but now he had real plans for his life. I had interrupted those plans, showing up at his parents' house, bringing my needy ass into his world. Throughout the 45 minute drive to his parents' house in Las Cruces where he still lived, he shouted, berated, and shamed me. He had never spoken to me or anyone else like that in

Alaska. I had seen him feeling depressed. I had seen him be harsh with my sisters. But I had never experienced his rage. I was devastated.

Karl and Bonnie, his parents, welcomed me kindly into their home. They told me I would share Linda's room. She was fourteen, a couple of years younger than me and a student in middle school. It was good that my parents wanted me to be safe from the violence in Anchorage, they said. I scanned their cluttered living room like a trapped rabbit, looking for the best escape route just in case, swallowing hard to try to remove the lump in my throat.

Linda was a bookish, likeable girl who didn't seem to mind sharing her room. All my belongings were in the battered suitcase I brought from Anchorage. The next day Bonnie took me to the local high school and enrolled me. My head felt like it would explode with questions and fear. Alex went through sharp mood swings, sometimes in the same hour, alternating between the charming man I remembered, to a brooding, angry presence who could not find joy. Who was this man I thought I knew? What would happen to my poor sisters now that I was gone? I was not able to go back to Alaska. I did not tell anyone in New Mexico about the violence that was there, at least not at first. But I began having nightmares in which the twins were drowning and I could not get to them fast enough. My stomach hurt all the time.

I stumbled through the next few weeks trying to adjust to my new situation. I never knew where I stood with Alex from one day to the next. Linda was my new best friend. I soon learned that although she seemed friendly the day I arrived, Mother, the name her kids used for Bonnie, had the same harsh, punitive mindset that I first saw in Alex. Daddy—Karl—was kind, sweet, and like every other member of the family, under Mother's control. I was astounded at how she took him for granted and ordered him around, and how he took it from her without a peep. I had never seen a man act like that with a woman, nor had I seen a woman behave that way toward her man. Daddy was gentle and respectful with me, which seemed to irritate the hell out of Mother.

My miniskirts bothered her a lot. So did my attitude. Having grown up mothering the twins and everyone else, I resented being told to put my jacket on because it might rain, or being asked what I bought with my own money when I went to the corner store. The more intrusive Mother was, the more I clammed up.

In the evenings after dinner I cleaned the kitchen, the pantry, the floors, the windows, everything I could get my hands on. I scrubbed with a fury, trying to wash away the anxiety that filled me more and more, day by day. In the pantry I organized all the jars of canned goods, the pet food, the cleaning supplies, everything that had been heaped up and forgotten. I quickly came to understand that cleaning frenzies were not part of their family culture. It was clear that I was not part of the culture. The brighter and more organized the kitchen got, the more delighted Daddy was with me and the more furious Mother became.

I had been there for a month when Mother sat Alex and me down and announced that we had to get married. Immediately. We were about to commit the sin of fornication, she said, and she would have none of that under her roof, and I was no longer welcome to live there as I had been doing. Daddy looked lost and sad, avoiding eye contact with me. I was dumbfounded. I had neither time nor privacy to fornicate. How could I be married and a junior in high school? Alex sputtered in apoplectic rage. Yet it was incomprehensible for us to defy Mother. I had nowhere else that I could go. Returning to Alaska was out of the question because I was broke and my parents would not let me come back. We would have to get married. Now Alex really was stuck with me. I had ruined his life forever.

The next day Mother called my parents and asked them to give written permission for me to marry Alex because without it, the marriage could not take place, because according to the law I was still a child and would be for some time. If I didn't marry Alex she was putting me out on the street because things weren't working out. Either way, I had to get out of her house.

A few days later their letter arrived, sending me into the bonds of matrimony with a man they despised, all framed as looking out for my well-being. They could not afford the airfare to bring me home, they said to Mother and Daddy. Golly, it would be better for me to go ahead and marry than to be out on my own, especially to such a bright young man from such a wonderful Christian family. They included a small check to help with the expense.

I did not know what else to do. I both loved and feared Alex, wanted to be with him and wanted to flee. I did not understand that he had two personality disorders, and I could not know that over time he would become increasingly violent. At least he wasn't a drunk, I reasoned. Nor did he have guns. He'd likely get a decent job and work it once he graduated. I could finish school, take summer classes, maybe graduate early and find a job. Maybe someday down the road I could become a beautician and make good tips.

We went to see the pastor at the Pentecostal church Alex's family attended, so we could plan the wedding. Pastor Johnson seemed kind and was soft spoken, a silver haired man who had already retired and then come back to serve the little church in his retirement. He quickly agreed to help us with the unexpected wedding. Mother sewed a simple little wedding dress from a length of white silk that Mike had brought home for me when I was thirteen and he returned from Viet Nam. I had kept that silk for a future wedding that I thought might take place in my twenties or thirties. It was smooth and butter soft, gorgeous, embossed with rice fronds.

Six weeks after I arrived in New Mexico we were married. When I told Pastor Johnson months later in his office, crying and shaking uncontrollably, that I was terrified, that my father strangled me and I thought I was going to die, that my sisters were in danger and I had nightmares all the time because I couldn't take care of them, that I was lonely and couldn't sleep and my stomach hurt and I felt like I was married to Dr. Jekyll and Mr. Hyde, when I said I didn't know what to do and needed help, Pastor Johnson patted my hand and said everything was going to be all right now that I was part of a good Christian family. He knew nothing about trauma.

So it was that I found myself in the third set of circumstances, married and a junior in high school, going to church twice on Sundays and once in the middle of the week, riddled with anxiety and awash in post-traumatic stress. Teachers at school got in the habit of staring at my belly because they couldn't think of any reason a sixteen year old kid's parents would let her get married other than a baby.

Once married we moved into a cockroach infested camp trailer on the edge of town where rent was cheap. I started cleaning house for Pastor and Mrs. Johnson so we could buy groceries. Alex got a part time job in the engineering department on campus. Every Sunday afternoon we went to Mother's house and sat and ate Magdalenas from the Mexican bakery while she smoked and complained about everything she could think of. I looked past her, fixing my eyes on the little placard that sat on the bookcase beside her chair. It said "JOY: Jesus first, Others second, Yourself last."

CHAPTER FIVE

Mothers and Daughters

DESPITE THE TEACHERS staring at my belly every day, it remained the same size and continued to ache from all the stress. It was weird being married in high school. I was out for a few days with the flu in April so when I returned to school I wrote a sick note from myself excusing myself. The school didn't know what to do with that so the guidance counselor had a word with me, but in the end he had to accept that I was my own mother in the sick note department.

    I also learned that if I would take a full load of summer classes and a couple of correspondence courses from somewhere in Oklahoma I could graduate at the end of August, a year early. So I signed up for all of it plus another part time job at a hole in the wall diner where I made hamburgers, five for a dollar, and mopped the floor. When I closed up in the evenings I took the pail of food scraps out back to feed the owner's chickens. His name was Chuck and his daughter, Liz was one of my best friends. She was a year behind me in school. Liz said I could ride her Welsh pony, Dinky, any time I wanted. Dinky lived with the chickens behind the diner and was just my size. I would saddle him up and off we'd go along the irrigation canals past farms and pecan orchards. He was an ornery little bugger who liked to buck and bite, which is why Liz wanted someone else to ride him, but mostly we got along just fine. Dinky and Liz were the bright spots in my days. Sometimes Alex's sister Linda, Liz, and I went swimming at the university pool where we played Marco Polo and shared secrets the way girls do. At the end of summer, I graduated without fanfare.

Soon I landed a better job at the local fabric store, which was intoxicating with possibilities. Between my Kenmore sewing machine (a wedding gift from Mother), ten percent employee discount, and the markdown table, I could make myself a new outfit for two bucks. We moved from the cockroach trailer to a concrete block apartment on campus, which seemed palatial in contrast. Alex had a desk job at the campus computer center working the night shift, plus a full load of classes during the day, so he was pretty much gone all the time, or asleep.

I could not afford to call my mother very often but we wrote letters. I grieved non-stop over my sisters, not knowing what was really happening. When Alex graduated we moved to Illinois for a year for his first job out of school. We returned to New Mexico after that, to Santa Fe, where Alex started a new job. I found work at Household Finance as a clerk typist.

We hadn't been in Santa Fe very long when my sister Julie, Jeanine's twin, called. She was in Colorado, she said, on summer vacation with one of her friends' family in their RV. They would be passing through New Mexico on their way to Texas. Could they drop her off to visit with Alex and me, she asked, and then on their way back to Alaska they would pick her up.

When Julie arrived for the visit I was ecstatic to see her again. She and Jeanine had just finished seventh grade. We spent hours talking, during which time Julie filled me in on the utter chaos of their lives, how they had bounced around to different houses and back and forth from Alaska to Idaho. She told me how she was now the target for our father's rage. I couldn't bear the thought of her returning to him as she described the fights, the gun, the failure of our mother to protect her. I begged Alex to allow Julie to stay with us permanently, and when he grudgingly gave permission, I called Mom to let her know that we wanted Julie to stay. She was all too happy to comply.

So it was that Julie came to live with us when she was twelve and I was nineteen. Like all our siblings and myself, Julie carried deep trauma from our family. I was relieved beyond telling to know that she was away from our parents, especially our father. Jeanine was still with them but had friends at the Baptist Church who I thought could help when she needed to escape. It meant the world to me to be able to look after Julie again, sewing a new wardrobe for her, styling her hair and bringing her to church. I enrolled her in the eighth grade. Soon Julie was a straight A student with a posse of friends. We loved goofing off together.

At that point I started begging Alex to allow us to legally adopt her. I wanted Julie to know that she belonged with me, that I wanted her, that she could finally breathe and know that her home was secure. Alex very reluctantly went along with the plan. But the day we prepared to go to the final meeting with the judge in which we would complete the adoption, Alex flew into a rage.

There had been tension brewing between Julie and Alex almost from the first week, with frequent disputes in which I wanted to side with Julie but was told by our fundamentalist church and Alex that I must submit to my husband in all things. Parenting a teen can be tough for anyone, but for us there were many layers of problems related to radically different cultures between Alex's family and ours. We were terribly young—I was still a teenager myself. But by far the biggest problem was Alex, who grew more and more resentful and jealous of the deep bond between Julie and me, which he did not understand. I had been Julie's mama until I left home. We shared the kind of closeness that people do who have been through war together. Alex's manner with Julie was exactly like Mother's way with her entire family—intrusive, negative, and harsh. His jealousy of Julie was frighteningly similar to our father's jealousy of all five of us kids, because he wanted Mom's undivided attention.

We postponed the meeting with the judge, trying to figure out what to do. Alex shouted "the deal is off!" during a fight, yelling that we would not adopt Julie and she could not stay with us anymore. So instead of adopting her Alex bought her a one way ticket back to Alaska. I was crushed.

Not long afterward I learned that I was pregnant. I continued to grieve over Julie and fear for her safety, but looked forward eagerly to having a child of my own.

I rode a Kawasaki 110 dirt bike to work at the time because the gas and insurance were cheaper than a car. Because of its bright green color and the noise it made when I gunned it, I named it The Green Hornet. Having grown up as I did with no common-sense guidance from adults, it only gradually dawned on me that pregnancy and motorcycles might not be the best mix. I was six months along when a pack of stray dogs, of which there were many in Santa Fe, came after me on the bike. I was on a gravel road in a hilly area. With no previous experience with stunt riding but ample adrenalin I opened the throttle full bore, popped a wheelie, went off road down an arroyo then flew back up again clearing the air by a good two feet, landed back on the road, spun a 360, then miraculously stalled out in an upright position. This was more than the dogs could take so they ran off. That day I sold my dirt bike to my boss, who was looking for cheap transportation. Mr. Hernandez was six foot two and looked like a giant grasshopper buzzing down the street, but he loved The Green Hornet, which pleased me.

When Anna was born three months later, she enchanted me with her large, luminous eyes and a head full of thick, dark hair. She was a cheerful, contented, elfin baby. Anna's future engineer tendencies began to show up when she was eight months old and would not go to sleep until her blanket was perfectly parallel with the edge of the crib. She began to walk long before she had any teeth, the first of which came in at fourteen months. She organized her toys according to size and color when she was eighteen months old. By age two Anna had a lot to say, including the time I told her to get away from the electric outlet to which she replied, "Don't worry about it with your mouth."

I wanted with all my might to be the mother for her that I never had. So I went to the library and checked out dozens of instruction manuals on parenting and child development. Some of the other women at church were also having babies. We helped each other through colic, mastitis, and all manner of new mother dilemmas. A few of them were Jesus People hippies who delivered their own babies at home in cabins they built with their own hands, and breast fed those babies until they were in kindergarten, which I thought was outlandish, but I never said so. Their funky Pippy Longstocking houses smelled like patchouli and they didn't believe in deodorant. I loved them with all my heart. There was a freedom of spirit about them that I longed for but did not have. Even though our church taught wives to submit to husbands in all things, these chicks had a mind of their own. In fact, I was pretty sure their husbands were scared of them. We got together every week to talk about God and pray. We drank a lot of herbal tea that they made from scratch. I never asked what was in it, but it tasted like stewed weeds.

My very best friend, Debbie, didn't have kids. She was tiny, maybe a hundred pounds, and married to a burly man who forced her to wear heavy makeup and dress like a hooker at night. He liked to tie her up with strips of old inner tubes and do unspeakable things to her. She played the violin at church where she wore long dresses that covered the damage. No one knew what went on at their house except me. I cried with relief when she divorced him years later. The church said she had lost her salvation but I was pretty sure she found it.

Anna was talking in full paragraphs when Julie reappeared. Our parents had announced that they were moving to Missouri and the twins had to find their own place to live. Some people from the Baptist Church had taken Jeanine in, but Julie had nowhere to go. Just as they had done with Mike, Jeff, and me when we were still children, they drove the twins out to find their own way in the world at age fourteen. Our father finally got what he always wanted, to have Mom all to himself.

Once again, I was overjoyed to have Julie with us so I could look after her. But the old dynamic started immediately, with tension, fights, and Alex's unpredictable rage. A few days after she arrived, Julie, Anna, and I were in the parking lot of our apartment complex, about to go to the mall. Alex rushed out of the house, demanding to know where we were going. I said that I was taking Julie shopping.

"What *kind* of shopping?" he shouted. I winced because the next door neighbors were in their front yard and could hear every word.

"Underwear," I whispered. "She needs new underwear."

"Give me those keys!" he spat through clenched teeth. "You two can't be trusted together on your own. I'll take her." Julie blushed furiously and said no, she would not go with him.

Chapter Five: Mothers and Daughters

When I disagreed and said Julie needed privacy for this kind of shopping, Alex went into a tirade, shouting about what we were and were not allowed to do, especially with his hard-earned money, and what the hell did we think we were doing, sneaking off without his permission. "Either I go and make the decisions or you're not going!" Alex screamed, face red, veins bulging, tearing the keys from my hand. Frightened, Anna began to cry.

Our neighbors, a young couple who were planting flowers in the little front yard of their apartment, stared at us, appalled. Julie and I fled back into our apartment with Anna, humiliated, Anna wailing at the top of her lungs. I would have to go with Alex later, without Julie, to get the underwear. He would throw some kind of fit about that, interpreting it as defiance on my part, but it had to be done.

This was the kind of scene we had several times per week, sometimes in front of other people, but mostly at home. Meanwhile at the church Alex served as treasurer, where the pastor and everyone else thought he was such a fine, responsible young man with a good head on his shoulders when it came to managing the church's money and wasn't it wonderful it was that he provided a godly home for his wife's kid sister.

I was near a breaking point, begging Alex for us to get help, when he finally agreed we could get some counseling. But it would be from our pastor, not some money-grubbing shrink, he said, glaring. Alex's wild outbursts were becoming more and more frightening because he had taken to throwing plates, books, whatever was at hand, at the wall to emphasize his point when he raged. I was terrified he would hurt Anna. We left Anna with Julie, and headed to the church.

Alex and I entered Pastor Braddock's office, with its walls lined with Bible commentaries and other books. There were golf clubs in the corner. He gestured for us to sit in the chairs in front of his desk, while he leaned back in his swivel office chair, rocking slightly, belly pressing tightly against the buttons of his shirt, tie loosened around his thick neck. His office smelled like pepperoni pizza.

"What's on your mind, young lady?" Pastor Braddock asked, literally looking down his nose at me from his position in the chair. As I began to describe the fights, the uncertainty, Alex's rage, and my fear, he cut me off. "Listen, young lady," he scolded, "Men need respect from their wives more than anything, and when they don't get it they naturally feel angry and lash out. It's your job to keep Alex from having to be angry with you, Julie, and Anna. The way to do that is to be more submissive and respectful toward your husband. You need to repent of your pride and rebellion." Turning toward Alex he said, "Wow, all alone with three females. No wonder you're having a tough time! Hey buddy, you need to continue to keep a firm hand, especially with your wife. You are the head of the house in the divine chain of command. It is God's will for every person living in your house and sitting at your table, to respect and obey you at all times."

When Julie was sixteen and Anna was two, I became pregnant again, followed by months of nausea and anemia. I didn't have knowledge of, or language for post-traumatic stress with triggers, flashbacks, anxiety, shame, and nightmares, but that is what Julie and I were both experiencing because of the constant tension, threats, and fights. We walked on eggshells the way we always had to do with our father. We didn't have fist holes in the walls yet, but every time Alex threw or broke something it was a message that one of us would be next. I began to have panic attacks. I developed colitis because the tension in our home was unbearable. Julie begged to stay with the friend from school again, this time for a few weeks, and Alex said she could go. She was in the final months of her junior year in high school. She and I privately agreed that at the end of the school year she would need to go back to Alaska, for her own safety, and because I couldn't take the stress anymore. I felt deep shame at having failed her yet again, but I was unable to stop Alex's terrifying actions.

By then our brother Jeff had returned to Alaska. He had joined a Christian commune called Maranatha Fellowship which had been started by some former leaders of Campus Crusade for Christ. It was patriarchal and authoritarian, but that was just the way things were, inside and outside the church. Jeff said that Julie could go back to Alaska and live in Maranatha's large communal house which they called the Big House. I was devastated to see her go, but glad for the fights between Alex and Julie to stop. I hoped they would be kind to her at the Big House.

A couple of months after Julie left, Kat was born. A team of student nurses came in to observe the delivery since I was one of the first women to use the new birthing center at St. Vincent's. They stood around me as I hollered and pushed, telling me what a great job I was doing. I did not feel great. What I felt was that my body had been taken over by an alien which was now forcing its way into the world at my expense. But between contractions I imagined myself as a quarterback running the ball down the field as the student nurses cheered me on. Dr. Rodriguez delivered Kat and immediately put her into my arms while he finished his work. I laughed and cried in wonder. She looked like a chili cheese dog with her red hair and flushed, vernix covered skin. She looked exactly like a newborn version of my mother. After they bathed her the nurse stuck a tiny pink bow in Kat's hair with a dab of lubricant jelly. My cheerleaders clapped and cried.

When Kat was eleven months old, we moved to a suburb of Denver where Alex started a consulting job with a new firm, one that would require us to relocate every 1-3 years. My dream of settling down in one place to raise our children so they wouldn't have to be uprooted over and over like I had, seemed more unlikely than ever. I sorely grieved the loss of my fearless hippie friends and their dubious tea, and Debbie, who as of yet had not left her violent spouse.

Though the constant fights with Alex diminished after Julie left, providing a measure of peace, the change was short lived. Soon his control, suspicion, and unpredictable rage were back, dominating our lives. It was a relief every morning when he went to work. I kept the house clean and made dinner so that it was ready when he came home every night, and did many other things to try to avoid making him mad. But there really was no way to know when he would explode. It would be several more years before I learned that there is a name for the pattern I experienced: the cycle of violence, and even more years after that before I could imagine doing anything to stop it.

It was intimidating to live in a city with six lane highways and houses as far as the eye could see. But the mountains were a comfort.

In time we settled in at Calvary Temple, a large, non-denominational, evangelical church. Like the city itself, the church seemed overwhelmingly huge with six thousand people in worship on Sundays. The lobby of the building looked like a fancy hotel. The eleven o'clock worship service was televised. A large, professional staff managed the many programs and departments, including the nursery, and the senior pastor ruled over it all like a benevolent dictator. Though intimidated by everything about the massive church, before long I joined the choir and in time learned to sing the alto part in Handel's *Messiah*, which I had never heard of before that, and I began to make a few friends. Since we only had one car which Alex drove to work, and the church was a forty-five minute drive from our house, choir practice was the one midweek event I could attend. One day a week Alex let me have the car and gave me money to do the grocery shopping, and he took the bus to work, complaining bitterly about how slow it was. When he came home those nights, the first thing I had to do was give him the change from grocery shopping, along with the receipts, which he scrutinized for every penny I spent and every item I bought. If even a nickel was unaccounted for, or I had bought anything he thought unnecessary, there was hell to pay.

We had been in Denver for a year when the turning point came. It was as unlikely as the angel Gabriel showing up to tell a pimple faced kid that she was going to be the mother of God, and it happened at the dentist's office.

CHAPTER SIX

The Dentist

DR. WOLFSTEIN STARED INTO MY MOUTH in horror. Because we lacked dental care along with everything else, all my siblings and I had massive dental problems by the time we were old enough to drive. Everything from cavities in our front teeth, to missing bottom molars that then allowed all the other teeth to wander afield, to gum issues, too many teeth for a small mouth, bone loss, and oh so much more. The dentist found his voice and said, "You need several extractions, four crowns, many fillings, and braces for three years. If we do all of that we can save your teeth. Otherwise you'll need dentures within five years." I asked how much it would cost. The office manager crunched the numbers and handed me a piece of paper because the amount was too much to say out loud. Between the dentist and orthodontist it would cost more than a new car. But they said they could give me an interest free payment plan that would work with my budget. They assumed I had a budget, that I could make decisions about spending, like other adults. "It is always better to keep your teeth if you can," the dentist said. I looked deep into his eyes to see if he was a money-grubbing liar, but decided he was okay. I said I needed to think about it and get back to them, but in my heart I knew that whatever was cheapest would be the "choice" Alex made for me. The thought of making my own decision to spend that kind of money was outrageous.

When I went home I looked in the mirror. How would I look if the dentist and orthodontist had their way with my sorry teeth? That got me to thinking about how my life had been before I met Alex and before I got kicked out, how I was a straight A student at the top of my class, had begun to learn to play a few chords on my cheap Sears and Roebuck guitar, and loved to draw and paint. Best of all was my life at the rink, hanging out with buddies, speed skating, feeling like I was somebody. Despite Dad and all the violence, at least back then I was a self. Now after eight years of marriage to a money obsessed, abusive man with what I now know were two personality disorders, after multiple geographic moves with no say in the matter and the loss of friends each time, after being unable to look after the twins until they were grown, I felt lost. I adored mothering Anna and Kat, but with Alex's control, demands, and anger I felt suffocated. Now I needed major dental work and knew that unlike normal people in this situation I would yet again be pressured to give up what I needed because it would save money. The constant lack of access to funds for necessary things like medical care, milk for the kids, and more, might have been understandable if we were poor. But we were middle class and debt free. Alex was a professional man with a decent salary. Withholding money was one of the ways he controlled me.

But my problem wasn't really about money. It was about power. It was about patriarchal, evangelical, fundamentalist religion in which Alex demanded that I ask his permission for every decision, from buying groceries to the smallest detail of personal care. As a woman I was under my husband's authority, and according to that theology I could not be trusted to make a wise decision about a single thing. We had no family budget. All the money belonged to Alex. All the decisions were his. After the experience in Pastor Braddock's office I gave up on asking for help from pastors or the church, for what my life had become. I felt subhuman, that I was no longer me, that I had become invisible and mute, and for what? Nothing I did made any difference in Alex's rage and mood swings.

Turning away from the mirror I made a decision.

The next day I called the dentist and said I wanted the payment plan and stated the paltry amount that I thought I could manage each month. It would take me a very long time to pay for my dental work but I could babysit and sew for people, which would cover a fair amount. Insurance would pay a tiny portion. It would take all the courage I could muster to face the atomic rage I knew would explode from Alex the minute I told him I needed extensive dental work and that we were going to budget for part of it from money that he earned. I would have to tell him that I already chose the more expensive option of treatment. But I had already made the series of appointments and I absolutely was not going to change them, no matter what he said.

For the first time in our marriage I drew a line in the sand.

This was the beginning of my slow process of regaining agency, as if I had been in a psychological, emotional, and spiritual coma and awakened. Now it was time to learn to think, walk, speak, and feed myself all over again. It was terrifying. And exhausting. I was twenty-six years old.

After weathering the rage that followed the dental announcement, I started intentionally doing small things that would help me pick up where I left off when I was fifteen so I could become me again. None of these things were earth shaking or immoral. Looking back, it is astounding how anxious and guilty each step forward made me feel. For example, I created a little art studio in the basement where I used books from the library to learn how to paint with oils. I bought the art supplies with money I earned from babysitting the neighbor's children. I felt ashamed and selfish for painting, for doing something "useless" just because it gave me joy. But it felt so good I did it anyway. Then I took my old skates to the bike trail at the park. It wasn't a third space like the rink had been, but the exercise felt great. Anna rode along on her little bike with training wheels and I pushed Kat in the stroller, gliding along the tree lined path. I gradually took back control over how I dressed and how I styled my hair. I stopped asking permission for every move I made as if I were a five-year old child. Instead of giving Alex the money I earned babysitting and sewing, which is what I did previously, I started saving it so that I had my own money for buying fabric or getting a cup of coffee on grocery shopping day, and didn't have to account for every dime. Each little advance into healthy adulthood made me feel like the whore of Babylon, but I was on a roll. I weathered the conflicts and pressed on with braces and headgear, roller skates, paint, and two preschool kids.

Chapter Six: The Dentist

After a year of making these self-care decisions I attended a conference with Alex that was sponsored by his employer. Spouses always went because the annual meetings were held at resorts with fancy hotels, pools, and shopping. Not one person recognized me, I looked so different from the previous year. At the banquet table that night Alex's boss and his wife said they thought Alex had divorced and that I was his beautiful new bride. I laughed and took Alex's hand, but he scowled and pulled away. That night in our room we had a huge fight because he said I was too attractive now, and his colleagues, all men, were looking at me. That experience was the beginning of what became Alex's increasing jealousy and paranoia that I would leave him because I was becoming too independent.

Then I hit the motherlode. I discovered that I could take college classes from Indiana University through the mail. The program had been designed for incarcerated persons, but now and then they let other people in, too. From the time I graduated high school I longed to go to college but each time I brought it up Alex said I was not allowed to go to school or work outside the home. It would cost too much money for tuition and childcare. Besides, we would probably be moving again which would disrupt my program, he said, and then I would have to pay exorbitant out of state tuition if I enrolled in a new school wherever we moved.

The fundamentalist church also said I must stay home but for different reasons. Working women were the bane of society, causing the destruction of God's ordained order in marriage and home, leading to mayhem and all manner of wickedness, everything from homosexuality to abortion. Godly women were submissive, happy wives and mothers who did not leave the home to work for money. They were thrifty and knew how to stretch a dollar, and never wasted a penny of their husbands' hard earned income.

Through the prison program I saw a way that I could go to college and possibly someday earn a degree no matter where we lived or how many times we moved, while I was still a godly woman who stayed home. I could take one class at a time so it wouldn't be too expensive, and I could pay for it with money I squirreled away from babysitting and sewing for people. I signed up, filled with guilty joy. In due time my course packet arrived in the mail. The class was Geography of North America. I tore the envelope open, ecstatic, burying my face in a textbook, inhaling its fragrance.

My brain felt alive in ways it hadn't since I was fifteen. When it came time to take the final exam I went to the local high school where it had been sent so that the office staff could proctor it. As I entered the building and headed for the office a teacher stopped me and demanded to see my hall pass. I smiled through extensive braces and explained that I was twenty-seven and taking a college course for which the exam was being proctored at the school office. He stared at my pubescent looking self suspiciously but finally let me go.

I aced the exam.

CHAPTER SEVEN

The Principal

THE JOURNEY OF BECOMING HUMAN AGAIN held yet another surprise. I began to have urges to invite neighbors over to study the Bible, and pray, and talk about life. I was uninterested in the women's groups at church, even if I'd had a car to get there. They seemed to care more about raising money for projects than they did about Jesus. I doubted they would know what to do with a woman who is starting to have a lot of questions about God and church that godly women don't ask. What I wanted was something I could sink my teeth into spiritually, something challenging and real. I also longed for the community of my former hippie friends. Between my kids, other kids I babysat, the prison class, and cleaning house I didn't have time to act upon these urges. But they did not go away. They were a fire kindled in my belly that would take years for me to understand.

Over the next two years we moved twice, first to Lincoln, Nebraska, then Toledo, Ohio. In 1981 Anna started first grade in Toledo then skipped to second because she already knew everything from first grade. She had been reading for two years. The new grade didn't help much at all but the school couldn't think of anything else to do with her. Kat, who was three, could easily read and do all of Anna's second grade homework. She was beginning to play the piano by ear with melody and chords. She loved to sit on the floor by the stereo listening to music, while she drew pictures of her Sesame Street fave, Don Music.

I thought the kids were early learners because they watched Sesame Street and because I had been reading to them daily since they were born. I knew nothing about gifted children. Decades later I learned that Anna was actually a twice-exceptional child, both gifted and challenged by Asperger's Syndrome. The lightbulb came on as to their giftedness when a professor for one of the correspondence courses assigned an essay about gifted kids in public schools. As I read it I recognized with a shock that it was describing my children and Anna's school. Anna had just gotten in trouble for throwing a book across the classroom and shouting that the book was stupid, school was stupid, and the teacher was an onion, which was the worst insult she could think of.

I got called to the principal's office when that happened. She had the longest fingernails I had ever seen. It was hard to keep my eyes on her face. Anna told me the principal grew them out so she could use them to check kids for head lice. I told the principal about Kat being able to do Anna's second grade homework and Anna hating school because it was so boring. Thanks to the recent essay I had read, I had learned there was something called a Country Day School that would be ideal for Anna but, I said, it was more expensive than college so that was out. Home schooling her was illegal because I didn't have a college degree or teaching certificate, which was required in the State of Ohio for home schooling parents at that time. I asked the principal if there was some kind of enrichment program for kids like mine. She told me the school district couldn't afford an enrichment program and if I wanted one I would have to create it and run it myself. I said, "You mean if I design a program for your school, you'll let me run it?" She nodded but said, "You'll have to do it as a volunteer. I can't pay you." I said, "I'll be back soon."

I returned to her office a week later with a draft of an enrichment program. Some books in the library helped me cook up a plan. We could meet once a week for an hour, and the class could be for first through third grade. It would be an interdisciplinary, immersive enrichment program with a thematic approach: food. The students would practice solving real life problems around the production, preparation, and distribution of food. We would draw from community resources, have guests, go on a field trip or two if I could figure out how to get the school to back it. In the process kids would be able to indulge themselves to their heart's content in higher level math, reading, and science, and have plenty of fun with art and music, to boot. The whole thing was a long shot but I thought what the heck, let's give it a try.

The Principal was stunned to see me back. She did not think I would return, much less with a program. She reviewed my handwritten plan of action on 8.5 x 11 notebook paper, eyes brimming with defeat, lethal nails pressed to one side of her face. It was time for her to keep her end of the bargain, including buying twenty-one copies of *Good for Me*, the book I chose as our text. To her credit, she kept her word. We launched. We had a blast. I couldn't remember when I'd had so much fun. The Principal seemed relieved that I was out of her hair.

Meanwhile I stepped up extra learning opportunities for my girls to help their busy little brains heave a sigh of relief. I took them to kids' programs at the Toledo Museum of Art. They went to every children's event at the public library, and Miss Mary the children's librarian became our new BFF. We went to rock and mineral shows run by nerds. If it was cheap or free, we were there. I gave Anna broken clocks, dead small appliances, and a screwdriver so she could dismantle them and play with the guts. We got a little book, *Things to Make and Do*, that had directions for dozens of science experiments, art projects, musical instruments to build for yourself, and everything else to spark imagination. I found a piano teacher for Kat, who though missing one finger, was a passable teacher. Anna built a large, elaborate doll house from cardboard boxes, Styrofoam packing material, scraps of fabric and egg cartons. She populated it with a nightmarish family of cicada husks. There were massive bugs lying on their backs in all the beds, their horrible legs curled up in repose. Others sat at table like gargoyles, their claws holding fake food the dreadful mother prepared at her cardboard stove.

As the semester wound down at the elementary school I heard many complaints from the enrichment kids about not being allowed to go outdoors for recess. Anna confirmed this was the case. They were like miniature prisoners, she said grimly, locked within their own school. When I asked other parents about it, they said there was a policy preventing children from going outdoors during the school day.

The principal told me the same thing when I asked her. No one could tell me the reason for the asinine policy. By then I had learned about the Suffragettes in my history class for criminals. Inspired, I started a petition among the parents, going door to door, which I then took to the principal to collectively demand a policy change. Horrified and nervous lest I call the superintendent, she promised to see what she could do if we would stand down.

Then she abruptly asked, "Don't you paint? Some of the pupils said you're an artist." I said I was a total beginner with no training and cheap tools, nonetheless I could show her my paltry efforts if she liked. She said, "I would like to buy one. Tomorrow." It occurred to me that she was flattering me so I'd keep the petition on the down low instead of sending it to the superintendent, or worse, the paper. But I liked the idea of cold cash. The principal kept her word, paying fifty bucks for a small snowscape featuring a trapper's cabin, a scene conjured from memories of Alaska. I pocketed the filthy lucre from this exchange even though there were cheap brush hairs stuck in the paint.

Before I could give the principal any more migraines or see the petition turn into a playground full of kids, Alex came home from work and announced that we were moving to Canada. Unlike previous moves, I was ready to hit the road. Life in Toledo had been a complicated mix of mothering people with baby teeth who had better instincts for math than I ever would, trying to cope with Alex, and fighting off anxiety by working myself to death: the enrichment program, the US History course, painting landscapes on the front porch, taking a class in basic auto maintenance so I could tune our 1976 Ford Fairmont, and mowing the grass in our neighborhood park when a bond didn't pass and the park turned into a jungle. I couldn't skate anymore because there wasn't anywhere close by to do it. But push mowing the park was a pretty good way to burn the adrenalin off.

CHAPTER EIGHT

O Canada

WE ARRIVED IN LONDON, ONTARIO on Valentine's Day, very fitting in that I immediately fell in love with the place. I was delighted with everything about it, from Storybook Gardens to chip trucks selling poutine—the uniquely Canadian cholesterol laden snack with heaps of fresh cut French fries smothered with brown gravy and mozzarella cheese. We joined a large Pentecostal church close enough to walk to. The elementary school was just behind our house.

I offered to set up an enrichment program at the elementary school similar to the one I had developed in Toledo, smiling with my newly renovated pearly whites. The school administration was thrilled. This time I networked with faculty at the University of Western Ontario and local small business owners to develop several interdisciplinary, thematic programs focusing on robotics, fairy tales, and folk art. A team of parent volunteers from the school joined in to help. Somehow I became their leader. The best moment was when a nine year old boy, Ivan, said after making a puppet on my Kenmore sewing machine, "My entire life I have wanted to sew. All my dreams have come true."

My increasingly volatile marriage was like a terrible version of the nursery rhyme about the little girl with the little curl in the middle of her forehead. When Alex wasn't raging the contrast felt good, but when he was it was horrid. The problem was, the more alive I became, the more inner freedom I experienced, the more I came home to myself and spoke up for what I wanted and believed, the more frequent, intense, and long-lasting the horrid part was. Horrid meant Alex's rage, suspicion, doubling down on control, jealousy of my friends, demanding to know who I talked to every day and the content of those conversations, and hidden bruises on my body. I still had not learned about the battering cycle, or that battering can be any combination of emotional, psychological, spiritual, physical, and sexual violence. I had not heard of gas-lighting and other mind games that were part of my daily life. Nor had I ever heard anyone in the church speak from a pulpit to denounce these patterns of violence as sin. What little I heard was from male clergy like Pastor Braddock, who told women to submit to anything their husbands dish out because in being meek the battered partner might lead the offender to salvation.

My not-knowing was about to radically change.

It started when Anna came home with a letter to parents from her teacher. A film was going to be shown in class that would help protect our children from predators. Parents had to sign the form attached to the letter to give their children permission to see the film and could preview the film one evening the following week. On the appointed day I went to see it. The vignette was simple and age appropriate for children, with the abuse implied rather than explicit. An older man—a neighbor—groomed a child and then molested her. As I walked home another mom asked if I was going to allow my daughter to see the film. I heard myself tell her in a rush of words that I had been that little girl, that the film was my story, while my brain blew a gasket. I was grateful that it was dark as a huge wave of shame swallowed me. I had just told a perfect stranger one of the most painful secrets of my life. She looked at me, shocked, and said nothing. I hurried into my house where I shut the door and leaned against it as wave after wave of shame engulfed me. I thought I was going to be sick.

For years I had pushed memories of old man Dodson to the back of my mind, along with having narrowly escaped the porn deacon when I was thirteen. I tried not to think about being strangled by my father, and every other act of terrorism, bullying, sexual abuse, and other forms of violence from my childhood, only a few of which I have described in this book.

I was clueless as to the way toxic shame permeated every aspect of my life. I did not know how shame fueled the anxiety that riddled my days. It would still be several more years before I learned that shame was behind every single act of agreeing to my own dehumanization and subjugation throughout my life, as if that was all I deserved, especially from my spouse and the church. That night was the beginning of waking up to how trauma shaped me body, mind, and soul. My long, slow recovery began the day I made my own decision about the dentist, followed by a hundred other choices to get my life back. But I moved light years ahead when I finally named to another person, however awkwardly, some of the sexual abuse that I experienced as a child. By awakening to the trauma I began a journey that would eventually lead to incredible healing and abundant life.

The other thing I did not realize until decades later looking back, was that in every loving act of parenting my daughters—reading to them, sewing for them, teaching them to roller skate, providing dental care, giving them materials to build a godawful dollhouse full of bugs, and doing the best I could to protect them from Alex—I reparented the traumatized child within myself. In fiercely protecting my daughters from information and experiences that were too much for a child to bear, I gave the little girl within me permission to rest. She didn't have to carry the burden of adulthood anymore. That child reveled in a thousand ordinary things that my kids were able to take for granted.

Our large Pentecostal church was slightly more progressive than any of the others we attended before moving to Canada. By this I mean there were even two women pastors on staff who were responsible for children's and women's ministries. Both Alex and I joined the choir, where I quickly made friends with a handful of women. I was happier than I had ever been since marrying Alex, because I was functioning as an adult and increasingly making my own decisions, and I loved my new friends and our new life in London.

We had been in Ontario for just a few months when Alex exploded about the checkbook not balancing. We were off by fifty-seven cents in comparison to the bank statement, and he demanded to know what I had done with that money. He then insisted that we both go to the bank to compare our checkbook balance with the bank's. Embarrassed beyond words at his hysteria over the missing change, I watched the bank clerk calmly demonstrate to Alex where the mistake was in how Alex balanced the checkbook. The moment we got in the car he slammed the steering wheel, swearing and screaming. The next day I told him we absolutely had to get some counseling because I couldn't take all the stress, and his anger was very bad for our children. We could go to the church for it, I said. Maybe the senior Pastor would see us, I added. And because we were members of the church the counseling sessions wouldn't cost anything, unlike seeing a therapist. He grudgingly agreed to go to one session.

That is where I met Betty. In addition to being the pastor over women's ministries, Betty was the pastoral counselor for the church. Our appointment with her was at six in the evening, on a cold, miserable day. She met us at the church door, unlocking it so we could come in. After we settled into chairs in her small office, Betty asked us why we had come to see her. She turned to me and said, "Elaine, why don't you tell me first, and then Alex can tell me the situation from his perspective." I chose my words carefully, having learned over the years that in all likelihood I would be blamed for Alex's behavior and moods. I deliberately understated the stress and anxiety I felt over Alex's unpredictable rage, his control, and abuse, framing it as a byproduct of his work stress. When it was Alex's turn to speak he scowled, blamed me for being too independent now and not respecting him the way I used to, which caused all the fights. He talked and talked, much more than I expected he would. I kept my eyes on his face the whole time he talked, which is what for many years he had demanded I do as a sign of respect in his presence.

When he was finished, I looked at Betty, exhausted. Her eyes were fathomless, her face composed. After a moment she said in a gentle but firm voice, "Alex, you need long term therapy." I don't remember a word she said after that. All I can remember is that she looked into my eyes with compassion, with knowing, and I felt seen, heard, and believed. For the first time in the fourteen years of our marriage, I felt that someone in the church who had official authority, did not want me to sit down and shut up, and could see what was really going on.

Alex threw another fit in the car on the way home, saying that he would never go to therapy with Betty or anyone else when I was the problem. I barely heard anything he said because I kept reliving the moment when I knew Betty saw my heart and believed me. I wanted to weep with relief.

A few weeks letter Betty called to invite me to come to a "Bible study and prayer group for special ladies" that was by invitation only. I was very happy to hear from her, but did not want to go to the group because I was tired of trying to fit into a mold for godly women. But in time, after having coffee with me a few times, Betty prevailed and I agreed to go.

Betty's teaching was deeper and more powerful than any preaching or teaching I had ever experienced. She was completely different from any church lady I ever met. Although she loved her husband and always treated him with respect, she was her own full-orbed person. I had never met anyone with her depth of wisdom.

Betty started inviting me to go with her on pastoral care visits, and to shadow her as she planned retreats and carried out other leadership tasks. Her primary areas of responsibility in the church were women's ministry, discipleship formation and pastoral care and counseling. After a year Betty stunned me when she asked me to take over leadership of the women's group. I resisted at first, feeling inept and unqualified. But she kept at it until I caved. She wouldn't attend, she said, but she was there any time I wanted to talk about what was happening, or if I needed help thinking things through. My buddy Mary Ann helped, making coffee, organizing hospitality and giving me courage.

At first the group dwindled down to a handful because Betty no longer led it and most of them were Betty groupies. I was the extremely nervous new kid on the block. But soon there were forty or so women from all over the city, and because of the University of Western Ontario where some of the women's spouses worked, some were even from other parts of the world including China, India, Australia, and South Africa. Almost none of the new women were from the church. I'm not even sure how some of them heard about the group. We met on Tuesday mornings for two and a half hours. Mary Ann and I named the group Dayspring to suggest a new day is possible for anyone. The meetings began with a few songs accompanied by my guitar. Then I would teach from the Bible for a half hour. The women then gathered into small groups to discuss reflection questions I gave them based on the teaching. They prayed for each other and left, collecting their kids from the nursery. In between times we stayed in touch and encouraged each other in practical ways, helping out when there was sickness or stress. The arc of the teaching for the year was what it means to follow Jesus.

Toward the end of that year five of the women came and asked me to baptize them. They said they wanted to follow Jesus now that they knew what that meant. I told them I had never baptized people but I would find out if I could. When I asked Betty what to do, she said that she would help me, which was a good thing because I was the size of a grammar school child and they were all full grown women. We held the baptism in the pool in my back yard. Afterward we had a big party. Without realizing it, I had planted a new congregation that met in the church building on Tuesday mornings, and I was functioning as its pastor.

Around that time I began to experience God's repeated and compelling call to go into ministry. The call included three parts: ordained pastoral ministry, preparing leaders for the church through theological education, and some kind of role of speaking to the church at large. It seemed terrifying and absolutely impossible, in no small part because of Alex. Yet the call came again and again. Finally I went to Betty to tell her about it. I was a nervous wreck. I told her haltingly what I was experiencing in dreams and prayer and as I read the Bible. I whispered what I thought it meant. I could barely make eye contact because it was all too much. Betty, who was a rather sober person, laughed hard. She laughed and laughed, wiping tears from her eyes. I was taken aback. "Elaine," she said. "I saw it the day I met you. I went home and wrote about it in my journal, but I couldn't tell you about it because you needed to experience it for yourself." For three years she had been waiting for this day, stacking the deck by exposing me to ministry, guiding me along with exactly the right balance of proximity and distance, never intrusive, always patient, treating me with respect in ways I had never experienced in the church or anywhere else. "Always say yes to God," Betty said, "and God will make a way for you." Then she said, "You won't believe where God is going to take you!"

But there was the problem of my little girl with the little curl marriage with the rules about staying home for the rest of my life so I wouldn't unleash evil in the world or spend unauthorized money or have friends who brought excessive joy to my life. There was the issue of my lack of an education other than a handful of classes from the program for convicted felons. To say nothing of the fact that I was still riddled with shame, and the anxiety that dogged my steps day and night. There was no suitable theological school for me to attend within the city even if I could cough up the money and enough guts to insist that I needed a real education and was going to work fulltime once I got it, by God. The biggest obstacle of all was that I could not fathom how I could ever answer this call when my husband was so volatile and cruel. I said yes to Betty and to God, but I had no idea how I could answer the call.

Three weeks later Alex came home from work and told me that we were moving to Detroit. He had a new job opportunity there with the same company, that was too good to pass up. I said I did not want to move, that we were landed immigrants and I wanted to eat maple cream cookies and sing *O Canada* until the Lord came back. I said the kids loved their school and were doing well, and there was Dayspring, and the enrichment program, and our house, and my friends. He said we were moving, and if I didn't go along with it I could divorce him but he would take the kids and make sure I never saw them again. This was the first time the "D" word entered the space between us. I did not doubt that he would find a way to take the kids away from me, to punish me if I ever left him. I could not endure even the thought of losing them. Three months later we packed up and moved to a suburb of Detroit. I was utterly bereft.

CHAPTER NINE

Mother Bumblebee

AFTER WE SETTLED INTO OUR NEW LIFE I enrolled in a Bible college from another state that had an extension program in Detroit. I thought that would be the next step to answering the call. I would take one evening class. The girls were now in fourth and sixth grade and I told Alex I was going to answer a call to ministry which required an education, so I could get a job like Betty's or the other female pastor on staff at the Pentecostal church in Canada, and that it would be sinful for me to resist the call. I had just secured a part-time, minimum wage job at JoAnn Fabric that would cover tuition. I concluded with "The job will not interfere with my ability to cook, clean, or look after you and the kids. I can flex my hours around my family's needs." He said it was a waste of time and money for me to go to school because no one would ever hire me, but now that I was a women's libber I would do whatever the hell I wanted, with or without his permission. "And don't think for one minute that I'll pay a dime for your so-called education," he said. "You're on your own."

The class was a total dud, but I loved the African American Church of God in Christ pastors with whom I sat every week, who were also students. They were as wonderful as my Pentecostal Canadian friends, who I missed with a pain that was physical. The instructor, a local white pastor, made sexist jokes every week as we made our way through the Book of Acts. He also patted me on the head and called me "young lady." One night toward the end of the semester he made yet another wise crack about women and I couldn't take it anymore. I yelled that his comment was offensive and his jokes against women needed to stop. He said I had a problem with male authority and needed to be healed. When the semester ended I high tailed it out of there, wondering how I would ever be able to answer God's call.

One Saturday morning while walking through our new neighborhood I came across a tiny American Baptist Church. The sign out front listed the pastor's name as Carol somebody. My body turned and walked through the open door of its own accord. A petite redhead came into the dimly lit hall and asked if she could help.

"I saw the pastor's name on the sign outside and wondered if the pastor is a male or female Carol," I blurted idiotically, my voice unnaturally high. I had begun to shake and my mouth went dry.

"Well. I'm definitely a female Carol," she said. "My office is right here. Would you like to come in? Would you like some coffee?"

For the next half hour I poured out the sorry state of affairs in which I found myself, racing through my history beginning with getting married but without saying I had been a child bride in a marriage arranged by violent and criminally negligent parents, to a violent and unwell man. I sped through all the places we had lived, ending with God had called me into ministry with three parts, and the pastor on staff at the church, Betty, said to always say yes to God and God would make a way, but the next thing you know we had to move to this godforsaken armpit of a neighborhood and when I tried going to Bible college to get an education this nitwit preacher patted me on the head and every week was his personal standup routine in which he insulted me and every other woman unfortunate enough to be there and by God I couldn't take it anymore and now I didn't know what to do but I saw the name Carol on the sign and it made me lonely for Betty and I just thought, I just wondered if you were a female Carol. Because I need to talk to a woman pastor.

With that I had to stop or I would break into wild sobs, and I truly hate crying in front of people.

The coffee Carol had given to me was untouched and now had gone cold. She left for a few minutes to replace it with a fresh cup. I scanned her office, swallowing the giant lump in my throat. She had an entire shelf full of scandalous feminist books that destroy people's faith and ruin the American family, like *Sexism and God Talk*. I saw an unfamiliar magazine called Christian Century and suspected it was filled with liberal propaganda. As if it were theology porn I fought the urge to open one of the feminist books to see what lurked inside. Carol returned in the nick of time with the coffee and sat down. She turned to me and said the words no one else had said, not even Betty:

"Elaine, you are far too intelligent for anything less than a real education. Go to one of the universities here, and there are several, and get a bachelor's degree in something that interests you, preferably in the humanities. Then go to a good seminary and earn a Master of Divinity degree. After that go for a Ph.D. in the theological field that resonates with you. That field will become clear to you as you pursue your M.Div. Get ordained in a denomination that routinely ordains women. With those credentials you will be able to answer every part of God's call that you have described. Don't let other people define you. Only God gets to define you. Go for it. I know you can do it."

I floated home from that encounter with the female Carol, marveling at how the doors of my imagination had opened wide. Maybe there was a way forward, despite Alex's contempt and resistance to my getting an education, and despite the condescending pastor at the Bible College. Our neighborhood wasn't so bad after all. I noticed the pretty flowers at the house on the corner. I smiled and said hello to the curmudgeon next door. I skipped a little. The next day I went to the library to find out where the local universities were, and what it would take for me to go to one of them. I tried to psych myself up for the inevitable fights that lay ahead with Alex as I took the next steps toward my vocation.

Within weeks I registered for fall semester at Oakland University, majoring in English with a minor in history. As I prepared to go to my first day of class I told Alex that dinner was already prepared in the crock pot, and I would be home in time to set the table and everything would be fine. It was unfathomable to ask him to prepare dinner. Anna and Kat, in fourth and sixth grade, joked that they hoped I got a lot of homework. I could tell they were proud of me.

As it turned out, the three of us did our homework together over the next four years as I studied Shakespeare, satire, creative writing, art history, the history of Nazi Germany, linguistics, and so much more. I made little history flash cards which I pored over before driving to class three mornings a week because the modern European history professor, a grim Ukrainian, started each class with a quiz and I wasn't about to let myself fail after all I had been through to get to go to college. It was absolutely invigorating to be in school again.

The girls progressed from elementary school to junior high, then high school. On weekends we went on bike rides and walks through our neighborhood, and I assumed leadership of the youth group at the little evangelical church we attended. Alex resented my newfound freedom, especially that I had friends he never met that were not from the church. When I won a merit scholarship that would cover half the tuition for Spring semester my second year, he took my scholarship money and bought himself a computer, telling me I could go find money somewhere else to pay for tuition, that he deserved the computer for putting up with how I abandoned the family to pursue a women's lib pipe dream of getting a job for which no one would ever hire me. This began a pattern at least once a semester in which he swore I would not go back to school. Every time that happened I became more determined to go.

I continued to do all the housework and cooking, and put on what I thought was a good front at church, but in my heart whatever love had once been there for Alex, had been destroyed by years of abuse. Divorce was unthinkable because I believed I would never be able to get a job or be taken seriously as a ministry professional if I were divorced. It would not matter why a divorce happened, I reasoned to myself. I would have to stay with Alex no matter what, for the sake of the call. Yet I longed to be free of the violence, and to have a peaceful life without Alex's drama and without having to walk on eggshells or fear being humiliated by my husband in front of other people.

In 1990 I graduated summa cum laude. Anna and Kat made up lyrics for the occasion, sung to the tune of I'm Bringing Home a Baby Bumblebee: "I am a Mother Bumblebee, graduating from the university, When I graduate you'll be so proud of meeee, bzz bzz bzz bzz bzzzzzz."

They did this because my school colors were black and gold and because they were smart alecks. The song was stuck in my head for weeks.

Several months later I enrolled in Ashland Theological Seminary, which had an extension campus that met at Wayne State University a half hour from our house. A handful of the African American Church of God in Christ pastors were there, too, also having ditched the other program. Between scholarships, working ten hours a week at the fabric store, and insisting that twenty years of unpaid labor in cooking, cleaning, and raising the children made me half owner of the family finances, including funds I needed for tuition, I paid for my education. By then I had my own shelf of feminist literature, because on top of everything else this mother bumblebee had now taken a course in feminist theory.

CHAPTER TEN

Seminary

By the time I went to seminary I had already begun to study feminist theory and a smattering of feminist theology. I had actually read *Women Who Run with the Wolves* and found it enlightening, and God didn't smite me. I even read an occasional issue of *Christian Century* which wasn't at all what I first thought. So my horizons were expanding. But the class that changed the course of everything happened at the end of my first year.

Up until then all my classes were in Detroit at the extension campus at Wayne State. Toward the end of Spring term I saw an announcement about a May intensive on the main campus: Integrative Seminar on Evil. It was a three-hour drive one way to the main campus in Ohio, making it impossible to commute and return home on the same day. Housing for commuters had been arranged at University dorms since undergrads were out for the summer. Some of my new buddies and I signed up, not knowing quite what to expect from a class on evil. But the one-week format would enable me to complete another class in a short amount of time, and give me a chance to experience the main campus.

The week passed quickly. Each morning before class we had an option to participate in faculty led small prayer circles in which we offered thanks for the day, prayed for our class and professors, and prayed for our families back home. I went to the prayer group led by one of the Old Testament professors, Dr. David Baker. His warmth and unassuming manner impressed me. He had written important Bible commentaries and was fluent in eleven languages including ancient

Ugaritic, but he was far more humble than most pastors I had known. What struck me the most was how respectful he was toward women students. He was as interested in our comments as those of the men.

The class was large, with at least sixty students. A dozen or so faculty including Dr. Baker, taught from a wide range of theological disciplines. There were lectures and other learning experiences, from ancient philosophy to liberation theologies of structural sin, to doctrines of atonement. We read Shakespeare, listened to protest music, and viewed images of famous works of art. On the final day a petite, very feminine woman who had been sitting across the room all week, who I thought was another student, went to the front of the room to teach. Her name was Morven Baker. She was Dr. Baker's wife, a therapist whose expertise was in recovery from sexual abuse and domestic violence. She worked at a counseling center in town and was on staff at the seminary. My heart leapt at the familiar Canadian accent when she began to speak. Then for the first time in my life I heard a Christian leader speak from a podium about the evil of sexual abuse and domestic violence, and how the church perpetuates instead of prevents and heals the violence.

When class was over I rushed out into the crowded hall, looking for her. She was on her way out the door when I spotted her. I called to her, "Marvin!" wondering why any parent would name their sweet little girl Marvin. She turned. "Yes dear?" she said, sounding just like Mrs. Doubtfire. "Oh, and my name is Morven." She smiled warmly. "It's Scottish."

"What you talked about in class, the things you said. That was my story. I have never heard anyone in church talk about sexual abuse or domestic violence. I'm stunned. I don't even know what to say," I said, swallowing the lump in my throat.

"Oh, dear, I am so sorry for what you endured," she said. "I noticed you all week and kept feeling drawn to you, as if we were supposed to meet and become friends. I have to catch a plane now, but when I get back next week why don't we have lunch? I'd love to get acquainted." We exchanged phone numbers and I went back home, pondering the week in my heart, wondering what God was up to. I read my notes from Morven's lecture over and over.

Later that summer Morven and I met for lunch. It wasn't easy because despite her incredible healing gifts she was, as they say, directionally challenged. I drew a complex map with little buildings and landmarks to help her find her way to my house. We quickly became close friends. She had a Scottish name because she was born in Edinburgh. Her family immigrated to Canada when she was a wee lass. She and David met when he was a student in Vancouver. They had two kids the same ages as mine.

When school started in the fall, I began attending classes on the main campus, commuting down for two days per week and staying in a dorm. Morven and I often met for a meal or coffee. After the term ended Morven and David surprised me by inviting me to stay in their home in the future when I commuted to campus. It would be more comfortable for me, they said, and they refused to let me pay for room and board.

Never had I experienced the depth of hospitality the Baker family offered to me. They became family for me. Adam and Emily and my daughters soon became friends. Emily gave me the nickname "Mommy Junior." I had been staying with them weekly for several months when I noticed a framed photo of me nestled in among a table full of their family photos. I sat down and cried until I couldn't cry any more, grateful no one else was there.

By this time, the fall of 1992, my sister Jeanine had finished going through therapy to recover from the violence of our childhood and had begun a master's degree in counseling. We had been constant companions as Jeanine went through therapy while I was in college, even though living thousands of miles apart. Just as I was throwing off the shackles of patriarchy in my context, she was doing so in her life. We spoke and wrote to one another often to share what we were learning, she in psychology and me in theology, and to console each other when we faced criticism and resistance from those in our churches who didn't like that we were budding feminists.

Chapter Ten: Seminary

Meanwhile I devoured every class. The combination of intellectual rigor, enriching spiritual formation groups, the homely hospitality of the Bakers, ongoing healing conversation with Jeanine, and deepening spiritual friendship with several other students was utterly transformational. I had entered a new world filled with light, affirmation, and hope. Just as the female Carol had predicted, I began to have clarity about where to focus my future doctoral studies. I would do integrative work with spirituality and systematic theology. I would need to go to a Catholic university to do that.

There were nights when God's presence and unfolding path were so palpable that I could not sleep but lay awake feeling astounded until the sun came up. Unlike most of my experience of church in which men were in the driver's seat about every single thing, in seminary women were treated as equals. Our gifts, thoughts, and work were honored just as much as the men's. Women preached in chapel along with the men. Many of my classmates were United Methodist women who were already in the ordination process. Even though most of the faculty were men, they intentionally mentored women students so that we would fully embrace our calling, wherever that would lead. David Baker helped me connect to theological societies so that I could begin presenting papers at guild meetings. He introduced me to editors so that I could begin to imagine publishing my own books someday. When it was time to apply for doctoral programs, he helped me know how to put my best foot forward. Another professor, Dr. Flora, took me on as his teaching assistant so that I could gain experience grading papers and doing other tasks that would be mine as a future professor. Like David, he became a trusted mentor whose humility and deep spirituality made him a favorite of students, faculty, and staff.

Then came the sickness. The tick bite happened at a church camp where I served as co-director for a hundred fourth through sixth graders. My co-director and I created the curriculum for the week ourselves, using a mad scientist theme. He was Dr. Watt and I was Dr. Volt. We wore lab coats and had the time of our lives other than rushing a kid to the ER because he nearly severed his finger with a hatchet. When I returned home from camp I noticed what I thought was a bug bite that had become infected. There was a bullseye rash around the lesion. Having never heard of Lyme Disease I put triple antibiotic ointment on it and went about my business.

A couple of weeks later while heading to a family gathering in Oregon with the girls, who were in high school at the time, I suddenly became very sick with flu-like symptoms during a layover in the airport. I was dizzy and weak, and had to lie down at the gate. After arriving in Oregon I was too exhausted to do anything but lie down all week. When I was awake I had a headache that wouldn't stop. Most of these symptoms dissipated as I returned home to start a new school year.

But I continued to feel exhausted all the time, so tired that I had to take two naps to get through the day. Before long I began to have neurological symptoms—tremors that made it hard to hold a cup or to walk. I developed double vision at night, and peripheral neuropathies so that my hands and feet alternated between feeling numb and experiencing what felt like electrical shocks. Then I developed heart palpitations and arthritis.

When I sought medical help from our family physician early on, she asked, "Do you have teen age children?" I thought it was a weird question but said yes, as a matter of fact, I did. "You're repressing anger," she stated, staring at me without blinking. "You need to see a mental health professional." She handed me the business card for a psychiatrist. I climbed down off the examining table, wobbling with tremors. I wanted to wipe the smug assumption off her face but instead got dressed and went home.

I then went to a neurologist who conducted a number of tests. He said he thought I might have multiple sclerosis but that I would need a spinal tap and an MRI to be sure. My head spun at his words. How could this be? As an afterthought he asked if I had been bitten by a tick in the recent past. Trying to get past the multiple sclerosis words I searched my memory. I vaguely recalled the bullseye rash from camp. Yes, I said, I had been bitten by something that could have been a tick. I told him about the rash. He asked if I'd had flu-like symptoms afterward. Yes, I had. At that point he said it was possible that I had Lyme Disease rather than MS, but the tests for Lyme were notoriously inaccurate and many doctors were skeptical that it was a bona fide disease. I got the feeling that he was one of those doctors.

He ordered bloodwork to test for Lyme Disease. After leaving his office I went to the library to find out more. I discovered that Lyme Disease often masquerades as MS, heart disease, and arthritis. The book said nothing about Lyme mimicking repressed anger against your kids.

When the neurologist called a few days later he said I tested positive for Lyme, but inexplicably then said he was still leaning toward MS. He sent me to an infectious disease doc to get another opinion. She ordered the same blood test, which also returned positive for Lyme. She said there were quack doctors who made big bucks by diagnosing people with Lyme Disease and then made out like bandits by prescribing lengthy treatments that were unnecessary. It was very clear that she belonged in the group of docs who had trouble believing in Lyme Disease. She hospitalized me so that I could get started on a two-week course of intravenous antibiotics just in case it was Lyme Disease, but along with the neurologist she was convinced I had MS. While in the hospital, she said, I could also get the MRI and spinal tap. Unlike the dubious Lyme Disease, MS was a known and trusted affliction. Instead of prescribing the kind of antibiotic for the length of time that the "quack" doctors successfully used to treat Lyme Disease, she ordered a two week course of penicillin. As it flowed into my veins I promptly went into anaphylactic shock.

The next day while I was in the hospital covered with a rash but now able to breathe, I received a call that my daughter Kat was being brought to the ER with what seemed to be appendicitis. They gave her pain medicine and scheduled her for an appendectomy. In an unprecedented move they allowed her to be in the same room with me the night before surgery, since the other bed was open. Early the next morning during surgery the doctor discovered that rather than appendicitis Kat had a rare, life threatening condition, ovarian torsion, in which her ovary had become gangrenous. She got to the hospital just in time. Another twenty-four hours and she wouldn't have made it.

A few days later I went home with an IV pole so I could complete my infusion therapy myself, with regular visits from a home health nurse. Kat also came home to recover from her surgery. I had barely been home a couple of days when I developed excruciating pain and had to be rushed back to the hospital, where I was diagnosed with gallstones caused by the new antibiotic. The skeptical infectious disease doc stopped the Lyme treatment once and for all, even though the neurological symptoms were worse than ever. I began to wonder if I would recover. It was hard to imagine being able to finish my degree, much less go on to do the three forms of ministry to which I had been called. When Jeanine came from Alaska to help me I was in a state of near despair.

Throughout this time I was on medical leave from the seminary. Yet the seminary came to me. I received hundreds of kind wishes, cards, and phone calls from other students, faculty and staff. The Dean and one of the professors even made the three hour trek from Ohio to my hospital room to visit. My Detroit African Methodist Episcopal buddies organized a prayer chain that reached across the nation. The Brahmin friend said the Lord had shown him in a vision that the Devil was trying to kill me, but would not succeed. He wept, fasted, and prayed. Morven and David stayed in touch every day.

In the midst of all the chaos surrounding my illness, my marriage moved to a permanent state of horrid. Alex fell apart, undone by the combination of my illness, my unwillingness to cooperate with abusive dynamics anymore, and the volume of support I received from dozens of friends he had never met and over whom he had no control. He became increasingly physically violent and irrational, terrifying Kat and me. I was grateful Anna was away at college where she was safe.

I could not have survived those days without Jeanine's constant support, and the compassion of seminary friends. The final straw was when Alex insisted on giving me my IV infusion one morning, which required injecting a syringe full of saline into the IV line, followed by starting the IV drip for the medicine. I had never allowed him to touch the picc line site or help with any of the medical procedures because I feared he would intentionally hurt me. I started to protest but he grabbed the syringe from my hand and jammed it into the IV port, forcing the fluid into my vein too fast. I screamed for him to stop, that he was hurting me. He jerked the needle out and threw the syringe against the room where it hit the wall and broke, shouting into my face that he was sick of me, sick of my friends, sick of everything. The last thing he said before storming out the front door was, "Don't they know I'm the victim in all this? I'm the one who needs support, not you! They should be coming to see me, not you!" In that moment I knew I had to escape and take Kat with me, as soon as possible. I was too exhausted to do anything but try to survive until I could leave.

As his rage grew worse, I began making plans to leave. Like battered women everywhere who leave their violent partners, I needed support from friends who would help me be as safe as possible while I left. The most dangerous time for a battered woman is when she tries to leave her partner. That is when she is most likely to be seriously injured or killed. My safety network included a police officer who was a fellow student at the seminary, and several friends including Morven and David, and Jeanine.

A few months later, when I had regained enough physical and emotional stamina to do so, I filed for a divorce and we separated. I was unspeakably relieved not to have to call the police in the process, even though Alex's reaction was dreadful. Leaving was the hardest, most frightening thing I ever did in my adult life. Part of what made it so hard was that I had compassion for his mental illness, but also knew he was intentional in his cruelty and that he took pleasure in causing pain. It took nearly two decades to stop being afraid of him after I left. By the time the divorce was finalized the following summer, Alex and I had been married for 23 years. I was thirty-nine years old.

CHAPTER ELEVEN

A New Beginning

Kat and I moved to Ashland, Ohio, walking distance from campus. She was a junior in high school. Anna was in her first year as an engineering student at Princeton University. She had graduated at the top of her class, having broken all academic records in the history of her high school. She was offered large scholarships from all five top tier schools to which she applied, including MIT. In the end she chose Princeton so that she could also study poetry.

Father Michael, an Orthodox monk who had come to the seminary so that he could translate ancient texts, helped us move into our little apartment in Ashland. Along with a group of other friends he moved furniture and boxes, then took a bottle of holy water and sprinkled every room and all of us who were gathered. He gave Kat and me an icon of Christ Pantocrator, a beautiful ancient image in which half of Christ's face seems masculine and half feminine. "You are safe now," he said. "Welcome home." Other friends brought linens, casseroles, flowers, and groceries. "We love you," they each said in their own way.

Our little apartment was on the edge of town, nestled in a hickory grove. I could look out my bedroom window and see a lovely rock bottom creek. At night, even though it was the dead of winter, I slept with my window open a little so I could hear the comforting sound of the tumbling water. Our apartment was adjacent to the large city cemetery, where I walked almost every day among the graves, weeping and wondering how I would ever be able to work in the church or in theological education when I had committed what I had been taught was the unforgiveable sin of divorce. Every church I had attended from the time I was sixteen, made it clear that the only legitimate reason a Christian can get a divorce is if their spouse had sex with someone else. And even in that situation, after the divorce the person who was wronged by their former partner's infidelity was not allowed to remarry, because to do so would be to commit adultery. This teaching was based on a patriarchal interpretation of Matthew 5:32.

By the time I got divorced I knew that interpretive logic was flawed because I had taken every Hebrew and Greek class available and had conducted in-depth studies in the original languages, of every scripture that was used by the evangelical church to forbid divorce and to permanently judge and exclude divorced people. I learned that from a scriptural standpoint, multiple forms of covenant breaking can kill a marriage and warrant a divorce for the wronged person, including every form of domestic violence. The anti-divorced people interpretation I inherited from the fundamentalist church was based in patriarchy, which by this time I knew was evil. All this research and awakening to new understandings in how to interpret the Bible, were crucial to the process the process that enabled me to finally leave my violent marriage.

Despite knowing that God was with me and helped me to say "no" to abuse, it was hard to imagine a denomination that would accept me, that would also appreciate my love of Jesus and my love for the Bible. At the grocery store I felt as if a large, red "D" was branded on my forehead. I wondered if I looked as broken as I felt. A few former friends from the conservative church I attended in Michigan wrote accusatory letters, telling me I was no longer a Christian, that I was damned, and that I should be ashamed of myself. Yet others were supportive. A few people said, "We wondered how you put up with him all those years. Thank God you are free." The comment that meant the most came from the pastor's wife in Michigan, a few months after I moved to Ohio. She said it when she and her husband came to visit. "Your eyes look different now. They used to look sad all the time, even when you laughed and smiled. Now they are at peace."

I got a part time job as a youth director at a local United Methodist

Church so we could pay the light bill and have something to eat. Although I had been taught in my fundamentalist days that mainline churches were not really Christian but were filled with liberals, feminists and godless humanism, my United Methodist seminary friends clearly loved Jesus, as did the pastor and congregation at Emmanuel United Methodist Church, where I worked. But to join the UMC and enter the ordination process, after graduation I would need to take required additional classes in Methodist history, doctrine, and polity. Since I adored the faculty and Dean, Dr. Mary Ellen Drushal, I didn't mind at all. By this time I was pastoring three small, rural churches in East Ohio near the Pennsylvania border. I could drive to class and return home the same day.

The neurological symptoms from Lyme Disease had diminished somewhat before I moved to Ohio, but within a year they came back with a vengeance. After doing some research I discovered a prominent rheumatologist at the University Hospital system in Cleveland, who had expertise in treating Lyme Disease. When I went to my first appointment and poured out my story, he apologized on behalf of arrogant doctors everywhere who get caught up in politicized arguments that make them lose sight of the needs and dignity of their patients. I was astounded. He then asked me what I had done that gave me strength and hope throughout the long journey of illness that never quite went away. I said that prayer, and the love of friends and family sustained me. I told him I knew God had called me to ministry and most of the time I believed God would bring me through. When I couldn't believe, my friends and family believed on my behalf. The nurse said, "Amen!" which startled me. I had never been to a medical professional who said anything about faith or who treated patients and their spirituality holistically.

Soon I had a picc line—a port that stays in place throughout the weeks or months of IV therapy—in my arm for the infusions, and a shiny new IV pole, and the right antibiotic that would treat the disease without sending me into anaphylactic shock or ruining my guts. For six weeks I made the trek to and from school with my IV pole and meds so I could give myself multiple infusions each day. Because of the exhaustion and need to take two naps per day, the Dean invited me to stay at her home where it was quiet all the time. By the time the six weeks was up I was already beginning to feel the difference. Within a few months I was almost symptom free. At my final follow up visit the rheumatologist, his nurse, and I all rejoiced. I still can't believe they said "Praise the Lord," right there in his office.

CHAPTER TWELVE

Us and Them

MY THERAPIST, WHO WEIRDLY ENOUGH looked exactly like the celebrity shrink at the time, Dr. Joyce Brothers, suggested that I let my feelings out in a controlled environment that was safe. So instead of driving too fast or eating the entire carton of ice cream, or taking a ball bat and, well, never mind about that one, she advised that I get some newspaper and let 'er rip. "Make sure you are in a safe, private place where you can express your feelings verbally, without fear of interruption or being heard. Let the anger surface. Let the grief come. Allow tears. Tear the paper, wad it up, throw it, whatever helps you to physically discharge the anger that your body has held for a long time. Verbalize your hurt and anger while you do this."

I thanked her for her suggestion, pushed my glasses up on my nose and said I would give it some thought. I always said "give it some thought" to her because my default when emotions get tricky is to go Vulcan. It's not a conscious move that I make. It's as if I have an inner dentist with a giant syringe full of emotional novocaine. Suddenly I'm calm and think a lot of logical thoughts even though everyone's hair is on fire. But sooner or later the novocaine wears off. By the time I sat in Dr. Brothers' doppelganger's office I had reached my limit with numbing out. Part of healing from trauma is learning to feel again. She was helping me get in touch with the anger I was ready to feel.

The year was 1997. I had finished seminary two years earlier and was in my first appointment as a pastor in the East Ohio Conference of the United Methodist Church. By then Alex and I had been divorced for several years. We separated when I was in the final lap of seminary studying the hitpael in Hebrew and healing from childhood trauma. Our daughters were in high school and college by then, brilliant, funny, gifted girls, the apples of my eye. The divorce was hard on them, even though they understood why it was necessary. Seminary friends saw the three of us through that cataclysm, every step of the way.

Because of the divorce I had become, as I expected, persona non grata in the evangelical church where I had been working toward ordination. It didn't matter why the divorce happened. There was no contextualization for people who could not be together anymore because it was so destructive, or because one of them was a sadistic bastard, or crazy, or because of betrayal or one of the partners came out of the closet after years of painful denial, or any other complexity in life. Divorce was always interpreted as evil, period, deserving of eternal damnation and like sin in general, mostly the woman's fault.

That theology fit very well with the philosophy I absorbed from country music and my parents when I was a kid. Stand by your man, Tammy Wynette wailed, no matter what, even if he strangles your children and threatens them with guns and breaks their jaws, even if he beats your babies in their cribs. Take what he dishes out and treat him like a king. You can resent him, but you always keep coming back for more.

The truth is that sometimes divorce is necessary, and it doesn't have to mean either person is evil. Nor does it mean it is always both people's fault. Divorce happens even to spiritual people, yes good, God loving Christians, including pastors, theologians, seminarians, and workaday Joes. Divorce happens to all kinds of decent, exhausted, fragile, lonely, beat up people in this world for whom there is no other way to resolve the agony of a relationship that will not ever work, that has become death-dealing. Ending a relationship is a mercy at such times and should be gone through with as much kindness and compassion as possible, for everyone concerned. Divorce is always hard, always painful. It reverberates through every single relationship in a person's life. What divorcing people need from the church is support.

After the divorce when I found my way into the United Methodist

Church, I was welcomed enthusiastically, and treated with respect. It was a huge relief to be able to answer God's call without having to navigate inappropriate questions about being divorced, or to have to prove that women can be pastors, or any other bigoted nonsense that had marked my path thus far. The female Carol was right, it was best to affiliate with a denomination that routinely ordained women. And I had come to love the Wesleyan theology of the UMC.

Though my life was so much better than it ever had been, now that I was free to pursue my vocation, I still had some hard work ahead in order to move through the next level of healing. After a brief rebound relationship that never could have worked, I became acutely aware of need for further healing. A friend gave me a copy of Richard Rohr's book, *Everything Belongs*, with its wisdom about self-compassion, which opened me to being more present to myself and what I needed in order to thrive. Along with Richard Rohr my mother's voice was in my head saying I needed some goddamn peace and quiet.

But to get there I had to go through some pain.

Because my pastor salary was fifteen grand a year, gross, which even then was below the poverty line, I needed to go to the county mental health clinic to find a therapist. There I could take advantage of the sliding scale fee structure so that I would not have to choose between eating and getting help. Having never gone to a county mental health clinic before, I didn't know what to expect. I wondered if I might get a greenhorn half my age, for whom this was their first job, or someone who thought all pastors were idiots. But I knew that I had to take that risk. I could no longer put up with abusive relationships, institutions, or theology. I had begun drawing firm boundaries about such things, which caused pushback from certain other people, which infuriated me more than the situations deserved. I needed help.

The parsonage where I lived was in a tough neighborhood in East Liverpool, Ohio. Though shabby and bedraggled on the outside, the old manse had good bones. I loved the high ceilings and the beautiful oak window casings, and the black and white checkered tiles in the bathroom. At one time that neighborhood was a great place to raise a family. People could earn a decent living at the potteries, factories, steel mills and small businesses that contributed to a thriving economy. Then outsourcing happened. One by one the potteries and mills closed, and businesses were shuttered. This happened up and down the Ohio River Valley.

As is so often the case in communities that collectively lose their livelihoods, a new set of industries showed up. Now a toxic waste incinerator near the elementary school provided jobs and burned something at night that sent people to the ER because they couldn't breathe. Chemical factories provided jobs and spewed God knows what but it made the paint fall off the houses. My neighborhood was riddled with drugs and crime and kids raising themselves. There was a busy crack house across the alley from the parsonage.

My new neighborhood was both alien and familiar. I grew up in poverty with the kind of neglect, abandonment, and violence the kids in my new neighborhood faced, but I had never lived by a crack house or in an urban setting of this kind, immersed in hazardous waste. I suspected my neighbors thought I was highfalutin because I showed up with a decent, if old car, and I was a pastor who carried a briefcase and wore a suit. The three small churches I pastored were several miles out of town, not in the neighborhood, so I was gone most of the time and didn't interact with neighbors much. They had no idea about how I grew up.

My colleagues and congregants thought of me as a polished, professional woman with a great future. The district superintendent described me to others as a rising star in our denomination. It helped that by then I had even learned to use table manners. When hosting dinner parties, for example, I had learned to say things like "May I freshen your beverage?" instead of "Hereyago, let's fillerup." I did not talk to them about my history as a child or my long and painful marriage to Alex, or the trauma of divorcing him. Honestly, I wanted to move on. I tried to get away from my own story. But stories have a way of following us, and all that anger that had been stashed in a deep freeze was beginning to thaw.

So it was that on a cold, rainy morning I stood in the middle of the living room doing my homework from therapy, wailing at the top of my lungs. I cried so hard it felt as if my body had turned inside out. The agony of a thousand memories poured out, from preschool years all the way to the present, for the neglect, abandonment, rape, assaults, contempt, control, exploitation, frustration, lost opportunities, toxic religion, sexism, pervasive anxiety, and shame. I felt utterly Godforsaken. Heaps of torn, crumpled newspaper and wads of soggy tissue surrounded me.

Someone pounded on the door. It was a fist, not a polite tap. I froze, mid-wail. The pounding became more frantic. I had to answer it. I went to the door and opened it a few inches. There was the scrawny little woman who lived in the crack house and sold her body to support her habit. Her teeth were shot and her hair looked like a bird's nest. She was in need of a shower. I had waived to her a time or two but we had never had a conversation.

"Honey, are you awright?" she asked, peering past me into the house. She pushed the door open wider and stepped in, looking around with a fierce glint in her eye, her boney hands balled into fists. "I was walkin' by and I heard you a cryin'. What's goin' on, baby?" I realized with a shock that she had come to take on whoever was in there hurting me.

I assured her that I was okay, I had been crying over old hurt from long ago. I thanked her for stopping to check. With one last scan of the room to make sure no one was lurking in a corner, she said "Awright then, honey, you take care," and left.

I was not Godforsaken. The Bible says that Jesus was a man of sorrows, acquainted with grief, that now he is a high priest who has gone through every kind of temptation we have and every kind of suffering so we can be sure that when we call upon him his seat of authority is mercy and grace. And I believed all of that. What stunned me was how he came to me through the crack house lady. I didn't know that was allowed. That street angel wrecked my theology.

Don't get me wrong. I loved my seminary experience more than words can tell, not only for the intellectual and spiritual challenge but also for the kindred spirits I found there, and the mentoring and encouragement of professors. I also loved studying Hebrew with a bunch of smart aleck future pastors who came up with a way to practice our vocabulary by saying rude things in Hebrew, such as "You can put that where the moon don't shine." Some of my favorite classmates included a former tight end for the Cleveland Browns, a psychiatrist who really was a Vulcan but was drawn to Christian mysticism, an African American pastor from the middle of Detroit who invited me to preach in her storefront Christian Methodist Episcopal church, and a wiry little fellow from the Brahmin caste who had a heart for poor people which caused him to run afoul of his aristocratic family. He spoke English in a flawless British accent and wept profusely when he prayed.

I learned so many things in seminary that to this day help me in my work. Even so, living with chronic, debilitating, hard to diagnose illness, multiple hospitalizations, an insurance company that didn't want to pay for treatment, doctors with a political agenda, unbearable stress at home, and going through a divorce after a long, violent marriage were some of the most formative educational experiences of my seminary years. Never again would I take for granted the ability to walk or to have energy for a full day's work. Years of Lyme Disease gave me compassion for people who suffer from chronic illness and because of the illness, depression and despair. The divorce opened my heart to all kinds of people who are judged and rejected by the church for deciding to be true to themselves and live with integrity, including sexual minorities. Most of all, I learned what it means to hold space with others who suffer in ways we cannot fathom.

Just as illness and divorce from a violent partner provided transformational learning experiences, my encounter with the crack house neighbor changed how I understood the Bible and the character of God in ways that no classroom experience could. That woman remains with me today in my heart and mind, a raspy voiced, hygiene challenged, street angel. She's there reminding me to listen to all my neighbors beyond the church, because God is speaking to me through them. God is with them, and in them. That's how she wrecked my theology. She knocked down the walls of the church, all the insider outsider categories, all the sanctimonious ways we use pious language to draw lines between "us" and "them." When she came to rescue me from whoever was hurting me, I learned there is only us.

CHAPTER THIRTEEN

How Old Are You?

"I CAN SEE HIM IN WATER. Or maybe on water. I can't tell." Bobbie said, eyes squeezed shut as she conjured the vision she had been given. "I dunno, there's water. He's been waiting for you. God is preparing him. He's almost ready." We were sitting at the table in my tiny apartment, drinking coffee. The apartment was so small there was no room for a sofa in the living room, so Kat and I had two Hobbit sized wingback chairs that she called the chastity chairs because it was impossible for more than one person at a time to sit in them. A TV the size of a lunchbox perched on a VCR player atop an end table, completing the living room ensemble. We couldn't afford cable nor did we have rabbit ears so we used the TV to watch free videos from the public library, everything from Riverdance to Lonesome Dove. I was a PhD student in Pittsburgh and Kat was an undergrad at Youngstown State University. Our apartment was in the sweet little town of Columbiana, Ohio, halfway between the two universities, making it easy for us each to commute. Between my meager grad student stipend, a fellowship, and ten hours per week as a youth pastor, and Kat's income from the local ice cream joint we just barely paid the bills.

Bobbie, one of my best friends, was the wife of the local undertaker who was also the drummer at the Pentecostal church. Bobbie looked like a Gelfling from *The Dark Crystal*—tiny, fragile, wispy blonde hair and huge eyes. She was a fierce prayer warrior who had visions, which is why she hastened to see me that morning. The Lord had given her a vision of the man he was preparing for me.

"What do you mean, water?" I demanded. "Is he walking on water? Surfing? What the heck?" I loved Bobbie to pieces, and I do believe God at times speaks through dreams and visions, indeed God called me to ministry through dreams and visions. But this vision seemed over the top. It was too vague. There was also the issue that I needed a long vacation from men.

"I told you everything I know," she said. "He's in the water and you'll know what it means when the time comes."

Soon I moved to McDonald, Ohio, where in July, 1999, I was appointed to serve as pastor for Woodland Park United Methodist Church. I had finished coursework for my PhD and was ready to prepare for comprehensive exams, then write the dissertation. It was time to go back to work fulltime and in the way of graduate students everywhere, juggle work, parenting, life, and writing a dissertation, fueled by gallons of cheap coffee. We said goodbye to our little apartment, the chastity chairs went to my new office, and as Kat put it, I "got some real furniture" for the parsonage. Kat moved onto campus at Youngstown State where she secured a post as resident assistant in one of the dorms.

McDonald was straight out of a Norman Rockwell painting, with its friendly porches and tree lined streets. I expected to see Jimmy Stewart running along shouting, "It's a wonderful life!" A one square mile village, it had been built by the Carnegie Steel Company in the 1920s to house workers for the new mill on the mighty Mahoning. The grocery store and bank were no longer in business by the time I showed up, but there were a few bars and a post office. Everybody said it was a great place to raise a family. The church was in the exact center of the village, beside the lovely Woodland Park with its gazebo, and across the street from Our Lady of Perpetual Help. The parsonage, three doors down, was a sprawling four-bedroom brick ranch with a fireplace and a full basement. I could have put three of our previous apartments on the main floor.

I had been on the job for just a few weeks when Kat came in, newspaper in hand. "You need to go test drive this car," she said. "It's what you've always wanted. Two seats, small, a convertible. My boyfriend will buy your clergy mobile." I looked at the ad. It was a 1996 Mazda

Miata, M Edition, 5 speed stick shift, midnight blue with tan leather upholstery, all the bells and whistles, like new, only 6000 miles, and at a price within reach.

"Sorry. I can't drive that car," I said. "What will people think? I'm already a petite, single, blonde, female pastor. What will they do if I peel out?"

"That's ridiculous!" she hollered, pushing keys and purse into my hands while shouldering me to the door. "You finally have a real job and real furniture and live in a real house. It's time for a real car, one that isn't for driving children around. Except for me. You can drive me. Maybe I get to drive it too, sometimes. Please. We're going now."

So off we went, Kat jabbering about engine specs and me clutching the high collar of my serviceable beige blouse. A few hours later we came back, delirious. Kat drove the beige Honda and I drove the Miata, full of conflicting emotions.

It was true, I had always wanted to drive a tiny car with 2 seats. When I was a child, Jeff and I played for hours every day in the dirt with small metal cars. My favorite was the Triumph. But now in my mid-forties, figuring out how to be myself, a pastor, and a theologian while navigating the impossible layers of shame and expectation placed on women in church and academy, well, it was a lot. I was pretty sure Jesus didn't mind if I had a fun car, but I wasn't so sure about the flock.

It would be different if my first name was Heath. Male pastors are expected to like sports cars. It helps them seem like regular guys, which supposedly can attract men to the church. Female pastors, well, not so much. Cars, clothes, hair, voice, weight, skin color, hobbies, everything is sexualized, scrutinized, and judged. When I was ordained many of the older women clergy in my denomination wore loose denim jumpers over long sleeved shirts, Birkenstocks, and what I thought of at the time as nun hair. It was their way of defying sexualization. They were pioneers, sheroes, the first women in my denomination to go to seminary, to be ordained, and to become bishops. They had to be tough to make it. The male clergy on the other hand, wore cargo shorts, Hawaiian shirts, and goatees. The super hip male clergy wore shoes without socks. I couldn't figure out what to wear. No matter what I put on in the morning, someone had something to say.

"Pastor, you're built like a gymnast." Said a sixty something man, giving me a slow once-over. I had on a pair of mom jeans and a baggy sweatshirt from my alma mater.

"Honey, every Sunday I wonder what's under that robe," leered an octogenarian after worship.

"You don't look like a pastor," said a forty-five year old congregant from his hospital bed, when I came to see him after his cancer surgery. He was still in a post anesthesia fog.

"What does a pastor look like?" I asked.

"Most of the clergy women are kind of, you know . . ." at this point he used his hands to indicate a large bosom on a buxom frame. "But you're so little and cute." Then he smiled lasciviously and tried to wink but failed because he was too tired to open the eye back up. I was wearing a billowy calf length skirt and tweed beige jacket with elbow patches and leather buttons. I pushed my horn-rimmed glasses up on my nose and tried to think of something to say but by then his other eye was closed, too.

Today's young clergy women rage against the machine by wearing sleeveless clergy shirts with a dog collar so everyone can see their righteous tattoos. They shave one side of their heads and spike the top like Woody Woodpecker. They're ready to kick ass and take names later. The sisters love liturgy and at the same time can blurt entire sentences in which nouns, verbs, objects and subjects are all variations of fuck. They drink Scotch, two fingers, neat, when they can afford it. Which isn't often. I worry about them. Despite their bravado, these women still bear the burden of systems that reward men just for showing up and objectifies and judges every move that women make. Only a tiny fraction of large churches are led by female senior pastors. Male clergy still make more money than female clergy who have equal education, more experience, and superior skills. Stained glass ceilings are real.

The day after bringing the Miata home I drove over to visit one of the homebound members, a sweet, affectionate, eighty-something woman named Nan whose breast cancer had come back with a vengeance. Nan was the first person I paid a pastoral call to upon taking up my new post. We instantly liked each other. On that visit as I prepared to leave she said, "Pastor, before you go I want to show you my chest where the cancer came back."

I was completely flummoxed. "Oh, Nan, you don't have to do that. I can imagine it must be very distressing for you to see what is happening to your body."

"It will make me feel better if I can show someone and I don't know who else to show it to. I can't show my boys. My sister-in-law Ruby is too squeamish. Please." By then she already had her shirt off. Nan peered up at me sadly as I beheld angry red tumors rising from the scarred ruins of her lost breast. After a moment she replaced her shirt. We sat and cried together.

Over the next several weeks I spent a lot of time with Nan. Normally I walked to visit my parishioners since everyone lived within the village, but when I got the Miata I drove so I could show her my new car. I thought it might make her laugh.

"Nan!" I announced through the screen door, "You have to see my new car! Well, it's pre-owned as they say, but new to me. It's a *convertible!*"

"Oh, I always wanted to ride in a convertible, my whole life," she sighed, looking longingly at the little beauty in her driveway.

I didn't know that she hadn't been out of the house in six months other than for doctor's appointments. She hadn't yet told me her son was in the process of arranging for Hospice care for her. "Well what the heck are we waiting for?" I hollered. "Come on! Let's go for a ride!"

It was a hot day in August so with the top down we sped off to Mill Creek, a huge metro park in Youngstown beloved for its shady picnic areas and flower gardens. "Oh I forgot my lipstick!" Nan cried. "No worries," I said, "You look gorgeous." We laughed at the sheer decadence of the moment.

I pulled into a parking lot so we could sit on a bench surrounded by flowers, glad for the cool shade. Birds chittered around us. Leaves danced in the breeze. Nan talked about raising her three sons with her husband, how they took their boys to Mill Creek on summer nights for picnics and how there used to be a small amusement park for the kids.

Now two of the boys lived out of town. "Randall's over in Niles," Nan said. "He's the assistant superintendent of roads with the county." At this statement she straightened for a moment and smiled shyly, visibly proud of her youngest son. "He's such a wonderful boy. He's divorced and don't have no kids, but he takes real good care of me. Comes over after work every day and cooks for me. He started with the county when he got out of the Army and stayed with it from then on. He was a bridge crew foreman for a long time." Her voice trailed away. I pictured a loud-mouth hard hat redneck with a beer gut and a soft spot for Mom.

There was a lull in conversation, then Nan abruptly said, "I'm about to die, pastor. The cancer's bad. Why don't we go ahead and talk about my funeral now?" So that is what we did. We planned the logistics of her funeral. We would use the hymn, Amazing Grace. I would preach. The family would help with the eulogy. I asked if there was anything she wanted to do, or anything she wanted say to anyone in the time that she had left. I asked what she loved about her life, and she told more stories about her family and friends, especially camping on the weekends. We talked about God and heaven.

Companioning people as they prepare for death is an unspeakably sacred and humbling part of pastoral ministry. Our conversation moved to silence, then after a time Nan said we should maybe go home as she was tired. She settled into the car and leaned back, eyes closed, spent from what turned out to be her last adventure in this life, and the daunting task of getting ready to die.

Twenty minutes later we pulled into her driveway behind a massive red F250 with the words "Trumbull County Engineer" emblazoned on the side. A very stern looking man stood beside it, staring accusingly at our windblown visage. He was slender and athletic, with salt and pepper hair and his mother's eyes. "That's my boy Randall," Nan whispered loudly. "The one I told you about." Then she giggled.

Randall was not pleased. "Jesus Christ. I come over after work and the door's open, the windows are open, there's no note. I look everywhere including the attic in case you climbed up there and hurt yourself. Or worse. I go to all the neighbors. Nobody knows where you are. I finally call Ruby. She says she thinks you went off with the new preacher." With the words "new preacher" his eyes swiveled to me. It was a very hot day. It appeared that my antiperspirant had worn off. Plus I was wearing shorts. They were beige, loose fitting, and only slightly above my knees, but still. I jumped out like a jack in the box, introduced myself, blithered something about the weather, got Nan out of the car and took off like a bat out of hell.

Over the next couple of months Nan's health rapidly declined. Occasionally Randall was there when I made pastoral calls, so after I visited Nan we would sit on the front porch and talk awhile, before I went on my way. In addition to not having a beer gut, Randall was nothing like the jerk I envisioned when Nan told me about her youngest boy. He was principled, quiet, and kind. Though he never went to college because of a reading disability, he knew more about music, art, and culture than most of the people in my academic circles. He had been spared from attending Sunday School as a child because the family went camping most weekends, but they attended worship at the campgrounds. His spirituality was deep and lively. Every day after work he cooked dinner for his mother, made sure she made it to the doctor, and in general kept her household afloat as her health declined.

Soon Nan was confined to bed. Hospice and a niece who took time off her nursing job to care for Nan, made it possible for her to remain at home. Then one frosty October night the call came. Nan was gone. We followed her wishes for every detail of the funeral, including me singing Amazing Grace with my guitar while trying not to bawl my eyes out.

About a week after the funeral Randall called. "I'm wondering if you'd like to have dinner tomorrow night," he said.

"I can't."

"Oh, well maybe another night?"

"No. I can't go out with you."

"Well why not?" he asked, very surprised. We had formed a warm friendship while caring for his mother over the past few months. It was very easy to be together, as if we had always been friends and only needed to catch up on details. He had begun attending church on Sundays with his Aunt Ruby, the squeamish one who lived next door to the parsonage and told him his mother had gone off with the new preacher. Ruby's house smelled of mothballs and was full of fancy tea cups and figurines. She wore a real fur coat in the winter. Ruby kept a sharp eye on me at all times, living next door to the parsonage.

"I can't go out with you because you attend the church where I am pastor, and there are rules against dating people in your congregation," I said primly.

"It doesn't have to be a date," he said, "We're friends."

"Yes, we are. I really wish I could go out with you, but I just can't," I said, and hung up the phone. I went and sat in the darkened living room thinking about how much I liked him. Should I ask him to go to some other church for a while? No, I couldn't do that. The older women in the church had known him from birth and adored him. He wasn't a drunk and so far as I could tell, wasn't into guns, either. Unlike Alex, he was gentle. My dog liked him. He seemed at home in his own skin. I felt at home when I was with him. I pondered his kindness to his mother, and his unassuming manner. My hand picked up the phone of its own volition.

"Okay," I said, "I'll go with you. *But this is not a date!*"

There was silence on the other end. Then, "I'll be there at six," he said.

At six o'clock sharp he knocked on the door. We got in the car.

"How old are you?" I blurted.

"What kind of question is that?" he said. "How old are *you*?"

The next day I called my district superintendent and told him I didn't know what to do. I had become friends with a man while providing pastoral care for his mother as she died and now he was coming to church and last night we went to a good Italian restaurant and ate pasta then walked in the park and I was pretty sure it was a date even though I tried for it not to be and now I had broken the rules because I dated someone from the church but he wasn't a member and only started coming regularly after I started caring for his mother so technically my relationship with him began before he came to the church but now he was there all the time and I guess I could ask him to go to some other church but that didn't seem like the right thing to do and

I didn't know what to do because I really liked him. I stopped talking when I ran out of air.

Gary, the DS, snort laughed. He said, "Well, where else are you going to meet someone? A bar? He sounds great! Just let the chair of the Staff-Parish Relations Committee know. The reason for the rule against dating congregants is in case things don't work out. It can become disruptive for the church. But this seems to be a different situation. Congratulations, and hey, have a good time!"

We got married the following summer in the gazebo at Woodland Park. A string quartet played for the wedding—Kat's buddies from the Dana School of Music where she was a piano performance major. We said our vows at 7 PM as the evening sun slanted through the hardwoods and the fireflies came out. Betty, who came from Canada with her husband Fred, told me the night before the wedding, "At first it was hard for me to accept, but God showed me your divorce from Alex was necessary. Randall is a gem. He will always be there for you and support your ministry. I, um, had a little talk with him about that," she concluded, giving me a fierce hug. There were many other friends at the wedding, too, including Bobbie and her undertaker husband.

The woman at Master Cuts got carried away and practically gave me a buzz cut for the wedding so what was left of my hair kind of had that helmet look like the clergy women with denim jumpers, but my white satin floor length sheath had a low cut back and was quite something. One of the old men from the church put his lips in my ear in the receiving line and said, "Nothing beats the contours of a woman's bare back. Thank you."

The reception was a front yard picnic at the parsonage. We didn't want speeches or toasts or any of that. We wanted comfort food. There were Italian hot sausage sandwiches, fried chicken, and biscuits. I found Bobbie and pulled her aside.

"Hey, remember your vision of the man in the water?"

"Of course! How could I forget?" she said, peering up at me through giant Gelfling eyes.

"Wait'll you hear this," I said. "That very same week when you came to see me, Randall was out on Lake Erie in his sailboat. He was *on the water*! He told me he was out there praying for God to send him the right woman. I asked him what he meant by "the right woman." He said, "Somebody who ain't afraid to pee in the woods." He said, "And then I felt at peace, that God was getting ready to send that woman to me. And then I met you." We laughed like lunatics while Bobbie praised the Lord, then I said, "Bobbie, we're going to northern Ontario for a fly-in fishing trip for our honeymoon. I told Randall that's what I really wanted to do. It was my idea. Because he's right. I'm not afraid. And you were right, God brought him to me. From the water."

CHAPTER FOURTEEN

Salvation

RANDALL REALIZED QUITE EARLY in our relationship that I'm a terrible workaholic, so he took upon himself the task of making sure we have fun on a regular basis. To this end during our first year of marriage he taught me to downhill ski at Peek N Peak Resort in upstate New York, which was just a half day drive from our house. "Drink a beer before you hit the slopes," he urged, rubbing a knuckle across the worry lines between my eyes, and steering us to the bar. "It'll take the edge off." He bought me a cobalt blue, fleece winter cap in the ski shop. It tied under my chin like a baby bonnet and sported a giant pointy black Mohawk on top, with "NO FEAR" emblazoned on one side. Somehow, by our third ski trip I managed to make it to intermediate slopes without injury. We celebrated my survival with a gourmet meal. Randall is a marvelous cook.

During warmer months we left work on Friday afternoons for overnight getaways at Geneva Marina on Lake Erie. It was a two-hour drive from the parsonage, during which time I discussed with him my sermon plans for Sunday, and he gave me helpful working man feedback. Randall had been sailing for many years before we met. Although I barely learned the difference between starboard and port, sailing was pure bliss. I wrote most of my dissertation in the little galley of the twenty-two foot Catalina while it was docked, because it was the most peaceful, uninterrupted location I could find to hunker down and write all day.

We hiked, biked, canoed, camped, went to Disney World, ate picnics in front of the fireplace at the parsonage, watched movies, and in general, went on lots of adventures. He cooked for us, several nights per week, delicious meals with beautiful presentations. It took two years for me to relax into so much love, and to trust he was never going to hurt me, be jealous, or try to control me or suffocate my soul. Sometimes when I was by myself, I wept with gratitude for this man God brought into my life.

When, the week before I graduated with my doctorate, I was offered an opportunity to return to Ashland Seminary to direct the Doctor of Ministry program, Randall said he would do whatever it took, including moving so I could answer my call. I was forty-nine years old. We bought a small farm near Ashland and made plans for him to retire early in a year's time so that we could eventually develop a retreat ministry for burnt out pastors who needed rest and spiritual support. This course of action meant we had to live apart for a year until he could retire, only seeing each other once a month because our jobs were a hundred miles apart. Even during that stressful year of commuting he made sure we had fun when we were together.

I had only been on the job at Ashland Seminary a few months when I learned that Mom was losing her vision due to macular degeneration. She had also developed a serious heart condition, COPD, and some other health problems. At eighty-three years of age her body was beginning to wear out. So it was that Randall and I did something that earlier in my life would have been unthinkable. We invited her to come and live with us.

By then Dad had been gone for over a decade. A couple of years before he died, Mom and Dad had moved back to Oregon to live next door to my brother Jeff. Even though they failed to take care of us kids and in fact committed crimes against us and threw every one of us out while we were kids, they expected all of us to take care of them in old age. And each of us agreed to try, because something happened when Mom and Dad were in their sixties that changed everything in our relationship with them.

At age sixty Mom became convinced that she wouldn't live much longer because our father was so out of his mind with booze and regret and mental illness. She drank heavily to medicate the pain of being with him. Between alcohol, smoking two packs a day for decades, and depression, Mom figured her days were numbered. She was so worn down by his constant complaints, moods, addictions, and desire to move somewhere else that she forgot she came from tough Appalachian stock where women smoke corncob pipes and live to be a hundred. So she spent every last dime of her meager retirement funds from her nursing job in Alaska, to buy a tiny house and acreage in the Ozarks so they could have some goddamn peace and quiet in what she thought would be her final few years. They moved to West Plains, Missouri because the cost of living was very low compared to Alaska.

They hadn't been there long when what neither of them nor any of us kids ever imagined would happen, happened. Dad fell off a ladder and broke his back while fixing the roof. While he was in the hospital recovering from his injuries he began to pray. He met Jesus. Dad was born again. He came home and did not lose his newfound faith. Once home from the hospital he started getting dressed up every Sunday so he could sit in his chair and watch the TV preacher. As real as his salvation was it couldn't quite cure him of his deep aversion to people, so he never went to an actual church. But he started reading the Bible, and found a measure of peace.

Now that he added the Bible and the TV preacher to his routine, Mom felt free to move past her disgust with stuffed shirts and judgmental bastards and go to church herself. She had already begun reading the Bible when no one was looking. And just like that their health improved. It didn't hurt that they got rid of all the liquor.

My siblings and I, who had been praying for our parents for years, were astounded. Suddenly our Christian faith was more or less acceptable to our parents. And in ways that had never been true before, we were all now welcome to come and visit.

Dad bought some cattle although he had never raised cattle, but there was an old barn and a fenced pasture so what the hell, might as well give it a try. He also raised Airedales for a while. Mom, always a sucker for his good looks, frequently pointed out how handsome he was in his Stetson and western boots. She planted a garden despite her morbid fear of snakes, of which there were many. She sent me the obituary and wedding announcements from the local small-town paper in her weekly letters because of the hilarious names she saw, her all time favorite being the wedding announcement for Elmer Fag Fog and Kissie Sue Baker. Our parents' previous life of fists, fury, guns, and liquor had miraculously run its course for the most part. My daughters were four and six at the time of my parents' conversion, so they never experienced the chaos and trauma that marked my siblings and my life with our parents. Anna and Kat loved our annual visit with Grandma and Grandpa on the farm. There were cows, puppies, and plenty of sweets.

Dad fell off the wagon once, after a good five years of sobriety, so I had to find people to take care of the kids who were in elementary school, while I went to help out. It was touch and go. The doc said we got him there just in the nick of time because Dad's organs had begun to fail. He was in rehab for a month. After that he never drank again.

They lived in Missouri for a total of twelve years, by far the longest they ever lived in one place, and they seemed happy there. But when Dad was diagnosed with congestive heart failure, they determined they should move back to Oregon so Mike could look after them. Dad had it in his head that eldest sons are responsible to care for their aged and infirm fathers, even when those sons have experienced nothing but cruelty and violence from said fathers their entire lives. I have no idea where Dad got such notions. It was unfair to Mike, and an all around bad idea, so no one was surprised that it didn't work. And none of us blamed Mike for that because he bent over backwards but it wasn't enough. Dad reverted to his old jealous contempt for Mike, despite dressing up and watching the tv preacher every Sunday. The folks went back to Missouri in a huff, but when Dad's health took a sharp turn for the worse, they returned to Oregon to live in a little apartment Jeff added on to his house, where they stayed put. Jeff had a couple of acres and raised emus, which Mom found highly entertaining.

Shortly after returning to Oregon, Dad was diagnosed with stage four lung cancer.

Dad had never been baptized after he came to faith, as he couldn't stand people or non-TV preachers, both of which are required for baptism. But as he faced his final weeks Mom told me that he would like for me to come from Ohio to offer the sacrament. By then I was a licensed pastor, living in Columbiana with Kat and the chastity chairs. I marveled at the thought of baptizing my father, who along with every other felonious crime he committed against us, strangled me when I was sixteen.

I arrived at their place a few days later, where I was greeted by Jeff's dog, the emus, and Morton the pot-bellied pig. I went into Mom and Dad's tidy little apartment with its familiar aroma of coffee, cigarettes, and Lysol. Dad, who had terrorized all of us throughout our formative years, was now eaten up with cancer, less than half his former size. His frail body leaned back in his recliner most of the time, with brief, hobbling trips to the porch to smoke. He refused medical treatment after his diagnosis because he wasn't going to let a fucking doctor hack, burn, and poison him. He'd rather die from the goddamn cancer. Now he wore pajamas, robe, socks, slippers, and gloves day and night because he couldn't quite get warm, and all he could keep down was ice cream. His skin was sallow and dry.

It was during a smoke break that I gently brought up his request for baptism. He looked at me, taking a long drag from his cigarette, eyes squinting against the smoke. "Can't do it," he said. "I've been a vicious man." I mostly listened and he mostly talked. He kept repeating over and over what a vicious man he was, as memories played through his mind. I put away my own memories because I had to. He did not speak to me as daughter. Now I was his priest, hearing his confession of lifelong, intentional, unremitting violence. I spoke of love, grace, forgiveness, the mercy of God. I said that love is God's meaning, not damnation, that God received him and would welcome him to heaven. It made no difference. He was unable to go through with baptism. I told him it was okay, the thief on the cross wasn't baptized and Jesus told him that very day they would both be in paradise. I told him Jesus loved him and that he would also be with Jesus in paradise, that he could count on it, that Jesus holds onto us when we don't know how to hold on to him, especially when we think we are too far gone. He looked at me with sorrow and shivered. He asked if he could go to bed because he was cold. That was my last conversation with my father.

CHAPTER FIFTEEN

Deep in the Heart of Texas

WHEN DAD DIED A FEW WEEKS LATER, I returned to Oregon to officiate at his funeral, something I never could have imagined doing. But it turned out it was possible, and I was able to do so from a place of peace. Mom stayed in Oregon a few more years during which time she traveled often to see us in Ohio, and to Alaska to see Julie and Jeanine. She even went to a family reunion in Kentucky to see cousins and siblings she had not seen in many decades. She spoke of how hard it was to get used to doing whatever she wanted, to jump in the truck and take off down the road whenever she wanted. Never in her life had she enjoyed such freedom. She became very active in a nearby church. She developed a deep life of prayer. As I watched her blossom after no longer being enslaved to Dad, I thought about how different her life could have been had she made different choices, had she decided to take care of us instead of enabling Dad.

So it was that when the time came that she was "old and feeble" as she put it, and needed more support, Randall and I asked her to come to Ohio. She did not want to live in our house but would be willing to live in a government subsidized apartment complex for seniors. A few weeks later she arrived by plane, with all her earthly goods following a few days later in the mail.

In her early eighties by then, Mom had macular degeneration, so she could no longer drive, which was a great loss. She also had a large aortic aneurism, heart disease, COPD, and a few other problems. After fifty years of smoking two packs a day she quit cold turkey because she couldn't justify to herself or Jesus the exorbitant price of cigarettes. Never mind the cost to her lungs.

After a couple of years on the job in Ashland, I was offered a faculty position at the Perkins School of Theology at Southern Methodist University in Dallas, Texas. The opportunity was too good to pass up. As Randall and I discussed how to get Mom to move with us to Texas, especially with her rabid contempt for Republicans, of which there are many in Texas, we decided to tell her that it would be best if we looked for a large house where she could have her own space and live with us. What with a new job and all, it would be less stressful for me to have her with us than to find an apartment for her and have to drive to see her every day. With her declining health we could be with her for constant support. Just as we made these plans and prepared to discuss them with her, Mom had an episode of atrial fibrillation, an emergency requiring hospitalization. The timing was less than ideal, but we needed to tell her about our desire for her to move in with us in Texas because we were leaving the next day to go house hunting in Texas.

Gazing up at us from her bed, Mom said with her soft Kentucky accent, "I know I always said to put me in the institute when I'm old and feeble. But I reckon I thought I could always take care of myself, and shit fire and save matches I never expected to live this long. As you can see," she said, gesturing at the heart monitor, "I'm not as powerful as I thought." She smiled sheepishly. "I reckon I could go live with you."

In Texas we bought a large, sprawling ranch style home that was already wheelchair accessible, to accommodate Mom. It was in a middle-class neighborhood with an increasingly diverse population. We were in Garland, a predominantly Latino city. Mom was intimidated by what she thought of as the opulence of the place. When we walked into the house the first time, she sat down abruptly, stunned. She took in the vaulted ceilings, fireplace, ceramic tiled floors, and the spacious suite of rooms that were just for her. "I don't know if I can live in such luxury," she said faintly. "I ain't never lived anywhere like this." She said the whole thing made her as nervous as a whore in church.

Before you know it, though, she was right at home. In the evenings after supper we all got in the backyard pool where she paddled around with her water wings singing Deep in the Heart of Texas. On the clapping part of the song she'd slap the water and laugh her head off. Mom didn't know how to swim and was terribly afraid of water, but the floaty devices gave her courage. Always an extravert, she quickly made friends with neighbors, the Jehovah's Witnesses who came to convert her, and the Terminex man.

Despite all of her health challenges she remained upbeat most of the time. As she put it, "I have a roof over my head, vittles, a good chair and prescription coverage. What more could I possibly want?" Mom loved to listen the TV preacher, Dr. David Jeremiah, every single day. She used a special low vision reading device that greatly enlarged the text of printed material, which enabled her to continue to read the Bible, the paper, biographies, mail order catalogues filled with cheap products, and anything else she could get her hands on. She read for hours every day, even when the macular degeneration had all but destroyed her eyes. She was fond of telling people, "The authorities say I'm legally blind. But really, is there such a thing as being illegally blind? I'm just asking."

She was a fervent Democrat and a political news junky who created a shrine in her room to the Obama family after Barack was elected president in 2008. There on the bookcase by her command center an entire shelf was devoted to Obama photos and memorabilia, while her own great-grandchildren's little pictures were shoved aside to make room for Sasha and Malia.

To keep her mind sharp in case she ever needed to pass a chemistry exam or save a life, she had laminated placemats with the periodic table of elements, the solar system, and the major systems of the human body, which she regularly reviewed with her reading machine. She also rehearsed the names of all the presidents of the United States going back to George Washington and could tell you when they were in office and whether or not they were conniving bastards. She drank dark roast coffee, high octane, day and night and slept like a babe.

One time on my way home from work after a very long day I stopped to get gasoline. Standing by the Miata my mind went blank and I couldn't remember our new zip code. The pump wouldn't accept my card until I did. I called Mom. She picked up the phone at once. "Mom, what's our zip code? I can't remember." She instantly rattled it off and asked in a worried voice, "Lainey, are you all right?"

Mom became an avid student of the Bible, pouring over the marginalia and asking dozens of questions when I came home from work. Her greatest joy throughout the seven years that she lived with us in Texas was to meet and befriend the steady stream of preachers, theologians, seminary students, and refugees who came to our home for meals and retreat. Mom counted among her new friends Brother Emmanuel from the Taize community in France, the Mayor of the City of Garland, Texas, several world renowned theologians, and six Congolese men who came to Dallas as refugees, who stood around her bed and sang to her in Swahili when she was hospitalized for A-Fib.

They all adored her. So did our entire neighborhood, Republicans and Democrats alike, with whom we shared monthly potluck dinners. None of them had any idea about our childhood or what we had to do to survive. They knew nothing other than a seemingly nice Christian couple with the wife's mother moved into the house on the cul de sac. One of them asked me one time in a nosey sort of way whether the house really belonged to Mom and she let us live in it so we'd take care of her, and said it was probably a financially advantageous arrangement for Randall and me. To all these people she was Dr. Heath's saintly mother, a loving friend who had plentiful wisdom and a generous heart. Dozens of times students would leave after spending an hour with Grandma, saying, "Dr. Heath, I now know where your wisdom and spirituality come from. How wonderful it must have been to have Grandma as your mother when you were a child."

She was also wildly funny. Her advancing spiritual maturity and deep experiences of God never made a dent in her lifelong appreciation for crude humor, nor did the church people manage to cure her profanity. Her nickname for Kat was CLS, which stood for Cute Little Shit. Sometimes when we prayed together in the evening she forgot herself and offered intercession for the greedy bastards in Congress. To her final days she could crack jokes that would make a sailor blush, and she knew by heart the lyrics of hundreds of back country ditties such as this one that she loved to sing with her brother Randy:

There was a woman from Boheath,
Who sat on her own false teeth.
She jumped up with start and said "Bless my heart!
I've bitten myself underneath!"

As she grew older, and in some ways more childlike it took more work to protect her from herself. It was like having an extremely smart, politically informed preschooler. By her early nineties Mom was on oxygen 24/7 for the COPD. She also had to use a walker because of what she always referred to as her goddamn knee. Sometimes instead of trailing the long tube of oxygen as she made her way to the bathroom and then having to wrangle the walker and the tube through the doorway, she would take off the tubing in her room and carefully drape it across the walker so the dog wouldn't lick the cannula. After peering around with her remaining peripheral vision to make sure she wasn't being observed, she would ditch the walker and take off, careening down the hall to use the toilet in newfound freedom. Sometimes she'd even sneak out to the kitchen like that. The problem was, without oxygen she couldn't breathe, so her escape never lasted very long. Now and then she just got fed up with all of it. "Shit and two's eight!" she would shout, shaking her head in disgust.

One day when I came home from work after a long day, and went to her room to check on her, she sensed my weariness. She beckoned me to sit down. Laboriously she stood, moved her walker behind my chair, took her hairbrush from the dresser and began to gently brush my shoulder length hair, braiding and unbraiding it, over and over. I have no memory of her brushing my hair since the twins were born.

"Tell me all about it," she said as she brushed. "What'd the goddamn Pharisees and Sadducees get up to today?" It was a joke she often used—referring to the two main Jewish sects in the New Testament as code for religious leaders acting like beltline politicians. I told her about this and that, slowly going into an endorphin induced stupor.

In this way in her final years, long after I thought it possible, decades after I stopped longing for her love or expecting anything from her at all, she offered herself to me.

We spoke many times in Texas about our histories, the neglect and abuse, the trauma. The worst conversation we had, by far, was when I told Mom about old man Dodson. "What the hell do you mean, he raped you?" she demanded, almost as outraged with me in that moment as she was the day it happened. For a moment I felt as if I were eight years old again, terrified, in need of a place to hide. "Why didn't you tell me? You mean that happened and you never told me? Why the hell not?" She screeched, setting off a coughing fit that required me to find her inhaler and help her settle down.

"Mom," I said hoarsely, kneeling beside her chair with the medicine. "I couldn't tell you. I was a traumatized, broken little girl, and you and Dad were drunk. He had the gun threatening to shoot Mrs. Dodson. You both shouted at me. All I could do was run and hide. You never asked if I was okay, if the old man hurt me. You never said anything about it the next day, or ever." At that point she started to weep in great, heaving sobs, cursing herself and her life, apologizing over and over. I felt myself going numb because I had to take care of her breathing, and her emotions. My own feelings had to wait until later.

It was excruciating for Mom to revisit our childhood, and very difficult for me, but she wanted to have these conversations and to come to peace with herself and all her young'uns. In this way, over those nine years of life together we were reconciled. I came to terms both with her culpability in our trauma, and with the hurtful limitations and circumstances that were not her fault, and with the trajectory of violence and dehumanization that spun out for me from my formative years and contributed to my vulnerability to toxic, abusive, misogynistic religion.

The hardest work of Mom's life was to forgive herself, she said.

Sometimes when church people were around she talked about our childhood and watching us grow up as if it had been a charmed existence with holidays, family outings, and joy. It was all a pack of lies, the small town Andy Griffith existence she longed for but never had.

At such times I could hardly bear to be in the same room with her, listening to revisionist history. But we got through it. I knew she was trying to cope and that was all she could manage on those days.

One time when I was saying goodnight to her, Mom asked, "Do you remember when we lived in that little house on Hauser Boulevard by the girls' reform school in Helena? You were four years old. You came in and said, 'Mama, when I grow up and you grow down, I'll take care of you. I'll be your mama.' I have no idea what prompted you to say such a thing. Do you reckon that was a prophecy? Because that's where we are now. You grew up and I grew down. And you're pretty much my mama now." I mumbled something from my sleepy stupor. Then she said almost to herself, "All those years I watched you raise your young'uns I wished I could have been your little girl."

We hadn't been in Texas long when Mom was diagnosed with colon cancer. She would need surgery right away, the doctor said, but he thought she had a pretty good chance of not needing chemo or radiation. A few days after the tumor was removed and we all rejoiced that she was going to be okay, Mom developed post-surgical complications. She required a second, emergency operation. At this point she hovered near death. She was having pulmonary trouble, and her kidneys were shutting down. Jeanine had come down from Alaska for the original surgery. Now before she went home we made a plan for looking after Mom, who was unconscious and on a ventilator in ICU. We didn't want her to suffer needlessly because of our failure to notice something we could do for her.

In addition to taking turns physically being at the hospital, we printed out an 8x10 photo of her at my PhD graduation ceremony. She looked very smart in the eggplant woolen coat, her hair styled elegantly for the occasion. That was the first time Mom ever came to a rite of passage in my life. She was never there for weddings, births, graduations, crises, or anything else. But Dad was gone by the time I finished my program, and Mom could travel as much as she liked. When she did come to my doctoral graduation she sat in the front row and clapped harder than anyone else. She jabbed the people next to her with her elbows and told them in a loud voice that was her daughter, the Reverend Doctor Heath. We placed the photo and some bullet point facts about Mom in size 16 font on the bulletin board in her ICU room. We wanted the staff to know something human and endearing about the unconscious old woman on a ventilator and in a coma:

- Hi, I'm Helen Heath, a retired registered nurse. I worked as a nurse for 50 years in hospitals like this one
- I love country music and being with people
- Here I am at my daughter, Dr. Heath's graduation
- Thank you for taking such good care of me. As a fellow nurse, I know and appreciate the amount of work it takes to help patients like me recover. Thank you for everything.

To the astonishment of most of the medical staff Mom pulled through. She spent three months in the hospital before she was ready to come home. I picked her up in my Miata, the top down to accommodate the oxygen tank, walker, suitcase, and the twenty-four inch animated frog that sang in Louis Armstrong's voice, It's a Wonderful World. We peeled out like a couple of wild thangs, ready to leave those months behind. The surgeon toasted Mom with champagne when she went in for her post-op visit. He said some of the other docs told him he was an idiot for investing so much in a useless old woman. But he told them to shut up, she was a fighter, she would live to die another day. And she did.

After that Mom had a personal care assistant thirty hours per week and a home health nurse who visited regularly. They worshipped her. She lived another thirteen years. After she turned ninety, she became more frail and was hospitalized several times for heart problems. She felt anxious whenever I traveled for work, which was often. She really wanted a daughter close by all the time, just in case. Jeanine and I talked it over with Mom and on Good Friday, 2012, I took Mom to Alaska. We boarded the plane with her oxygen, walker, and a suitcase with a week's worth of clothes plus her Big Mouth Billy Bass wall plaque that sang Take Me to the River. When we arrived, she stayed for a brief few weeks with Jeanine and her wife, Jackie, then moved into a senior apartment complex a five-minute walk from their house in Wasilla. Before you know it, she was campaigning for her fellow residents to re-elect Barack Obama, threatening to kneecap them if they didn't.

For the next five years Jeanine and Jackie looked after Mom every day. Julie, who lived an hour away in Anchorage, tenderly washed Mom's feet and gave her regular pedicures, and did whatever else she could to help. Though Mom was no longer able to leave her apartment much, she did attend worship and a Bible study at the local United Methodist Church. There she beguiled the pastors with her insightful theological comments and crude jokes, and frequent requests that they do the Hokey Pokey with her. "Because really," she said, "that's what it's all about."

When she was ninety-five and had been back in Alaska four years, Mom decided she would not be buried with Dad, who had been laid to rest in the National Cemetery in White City, Oregon, for over two decades. Mom felt guilty for spurning a free burial plot with Dad, partly because it was free and partly because of Dad. But by then she finally told herself and all of us kids the truth, that it was awful to be enmeshed with his violence and have her entire life consumed by his mental illness, cruelty, and needs. Though she still loved him and kept his photo on her bedside table, she saw no need to be trapped with him in the grave. He was with Jesus anyway, she reckoned, not in the ground, and she had saved up enough money to buy herself a spot wherever the hell she wanted. So it was that she purchased a niche for her future urn in the public cemetery in Palmer, Alaska, nestled between the Talkeetna and Chugach mountains.

Right around the time Mom decided where we should eventually lay her to rest, I received an email from an executive head-hunter. He said that I had been nominated as an excellent candidate for the position of Dean of the Divinity School at Duke University, one of the most elite theological schools in the nation. He asked for a phone conversation.

I thought some good-hearted pal sent a letter to them because he liked one of my books, thinking it would be a long shot but what the heck, it can't hurt to try. I learned much later that my nominators and advocates included several Bishops, former deans including one that had served at Duke for a long time, academic colleagues, Duke students and alumni, and pastors from within and beyond Methodism. I had been nominated by all of them because of my innovative work in theological education, and because of my prophetic voice in the church. They each believed I could bring necessary change to theological education at a time when the church and the academy needed to retool as quickly as possible for a very different future.

I read the email again and laughed hard.

That night I showed the message to Randall. "It's flattering to be asked," I said, "But there's no way I'm going to apply for this job at Duke. I'm not their type. They are very traditional, patriarchal, and institutional, which means they would be allergic to me. I'm a feminist, an innovator, and do my best work on the edges of institutions, creating experiments. I need elbow room. No matter what they might say now about wanting change, I would make them mad, they would make me mad, and it wouldn't end well."

Randall said, "You need to take this seriously. This is the third time in two years you've been recruited to be a dean or president of a school of theology. People recognize your leadership and vision. Somebody at Duke must see it, too, or they wouldn't have come after you. Pray about it." I didn't want to pray about it. So I ate chips and watched Poldark.

But Randall and my closest spiritual friend prevailed, urging me to seriously consider it. So a few days later I took time for retreat to focus on this new, unexpected possibility. It had taken decades to free myself and heal from abusive relationships and religious institutions. The thought of going to work in an environment known for its patriarchy and resistance to change was not what I wanted to do.

People scoff sometimes at those who claim to hear God speak. But that is because they have yet to perceive or perhaps trust how God speaks and what God says. God is always present, always listening, always speaking to us. As Betty taught me long ago, prayer is about gazing back into the face of Jesus, who always gazes at us with infinite love. Betty also taught me to listen to what God says when specific direction is given. "Always say yes to God," she said, "and God will make a way for you." And I had promised her I would do that.

While walking around that balmy Texas night with owls hooting softly in the trees, I heard from Jesus. The call was as clear and detailed as when I lived in Canada and Jesus asked the impossible of me—to say yes to threefold ministry when I had a thousand obstacles and no knowledge of how to overcome them. The outcome of saying "yes" to this call to Duke would be a gamble. But in Jesus' view, it was worth the risk to try.

I knew I had a choice, that I was not being forced, that I was being asked to get onto a rickety raft and go down level five rapids. But in the end I said yes, because what else could I do? Even as I said yes, my heart was pierced with knowing. This would be the hardest professional work I had ever done.

I called the head-hunter and applied for the job. Nine months later I was offered and accepted the appointment. I had broken a stained-glass ceiling. I became the first female Dean at the Divinity School at Duke University, one of the most elite educational institutions in America. This happened in the volatile south during the rise of Donald Trump's administration while waves of outraged protests swept academic institutions nationally around issues of freedom of speech, academic freedom, trigger warnings, Black Lives Matter, the #MeToo Movement, and more.

I was tasked by the President and Provost above all else to lead systems change so that the school would become truly diverse and equitable around race, gender, and sexuality. It was going to be a new day. Secondarily I was to guide the school in creating and launching a vibrant vision and strategic plan that made sense given rapidly changing contexts of the students. My expertise in emergence of new forms of faith communities, my experience with innovation in theological education, and my many strong connections across and beyond the United Methodist Church were just what the school needed, the President said. I would be able to guide the school with a steady but creative hand as it navigated the shifting sands of culture change.

I was installed during Opening Convocation, with President Brodhead introducing me and participating in the liturgy, which he said was not something he normally did with new deans. At the appointed time I strode to the elevated pulpit, stood as tall as possible so my Hobbit-sized self could see over the monolith, and looked out at the gathered community. We were in Duke Chapel, the internationally renowned Gothic cathedral whose African American architect, Julian Abele, drew inspiration from Oxford and Cambridge Universities.

It was time for me to bring the word of God.

There in the front were the upturned faces of the faculty, including some of the most distinguished theologians in the world. Jeanine and our brother Mike sat with Randall and a large group of our friends. I could scarcely believe we were all together in this place. I thought of the chaos of our childhood as I gazed at Mike and Jeanine, marveling at how far we had come from the time Mike had to sleep with an axe under his bed and we nearly lost Jeanine to failure to thrive. I thought of old man Dodson and Mrs. Dodson's eyes, of the many times I had been told one way or another to get the hell out, that I didn't belong. I recalled Alex telling me that my education was a waste of time because no one would ever hire me. I remembered the woman from the crack house who had come to save me with her fists, and wrecked my tidy theology.

That morning in Duke Chapel I preached from Acts 10 about Cornelius and the cloth being lowered from heaven and the Apostle Peter having to learn he had no right to call anyone unclean. I preached about Jesus coming to us in the very people we love to hate, the people we exclude and think we're doing God a favor. I preached about how God educates us.

Shortly after I was installed as Dean, Jeanine called to tell me Mom had developed what the doctor thought was lung cancer, but that in light of her advanced age and many other health problems, Mom decided not to receive treatment other than comfort care, and her time was short. I quickly booked a flight to Anchorage, arriving a few days later. I stayed at Jeanine and Jackie's lakefront house but walked through the wintry forest every day to the senior complex where Mom lived. We drank coffee, talked about everything under the sun, and laughed a lot. I wore my new Duke sweatshirt and told her all about my new job. Though almost completely blind at ninety-six, her eyes rested upon me, shining with joy at what had become of her oldest girl. Our hearts were at peace.

Mom died a couple months later, December 11, 2016. At her funeral the very last thing that happened was the pastor played a video Mom had recorded of herself, with help from Jeanine, standing next to where her urn would go in the cemetery. She told all of us not to cry too much, she was with Jesus now, and nothing is better than that. She then sang all the verses of "In the Sweet Bye and Bye," waved, and said "Bye-bye" in her sweet Kentucky voice, cracking herself up at getting in the last word at her own funeral.

Helen Madon, R.N. (1944)

Fred Heath, U.S. Original Paratrooper (1944)

Mom & Dad's Wedding (1944)

Elaine & the Three Legged Dog (1956)

Elaine, Jeff, Julie, & Jeanine (1961)

Mom, Jeanine & Julie (1962)

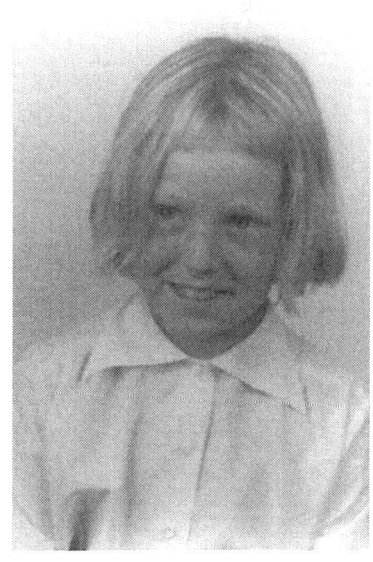

Elaine, Age 8 (1962)

Julie & Jeanine, Age 2, with Sister-Momma Elaine, Age 9 (1963)

Jeanine & Julie, Age 5 (1966)

Elaine, Age 15 (1970)

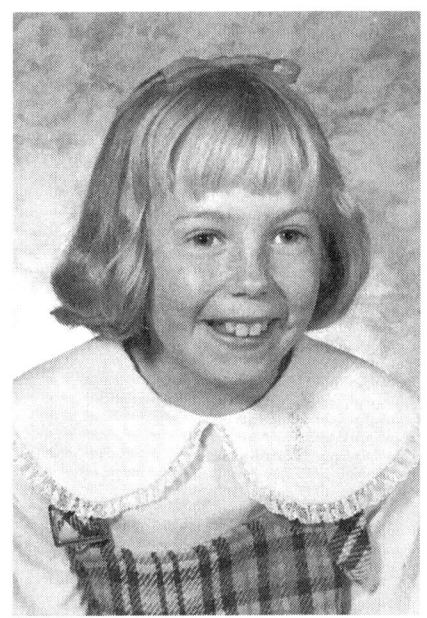
Jeanine, Age 9 (1970)

Jeanine, Age 15 (1976)

Elaine, Anna, & Kat (1976)   Jeanine, Age 25 (1985)

Elaine, Age 24, & Jeanine, Age 17 (1978)

Part Two

SHOWING UP TO LOVE

(Jeanine's Story)

CHAPTER SIXTEEN

Old Hands

MY HANDS HAVE ALWAYS BEEN OLD. From the day I was born they have been wrinkled with extra lines and dry skin. With each birthday that passes I slowly grow into them. Our mom told me as a little girl and throughout my childhood, "Neanie, I reckon you've always been old." I believe my soul is older than my hands. Even now, toward the end of my sixth decade, each birthday draws me to the age I've always been.

Sometimes I marvel at the abundance of my life experiences, rich with texture and depth. As a baby boomer born late into our parents' lives, I am connected to the Great Depression, profound poverty found in coal-mining-eastern-Kentucky, WWII, the American Dream, Vietnam, as well as the current day of instant technology, 24/7 news coverage, and the need to be virtually liked by all my virtual friends. Life is both more convenient and more complicated than when I was a child.

As children, we are told stories about who we are, about our unique contributions to our family, and what our potential role will be when we grow up. Our internal narrative and world perception are naturally formed in this way. Maybe a thousand times Mom told me that I was a blessing in disguise. As a little girl, I didn't know what that meant. Was it good? Was it bad? The blessing in disguise story was about my existence. At forty years of age, Mom found out that she was pregnant. Even though it was against the law, a few doctors she worked with offered her an abortion if she wanted it. She was very tempted, but decided to not terminate the pregnancy. Our father was extremely unhappy about her decision and as she said, "Your father hardly spoke a word to me the entire pregnancy." She went on to say, "It served him right when I had to have an x-ray because I was so large and there were two sets of vertebrae!" Within this unwelcoming story, she would include how she brought two bassinettes home and how amazing it was to have two babies, each under five pounds. Our father refused to hold us or to touch us for years. It was no surprise that when he eventually spoke to me, he often told me he wished I had never been born. I would later learn he told all of his children the same thing.

My twin sister Julie was born first. I made my appearance twenty minutes later. We had three older siblings, Elaine (7), Jeff (9), and Mike (14). Julie, as the family story was told, was a very happy baby, plump and dimpled, and she smiled readily and was playful and fun to care for. Julie was much more engaging for my brothers and sister, who my mother frequently relied on to entertain and care for us.

I, on the other hand, was a frail baby. My crying sounded like, "woo woo" which was the source of one of my many nicknames: Little Woo Woo. Mom said that I was a quiet baby, a sleepy baby, an unengaged baby. I was so detached that they had to wake me up to feed me and it didn't seem to bother me if Julie drank my bottle too.

When I was about eighteen months old, I got very sick and stopped eating. The doctor in the emergency room told Mom that he didn't expect me to live through the night. I was diagnosed with failure to thrive. I had given up the will to live. Years later Mom told me how I had hurt her feelings when I turned away from her when she came to see me in the hospital. Even as a baby, I was responsible for Mom's feelings. As mom would relay this story, she always ended it with, "I went home and yelled at Elaine and Jeff, you sonsabitches, put Julie down and pick Jeanine up! She will die if you don't start picking her up!" How was it my siblings' fault that I was failing to thrive? They were eight and ten years old. And how was it that at my dear twin's expense, I would now be held? What would it mean for her, that she had to be put down and I had to be picked up? Why couldn't we both be picked up?

It took a long time for me to recover from failure to thrive. My oldest brother, Mike, told me that he is haunted with memories of the skeletal baby Mom brought home, "Honey," he said, "you were so sick and thin. I'd never seen a toddler with cheek bones." My early narrative of not being wanted, not being held, not being strong was told to me repeatedly, countless times, which along with everything else we endured, created a deep sense of being inferior. How desperately I wanted to be good enough, upon which my very existence depended.

My sister, Elaine, had her seventh birthday a month after Julie and I were born. We called her Lainey. Even though she was just a little girl herself, Elaine cared for us with as much maturity and sacrifice as you can imagine. She fed us, changed our diapers, and played with us. She was our sister-momma and we were her living baby dolls. My earliest memories of Elaine are tactile. She had old hands, too. I felt at home in her hands. Corn Huskers and Avon Skin-So-Soft lotions were used in abundance. When I was scared, which was often, Elaine allowed me to sleep with her in her twin-size bed. Her only condition was that I had to put my head down by her feet and I was told not to kick her. She thought we would fit better this way as we shared the narrow bed. Because of this, I also got to know the skin on her feet, which helped me feel safe. It was a small cost to me to sleep with her feet if I could rest near Lainey.

Memory is a tricky thing. As a therapist, I respect memories that hide in the shadows and trust that when a person is ready to remember or know, they will. I am also aware of the potential for suggesting a memory or an interpretation of a memory. It is enough to deal with what we truly remember, even if it is a memory held in a muscle or in a sense of smell or on some other level of knowing.

Prior to age six, my memories are episodic snap shots of moments and feelings. For example, I do not remember being in a camper on the back of the truck with Mom when the Coleman stove blew up in her face, singeing off her eye lashes and eye brows. Nor do I recall being in the cab of the truck when our father shot a .45 pistol through the roof when I was a toddler. Or when Mom went to Arizona with a man during which time our dad took Jeff and Elaine to Michigan on the train when I was two, then returned to Dad with us when Julie and I were three. But these things happened and I hold them in my body's trauma bank. I also have sweet memories of my mother's red lipstick, powdered face, the smell of Avon "Here's My Heart" perfume, and her white nurse's hat held on with bobby pins.

There are memories that hold much more meaning in hindsight, that come into complete focus as I learned the whole story. When I was in first grade, we lived in a shabby clapboard house in Airway Heights, a small town outside of Spokane, Washington. Our father was unemployed, a sad, angry, scary man who sat day in and day out in his chair in the living room of our tiny house. When he wasn't ranting and raving, he was in a silent sulk that was full of danger. I stayed out of his way as much as possible. It was as if there were unseen trip wires around the house; the slightest real or imagined infraction would set him off. Jeff, Elaine, Julie and I all slept in a dank, smelly, unfinished basement, as if we had been sent to a child dungeon. Our brother Mike was in the army, fighting in Vietnam.

An older couple, Mr. and Mrs. Brown, lived across the street. They took my sisters and me to church with them. I loved that they gave us Life Saver mints during the service and we got to go to Sunday School with other children. It was there, in a room with fake mahogany paneled walls and chairs that were just my size that I learned Jesus loved me, that he loved all the children of the world. This gave me great joy and comfort, and was the beginning of a faith that remains to this day.

My sister, Elaine, was in 8th grade. Mr. Brown, a deacon, had a photography studio in his garage where he made portraits for graduating seniors. He began grooming Elaine, wanting her to spend a lot of time in his studio, where he pressured her to allow him to photograph her. Then Mr. Brown was arrested and sentenced for trafficking in child pornography. Elaine was lucky that he was arrested before things went further than they did, but she had to endure a traumatic police interview. The boiling waters of injury, and lack of parental protection increased the pressure within our tiny house. It was time to move, but this would not be the last time someone in the Church would prey on my sisters and me.

Moving was our way of life. Our parents perpetually looked for the elusive better job or home or life, always thinking that a change of scene would banish their inner torment. Alaska was a great place for folks looking for the mother lode of gold or other jackpot fantasies. It also served as a remote destination for those who wanted to cut off relationships with people in the lower 48 in the name of getting a fresh start.

The first time our family moved to Alaska was in 1957, before Julie and I were born. They lived in Seward and celebrated statehood in 1959 before moving back to the Pacific Northwest. A decade later, once again, we headed north to Alaska. Our father and brother Jeff made the journey first, looking for a job for Dad and a place for all of us to live. Jeff was a freshman in high school, but was often expected to function as an adult and help with yet another move. Having found a home for us, and having verified that yes, Dad had a job, Jeff returned to Washington to help the rest of us make the journey north. Julie and I turned seven somewhere on the Alcan Highway. One of the few pictures of us in our childhood features us standing beside the road with spectacular snowcapped mountains in the background. We are holding our birthday presents: a pack of Wrigley's gum and a plastic magic slate writing pad. After a week that felt like a month, our overloaded rig that we called The Crummy pulled into the trailer park where we would now live. We looked like the Beverly Hillbillies with Mom, Jeff, Elaine, Julie, and our dog Amigo. All that was missing was Granny's rocker and the chickens.

My deep affinity for mountains began in that trailer park which sat at the foothills of the Chugach Mountain range. We were in Muldoon, a neighborhood in East Anchorage. These mountains to this day remain a constant for me, anchoring me to the beauty and goodness in life. When I see them I know that I am home.

The next three years were the most stable years in my childhood. Our mother worked as a psychiatric nurse at the state hospital and when our father was sober and not pissed off with someone, he worked as a sheet metal journeyman. The mountains spread their wings wide over our lives like guardian angels, as did Elaine, who wanted us to learn how to be good girls as we grew older. If we broke a rule, lied, or did something she thought was naughty, she would spank us. Afterwards, she would point her finger and say, "I hope you're proud of yourself." We laugh about this now, and she still cringes about it. But how did we know that we needed limits? It was incredibly inappropriate that Elaine spanked us, but in spite of this we grew under her care. She was the one who would bathe us, brush our hair, and bring us small bowls of popcorn to eat as we watched Disney World on Sunday evenings.

Elaine also made sure we had fun. With her generous heart, she allowed us to go on dates with her. We made weekly trips to the roller rink with Julie and me jammed in the back seat of a car driven by one of Elaine's boyfriends. All of my senses hold memories of the roller rink. Feelings of anticipation were combined with the smell of metal ball bearings, sweaty skates, and stale popcorn. The songs "The Age of Aquarius," "Hey Jude," and "Cecilia" take me back to Friday nights when I heard the voice from the skating-rink booth say, "All skate in the opposite direction." Somehow Elaine's boyfriends put up with her kid sisters, and took us on many adventures to Thunderbird Falls or swimming at a local lake or to make Christmas cookies.

We also went to church and Sunday School with Elaine. There I sat in a circle with all the other third graders. One day the Sunday School teacher asked if anyone knew what salvation is. Well, I did. I wondered why the other children didn't know. There was a long period of silence and I tentatively raised my hand. The teacher called on me expectantly. I answered, "Salvation is where my mom buys my clothes." After a moment the teacher said "Why yes, in the same way old clothes are made new, salvation is God's way of making us new." I have always loved her for that.

During our father's drinking binges, he would start in the morning and go late into the night. His medication of choice was vodka. For breakfast he mixed it with orange juice. Later in the day, he put it in coke. You could smell it in his pores and on his breath for weeks at a time. When he sobered up, he didn't simply have hangovers; he went through retching, violent withdrawals. Getting sober often required hospitalization in order to manage the DT's.

It is impossible to keep a job when you are a profound alcoholic. A few years after returning from WWII, our father became friends with Bill W. and joined Alcoholics Anonymous. He experienced longish periods of sobriety with many short relapses knitted between. However, beginning the year before I was born, his periods of sobriety were fewer and shorter, with the longest lasting only a year or so.

There were many contributing factors that played a role in our father's addiction and mental illness. Both of our parents were nine years old when the Great Depression hit in 1929. They were profoundly impacted by poverty. Dad told stories about starving when he was a boy and stealing vegetables from neighbors' gardens. When he was a teen, he joined the Civil Conservation Corps, which offered him a chance to work outside and send money home to help his family. The CCC took our father "out west" from Ohio to Wyoming and Montana, which is where he fell in love with the Rocky Mountains. It was to those mountains that he would return again and again, looking for peace.

Later, Dad joined the Army and was one of the original paratroopers in the 1st of the 501st Company C. Eventually he traveled to Europe with 17,000 other soldiers on the Queen Mary. Our parents were married in 1944. They had met through mutual friends when Mom was attending nursing school in Toledo. Mom said to me once, many years later, "When your father came home from the war, he was a different man than I married." Indiscriminately and irrationally, the wounds and secrets he carried would spill onto his wife and children. So we moved around and around in Montana, Oregon, Washington, Idaho, Alaska, our father always seeking something beyond his reach, our mother having to find work so that we could live.

Along with Fred Flintstone and Ralph Kramden (played by Jackie Gleason), Dad shaped my early ideas about men. All three of them yelled when they came home from work. Fred Flintstone yelled at the top of his lungs, "WILMA!!!!" and Ralph yelled with a raised fist, "One of these days, Alice, POW, right in the kisser."

It was normal for Dad to be angry, loud, and cuss entire sentences of profanity. Coming home he would exhale loudly through his nostrils, slam his thermos and shoes down, and finally explode into a tirade of perceived injustices and insults that he had endured during the day. At any point something that had been okay the day before would not be okay today and we would be the target of his rage. After storming verbally for an hour or so, he would change into his pajamas and robe, which had been starched and ironed for him. He would then be served dinner on a tray in the living room so that he could watch the news and not have to engage his family. Later we might all watch Ralph Kramden threaten to hit his wife one of these days. This is what men got to do, even when they were sober.

Mom listened to Dad rant and tried to placate him in various ways. The eggshells she walked on were razor sharp. As a registered nurse she worked with psychiatric patients during the day. She came home to a mentally ill alcoholic at night. PTSD wasn't a thing anyone talked about back then. There was no way either of our parents could look honestly at the anxiety or obsessive-compulsive behaviors that poured out of our Dad. To help her cope, Mom drank a lot of beer, but she was a different kind of alcoholic than Dad. As a functional alcoholic, she drank every night to numb the pain of her life choices, but she was able to keep a job in spite of frequent hang-overs. The quicksand of codependency had a death grip on Mom before I was ever born, and now we all lived in the perpetual, chaotic doublespeak of love/hate, respect/rage, want/void. With a hillbilly twist, our mom could cuss almost as fluently as our father. While she deeply resented him, she also irrationally believed that he would die without her, that she had been assigned to be his personal savior. This belief was played out time after time with our mother literally choosing our dad over her own children's safety and security.

Our mother, Helen, was born in 1920, the eldest child of a coal miner and his wife in Harlan, Kentucky. She was an optimistic, intelligent, hard-working girl who had a keen sense of humor. As the oldest of six children she often had to live for a while with an aunt due to her momma being sick, or because it would mean one less mouth to feed in hard times. Mom didn't get to go to school in third grade because she had no shoes. Food, coal, and everything else that required money was scarce. Once her father asked her to go out along the train tracks at night to collect broken coal that had fallen off the carts because the family couldn't afford to buy coal. But she was too afraid of the dark so she helped herself to coal from a neighbor's bucket on their porch. When her father saw the big, fine pieces of coal he gave her a whipping for stealing and lying. Her parents were poor, but they were also proud.

When our mother entered high school, she left her family to attend Pine Mountain Settlement School, a boarding school run by missionaries for Appalachian children. She excelled in school, academically and socially. Like other students, she worked in the kitchen to help pay her room and board. The boarding school often hosted interesting guests. One visitor was so impressed with the biscuits, he asked to speak with the baker. Mom went to the dining room to meet him. He told her, "I'm Colonel Sanders and I've opened a restaurant called Kentucky Fried Chicken. Would you consider coming to work for me? Your biscuits are the best I've ever eaten." She told him, "No thank you, I am going to become a nurse when I finish high school." Throughout my childhood whenever we were flat broke and Mom had to hock Dad's gun to buy food, she would wonder out loud how our life might have been different if she had said yes to Colonel Sanders.

Pine Mountain Settlement School was not an accredited high school, so when our mother graduated at the top of her class she wasn't able to meet the admissions criteria for nursing school. Her beloved teacher, Miss Cold, had a solution. Miss Cold was already preparing to return to her home state of California. She offered to take Mom to live in her family's home so Mom could earn a diploma from an accredited high school with only one additional year of schooling. After graduating from Pine Mountain in 1938, she headed west with Miss Cold, graduating a second time a year later with a diploma from an accredited high school. She then was accepted into nursing school in Toledo, Ohio, which had been her dream since she was a little girl and watched the itinerant nurse come on horseback to see people in the coal camps. Little did Miss Cold know that her student would practice her healing arts in far off places like Alaska.

Miss Cold had a life-long positive impact on Mom's life. When I sorted through Mom's belongings after she died, I found a large bundle of letters from Miss Cold. They had stayed in contact, in spite of all my parents' moves. I found some letters written in 1968 and '69 to our Alaskan address.

As a third-grade student in 1969 in Alaska, I learned that not all teachers are cut from the same cloth as Mom's beloved Miss Cold. My teacher, Mr. Henderson, had a few strikes against him from the get go: he was a man and he scared the shit out of me. He was the teacher in charge, which meant he was the acting principal whenever the real principal was out of the building. He did not redeem my skewed perception of men with his stern voice, strict rules, and always groomed military haircut. Maybe it was the way he would use a baseball bat to hit the giant icicles hanging off the school roof during winter. Maybe it was the time he made me bend over and hold my ankles while he hit my butt with a wooden paddle.

It's true that I called the lunch-lady a kindergartner, but that hardly justified corporal punishment. After the public spanking I ran to my desk, buried my face in my arms and cried inconsolably. I was still crying when all the other students came in from recess. Mr. Henderson said in a stern voice, "Jeanine, that is quite enough. You need to stop it!" When I brought my head up, there was an amazing amount of snot connecting the desk to my face. Between the shame of paddling and the snot, I wanted to crawl into a hole and disappear. It wasn't many days later that I peed my pants in class because I was too afraid to ask to go to the toilet. One trauma led to another, both at home and at school.

When he was sixteen our brother, Jeff, quit high school. As an intelligent introvert he survived life at home by perpetually escaping into science fiction and adventure novels. Jeff thought high school was a waste of time. He took his GED and then joined the Coast Guard. About that same time our father's dad, Grandpa, came to live with us. Elaine moved into Jeff's old room and Grandpa moved into Elaine's room, which isn't saying much because the rooms in our trailer would be closets in many people's homes. The trailer was able to fit all of us, but Grandpa's increasing senility was too much to contain. Eventually, Grandpa was placed in a nursing home. On Saturdays, after we finished doing our laundry at the laundromat, Mom would take us to see Grandpa, bringing him gifts of cigarettes and chocolates. Mom was juggling more and more, while our father's addiction and grief demanded all of his attention.

By the mercy of the gods, my fourth-grade teacher, Miss Roberts, was a gentle angel who hugged her fearful students, read *Where the Red Fern Grows* to her class after lunch, and sang "Puff the Magic Dragon" while she played the guitar. She never corrected me when I lied during Show and Tell, sharing the exact story another student had just said about their father killing a bear while hunting. It was an obvious copy-cat move on my part. In hindsight she may have known my dad was home, drunk.

Elaine, now a junior in high school, met a handsome guy at the roller-rink named Alex. He was older than her, but that wasn't an issue in our house. Alex was on a college work exchange for the summer and fall semester. As with other boyfriends, Elaine let Julie and me tag along on dates, but this was the first boyfriend she had who came with his own apartment. There was something more serious about this relationship, but from my nine year old perspective it was just fun to be at his house making Christmas cookies or hanging out. Alex was very good at roller-skating, too. Elaine was heartbroken when his semester work was completed in Alaska and he moved back to New Mexico.

It was during this time that in conversation with Dad, Elaine referred to Grandpa as "the old geezer," which set off a chain reaction. I watched in horror as the rage in my father's eyes became violence, as he screamed profanity at Elaine and grabbed her petite body, slamming it to the floor. He straddled her, pinning her arms beneath his knees. She screamed and cried as he put his hands around her neck and strangled her. Was Elaine going to die? Somehow, I don't know why, Dad stopped. He punched holes through the paneled wall beside her room.

A few weeks later, my sister-momma left home forever. She moved to New Mexico to live with Alex's family. A few weeks after that, our parents signed permission for their sixteen-year-old child to marry. Elaine finished high school as a married woman in New Mexico. Julie and I were alone with our parents without our sister-momma, who had always been our buffer against Dad's rage.

I grieved like a child for her dead mother. The red patchwork quilt on Elaine's bed held my tears, my sorrow, my traumatized body. There was no comfort offered to Julie or me in words of explanation. No one seemed to notice or understand that my heart was broken. Nothing was said about Dad's behavior being wrong or violent or crazy or criminal. The narrative our parents concocted to cover the truth was that Elaine had to move because there was so much racial unrest at her high school. With this fiction, our parents justified their actions.

Chaos and unpredictability had always been the norm in our family. Nothing made sense at the time, and looking back the choices our parents made seem even crazier than they did then. The perpetual lump in my throat told me to stay alert. It didn't matter if my father was drunk or sober, he was out of control, ready to savage anyone who crossed him. I watched him the way you keep an eye on a vicious dog, noticing the moment his squinted eyes and sucked in breath announced another fit of rage.

Many decades later, after Mom died and my sisters and I cleared out her apartment, I found a letter dated Spring 1971. It was written by a psychiatrist, one of Mom's colleagues, to the Coast Guard requesting that Jeff be given an honorable discharge to help with his family. The psychiatrist wrote, per our mother's request, that our father was mentally ill, violent, and was threatening to kill himself. Jeff was needed at home to help his mother and little sisters. It was a family hardship issue. It was all true, but it was also false. Once again Jeff's future was hijacked by our parents' endless quest to move to the ideal location where they could leave their problems behind. Jeff's dreams were deferred as he returned to help us with yet another move. Like Mom with Colonel Sanders, I have wondered what our brother's life might have become if he had been allowed to stay in the Coast Guard.

Jeff moved Dad to Orofino, Idaho, that spring. Mom, Julie and I would make the trek after Mom sold our trailer, quit her job, and school was out. A person interested in buying our trailer walked through it and asked me why there was a patch on the wall in the hallway. I told them, "The patch covers holes in the wall where my dad punched it when he was drunk." After they left, Mom grabbed both of my shoulders, shaking me and yelling, "Don't tell people that! Our dirty laundry is none of their goddamn business!"

We must have been quite a sight with our worn-out, frazzled, fifty-year-old Mom driving an equally worn out station wagon with her senile father-in-law and twin nine-year-old daughters headed south to the Canadian border. It took a long time to make the journey, partly due to the distance of the Alcan Highway and partly because Mom needed a few extra days to drink a case of beer at a motel in Canada. We finally made it to the twenty acres of land and double wide trailer where Dad was waiting in Orofino, Idaho.

The Clearwater River Valley was beautiful, winding through the gorges with intermittent white water and trout pools. We called the property "Heath Mountain" because our trailer and acreage were on the top on one of many mountains eight miles above the town of Orofino. Mom found a job at the state psychiatric hospital.

Grandpa lived with us for a brief time, until a room opened up at an old folks' home down the road. He called me *boy*, which was irritating, because he couldn't remember I was a girl no matter how many times I told him. He would point out the window and say, "Boy, see the Indians on the top of the mountains across the valley?" I would tell him, "No, Grandpa. Those are trees, tall pine trees." I was told repeatedly what a good and gentle man Grandpa had been before he became senile. I wished I could have known the man that raised our father, and I wondered why in light of his kind father, Dad was so scary. I only knew Grandpa as an old man who saw Indians in trees, spent hours looking at leaves, and wanted to get home to Tennessee because he needed to feed his mules.

Jeff had done his duty to our father and then some. Honorably discharged from the Coast Guard, this twenty-year old son helped him move, find Heath Mountain, and completed projects to fix up the place, all the while enduring insults and angry outbursts. The small workshop with a lean-to was done. The entry way was paneled and the porch was painted. The trailer was skirted which included a small access door. All this time, Jeff's wavy brown hair was growing long and his patience short. When we finally arrived in Orofino, he had had enough of hearing our father say, "You lazy good-for-nothing piece of shit! You'll never amount to anything!"

Before Jeff hit the road, he spent some time with Julie and me. There was a small beach and swimming hole nearby on the Clearwater River. We had made a few trips there. It was fun to watch Jeff float the current as I stayed close to the shore because I didn't know how to swim. The last time we went there, Jeff didn't swim; he sat near the car, smoking Marlboros and planning his escape from Dad. This time there were more people. It was a warm day with several families playing at the swimming hole. I must have stepped into a dip on the river floor or maybe the current pulled me too far. Suddenly, I was over my head. Time slowed way down with each detail etched into my memory where it played itself out in nightmares again and again in the years that followed.

I told myself to push my feet down on the river floor propelling my body up. As I broke through the surface, I gasped air and yelled, "HELP!" before going down, and repeated the same down, up, surface, air, scream several times. How did I know to do this? Before going down, maybe the fourth time, I heard Julie scream my name. Up and down a few more times as my fear and exhaustion were giving in to the current. Suddenly, a man grabbed me. My arms and legs wrapped around this savior, who carried me to shore. By this time, Jeff was standing next to Julie. Looking pissed, embarrassed, and relieved, he told us to get in the car. We drove home in silence. It wasn't very many days later when Jeff moved to a nearby town.

Honeymoons only last so long. The newness of the move, the beauty of the land, the fresh start came to a violent end one night. Dad and Mom had been drinking and had been sequestered in their bedroom for the better part of a day. Julie and I had been instructed to leave them alone. As the day passed, it was odd and nice to hear laughter coming from their room. But passion can be a two-edged sword, sharp in its exacting of pleasure until it cuts you to the bone. Our parents' passion was like that.

We were playing in our bedroom when we heard raised voices and glass breaking. Our father yelled, "Goddammit, I'll kill you!" More loud sounds, like a body hitting the wall. Julie and I huddled together in the doorway of our room. I could see our mother's body through her nightgown when she ran out into the hallway. She was drunk, yelling "RUN, your father is going to kill us all!" Dad was right behind her, pistol in hand. He lunged and grabbed her by the hair. She fell. He fell, still holding the gun. Julie and I were beside ourselves. Mom rose to her feet, grabbing us. We ran out into the dark mountain night. There was no moon, no yard light. We could hear our father shouting "I'm gonna kill you sonsabitches!" We found the hinged door through the skirting around the trailer and crawled in as quietly as we could. There we stayed for hours, in terror, with a dry mouth and in absolute silence. We sat with spiders and beetles and God knows what, listening to Dad yell, listening to his foot-steps come and go, finally listening to silence. Sometime before dawn we crawled out and crept into the station wagon. The keys to the car were in the house so Mom could not drive us to safety.

Even as a nine-year old, I had already begged Mom to leave Dad a million times. She always agreed that our father was a mean bastard, but nothing ever changed. That morning in the car was different. It was one of the rare times when Mom made a choice to protect us. She told us, "Stay in the car. Your goddamn father has probably passed out." Quietly, she made her way into the trailer and found him on the floor of their bedroom, unconscious. The gun was a few feet from his hand. She grabbed it and put it in her purse, then returned to the car and said, "We're leaving. Your dad is passed out so I don't think he will wake up, but be very quiet while you put your clothes in a grocery sack. I've got the gun in the car." The three of us tip toed into the trailer, grabbed as much as we could, and drove away. Relief was a warm blanket enfolding us after the terror of the night. We drove on and on, toward what would become the worst poverty of our lives.

CHAPTER SEVENTEEN

Chaos Breeds Chaos

THE FIRST OF SEVERAL shit-hole trailers and shacks that we then called "home" was outside of Coeur d'Alene, Idaho. Mom found yet another job at Deaconess Hospital in Spokane, but this trailer was cheap so she made the half hour or so commute. It was July. Had it only been a month since we left Alaska? We stayed in this trailer for less than a month, but it was long enough for Julie and me to make friends with a family a few doors down. All of their names escape me except the dad, John. This family lived in poverty too, but there was sweetness and laughter between them. They loved each other and welcomed us. As was always the case for my siblings and me, we had to find adults who became for us the extended family we never had. It was that search for adult care that made us so susceptible to predators.

We didn't know our paths would cross again with John and his family, when we moved to the next place closer to Mom's job. The duplex was better than the trailer and was near the elementary school, but we had no furniture, so we slept on the floor. Jeff reappeared. He helped Mom with expenses and took care of us when she worked the night shift. Julie and I started fifth grade. After a few days in music class I was given a loaner violin. I carried it home overwhelmed with wonder and anticipation. I was going to learn to make music. That night, our mother said we were moving on her next day off to Post Falls, Idaho. My music education ended before it could start.

The dilapidated white shack sat on a frontage road outside of Post Falls, close to the Washington border. We settled into it for the remaining school year. Our landlord lived next door in a white, two story house with dormers and blue shutters, and a lawn. Out back, there were several broken-down out buildings, an irrigation ditch, and beyond that fields of wheat. Mr. Wilson's house seemed like a palace compared to our dump. I have often wondered how he lived with himself knowing the conditions in which we lived. The shack was poorly insulated, heated with an oil barrel stove in the living room. There was a small unheated addition that became two "bedrooms" by means of a thick sheet of tan canvas hung from the ceiling. Mom slept on one side, Jeff on the other. Julie and I had bunkbeds in a room you walked thru to get to the bathroom and the lean to. The bathroom was the only room with a door.

When we started at our new school, Julie and I were surprised and delighted to see that our recent neighbor, John, was now our bus driver. His family had also moved. John was the saving grace that year because the school was the worst of our childhood. Even though we were only in fifth grade, the school was run like high school with six classes and lockers in the hallway. It felt like a military bootcamp to me.

Being a new kid is always a challenge, but when you're a traumatized kid living in poverty and constantly on the move it is especially hard. Maybe it was Miss Burgess, the English teacher from New York who had big teeth and big glasses and gave me big red Fs on my papers. Maybe it was the pretty math teacher who maintained eye contact with me when she told the whole class that we needed to change our clothes and bathe more often. Maybe it was how the teachers called me by my last name because they couldn't remember I had a first name and didn't seem to know me at all. I stayed home as often as I could with bellyaches, headaches, and heartaches and could hardly wait for summer to come.

Violence, trauma, and near-death experiences have a way of making the brain go into a state of keen observation, noticing the slightest twitch, eye movement, or pause. By age ten, my old soul and old hands were as hyper-vigilant as any combat vet. Our mother worked the 3 to 11 shift, so we didn't see her much but when we did I watched her like a hawk. We left notes for her to read when she came home and she left inexpensive Spanish rice on the stove for our dinner. That was the year I became my mother's mother. I watched her drinking, depression, and being a victim of my father. I watched the rip current of codependence pulling her. I watched in horror as Mom began to have telephone conversations with Dad, who was still living on Heath Mountain. I saw her pay his bills and use what was left over for us. Every month I watched her hock the gun that almost killed us, so she'd have a little money to live on 'til payday. Somehow we kept going.

Being a twin was one of the great gifts of life because it meant having a constant playmate, one who understood your life. We were good friends most of the time. Being unsupervised, our adventures were only limited by our imagination. One of the ramshackle sheds in the back yard was still standing but the glass had long since disappeared from the windows. Discarded junk, dirt, and cement blocks cluttered the floor. Julie and I spent days cleaning it out, creating our own special playroom. We went swimming in the irrigation ditch, which smelled funny but was waist deep and warm enough. We used the rusted steel clothes line posts for monkey bars, swinging upside down with our knees over the top. When we could scrape up small change we walked several miles into town to buy candy and play on a real playground. As the weather turned cold we had to stay indoors.

That winter an epic blizzard brought a deep freeze, mounds of snow, and many days off school. The water pipes froze. Mom and Julie went to the landlord's fancy house with a bucket and cheap plastic pitchers to get water. This state of affairs coincided with running out of money to buy fuel oil. Julie and I were reduced to huddling under old green army blankets and quilts, where we watched cartoons on the black and white tv. Food was almost gone too, but Mom made corn bread in a cast iron skillet in the oven. We filled our empty bellies with corn bread and peanut butter, huddling around the open oven as the temperature in the house dropped below freezing. The water in the toilet turned to ice. Before long the toilet became an overflowing nightmare of human waste. Our mother was going through menopause, with heavy bleeding added to everything else. Not knowing what was wrong with her I assumed the worst, that our mother was about to die.

I do not remember when the house got warm again, or who cleaned the appalling bathroom, or when our mother explained to us about menopause and blood. But eventually all those things happened.

The merry-go-round of our life kept turning. One morning Mom didn't wake us up for school, which we didn't really mind. I thought she was tired, so we let her sleep until it was time for her to get ready for work. As her mother, I knew how much time she would need so that she would not be late. At the appointed time we shook her, touched her face, cried, but nothing would rouse her. We let her sleep awhile longer and tried again. We panicked. I have no memory of this, probably from the trauma, but years later Mom often told me that I called her workplace to ask one of the nurses to come to our house to help, because our mother would not wake up. We saved her life, because she had severe alcohol poisoning from drinking a six pack of beer and slamming an entire 5th of vodka.

I wore depression like a heavy winter coat. At night, laying in the lower bunk, I quietly cried, longing for my sister momma, the Chugach Mountains, the roller rink. When I went to school, I managed to make a few friends but no one knew the burden that I carried, because they did not come to our house, and I had been keeping family secrets my whole life. I lived with a constant sense of impending doom. At school, I felt stupid maybe even retarded. I was living into one of the labels my parents gave me—*the sweet little retard*—but I didn't care anymore.

My mouth began to hurt, then my cheek became swollen and hot. When you're a kid trying to survive crazy parents, dental hygiene isn't on your radar. I had an abscess. Mom said she could see the puss coming through the gum in the back of my mouth. Instead of taking me to an actual dentist, Mom stole a penicillin shot from the hospital and brought it home to kill the infection. She did this because there was no money for dentists, which were for rich people. The shot remained in the fridge for several days as I cried and begged her not to give me a shot in my butt. In the end, she neither gave me the shot nor took me to the dentist. Eventually my body successfully fought the infection. If I had been one of our mother's patients, she would have given me the shot without hesitation because when she was on the job she always knew what to do, and did it. But at home she turned into someone else who was overwhelmed with her life and often lacked the ability to offer basic care to her children.

As spring approached, our parents patched things up. It was decided that when school was out, Julie and I would live with Dad on Heath Mountain, while Mom continued to work at the hospital in Spokane until the end of summer. At that moment our father was working the program at AA again and had convinced our mom that he was sorry. I was scared as hell to live with him but even more worried that our mother would die without me to care for her. All of my begging to stay with her fell like pennies in a wishing well, hoping and praying that she would let me stay. It was another one of their schemes concocted by elusive dreams. Julie and I had no choice but to move back to the trailer on Heath Mountain to live with our father who had threatened to kill us, but this time without our mother to protect us.

We were surprised to learn that Dad was a much better parent without mom around. He kept a routine of chores, meals, and AA meetings. Julie and I played in the woods and with neighbors down the road. There was a young family with small children that lived at the edge of our property, who befriended Julie and me, letting us play with their kids and feeding us peanut butter and jelly sandwiches. Never mind that they used moldy whole-wheat bread.

They also took us to their Pentecostal church. It frightened me to death to see adults overcome with emotion. They would faint (*be slain in the spirit*), babble (*speak in tongues*), and grown men cried like babies. When Mom came for a long weekend, I told her about it. She explained, "Those people are like the snake handlers I watched when I was a young'un in Kentucky. We would climb on the roof of the Pentecostal church and watch them. When Mommy found out, she would bust our ass for going near those crazy holy rollers." I was scared of their church, but anything was better than being at home. There were other neighbor kids we found to play with, too, which helped to pass long summer days.

We had another new experience helping Dad tend a large garden that grew corn, beans, tomatoes, and peas. I learned how to use a lawn mower. We didn't have a TV, so we read the encyclopedia, the few children's books we owned, and listened to the radio. My favorite song that summer was by Three Dog Night, *"Jeremiah was a bullfrog, Was a good friend of mine... Joy to the World, All the boys and girls."* Like I had done with our mother, I kept a sharp eye on our father but for different reasons. Sobriety and routine helped, but his volatile temper was just below the thin surface. Julie pissed him off one day and just as he had done with Elaine, he threw her to the floor and pinned her down. In horror, I watched him reach back to take his hard-soled Romeo slipper off to beat her head and body with it. I screamed and cried, begging him to stop.

In alcoholic families everywhere, children are unfairly typecast from the time they are toddlers. In our family, Mike was labeled the hero, Jeff the chameleon, Elaine the responsible. I became the "good but pitiful twin." Julie, the scapegoat, didn't stand a chance. These labels were diminishing to each of my siblings and me, setting us up for needless pain and extra hardship in claiming our own voices and personhood later on.

That isn't to say being the good twin was easy. Watching a beating is almost as violent as receiving it, and there is irrational guilt for not being beaten, too.

The weight of single parenting and being sober was beginning to crack our father's resolve. Mom was still in Spokane when Dad got the call telling him that Grandpa died. That night Dad called me into his bedroom. He asked me if I would mind staying with him. He didn't want to be alone. Scared but obedient, I laid stiffly on the bed, while he sat with his back to me, slouching over with head in his hands and wept. Only a year before, this man had held a gun in his hands intending to shoot me. This year he asked for the comfort of my company. I remember tentatively touching the striped pajamas on his back telling him, "I'm sorry, Daddy."

I didn't know what to do; it all felt very dangerous and forbidden. Late into the night my father thanked me and told me to go to my bed. I felt honored and terrified for a long time. It wasn't many hours later that the comfort of Vodka numbed our father's grief.

The next day, in a drunken stupor, Dad asked us to get him more vodka. Scared of saying no, we did what all ten-year old kids do when their parents ask for a bottle of booze. We called Mom and she called a friend in Orofino, who delivered a full bottle of vodka to our doorstep. A few days later, Mom moved back to Heath Mountain and got her job back at the state psychiatric hospital. Whatever the year of separation was intended to do, it didn't work.

August was full of heat and visitors. Old friends from Montana stopped by for a few days. Elaine and her husband, Alex, came to visit for a week. Then Mom's sister, Irene, came to stay. It was unheard of for us to have company. Our parents put on the dog with these visitors and used a tone of voice that was meant only for others. It was exciting to meet a relative, but my already laser sharp intuition told me not to trust our aunt. I started watching her like a hawk, too. I lied and told her I didn't like to be hugged when she tried to hug me. At bedtime, I simply made a peace sign with my fingers and said, "Good night, Aunt Irene." It wasn't long before Dad and Aunt Irene spent the days drinking together while Mom went to work.

Chaos breeds chaos. There are some things you only know in hindsight and by connecting dots that you cannot connect as a child. Aunt Irene continued to stay at our house as Julie and I settled into 6th grade at Orofino Elementary School. She was there when we went trick or treating with friends that Halloween. The tension between the triangle of Mom, her alcoholic sister, and Dad finally blew up, with Mom, Julie and me suddenly on an airplane going back to Alaska and our Dad staying with Aunt Irene in Idaho. In my innocence, I didn't understand what this meant. I was just glad to get back to the Chugach Mountains and away from all that Heath Mountain held.

Mom's humility, fortitude, and inherent optimism helped us start again from all that wreckage. Before leaving Idaho, she contacted the parents of Elaine's roller rink friend, Laurie, to see if we could stay with them for a few weeks while she got a job, a car, and a place to stay. They welcomed us with genuine hospitality. We celebrated Thanksgiving with them.

After getting her job back at the state psychiatric hospital, Mom went to the bank for a car loan, but in 1972 a woman was ineligible for a bank loan without a man's signature. It didn't have to be her husband's signature; any man would do. Laurie's father provided his manly signature, co-signing the loan without hesitation. Other friends gave us sheets, blankets, and a few pots to cook with. When Mom received her first paycheck, we moved into a small trailer in east Anchorage and enrolled in school. During one of the thawing Chinook winds common in Alaskan winters, Mom found a muddy Teflon slotted spoon in the driveway. She sterilized it in boiling water, calling it the spoon of optimism. I still use that spoon of optimism, which I inherited, sometimes to stir spaghetti, and at other times as a talking stick in sacred circles.

By mid-December Dad and Aunt Irene appeared. We were all together again. All hell broke loose when Mom came home from work to find Dad passed out and her sister partially dressed, dead drunk on the floor. At that point, Mom called the police and told them they better come quick before someone got killed. I still remember the police officer's expression when he looked at me as he hauled my cuffed aunt out the door. His serious eyes were filled with sorrow and strain from understanding what he was seeing, but unable to really do anything but take my drunk aunt away from our trailer. I can still hear our father puking his guts out as yet again he went through withdrawals toward sobriety. As soon as he was sober, Mom sent him back down the Alcan to find another piece of property in Idaho.

We moved three more times to three more shit-hole places before I went into 7th grade. Well established now in my care-taking role, it was common for the lump in my throat to grow large as I watched Mom drink herself into a raging, inconsolable state. One late summer night in the land of the midnight sun, while standing in the middle of the narrow trailer park street, Mom ripped off all her clothes and threw her wedding ring on the ground. Crying and pleading, I begged our mother who was down to her bra and underpants to please come inside. What had become of our mother? What would become of us?

CHAPTER EIGHTEEN

Good Enough

BEING SAVED FROM DROWNING counts as a miracle, but finding a giant bag of good clothes in a ditch just in time for seventh grade is pretty high on the list, too. We lived on the outskirts of Anchorage in what we called the cow shit house. The exterior was covered in dry tar paper, which looked exactly like the name we gave it. One afternoon mere days before school started I was walking our dog, Amigo when I noticed a large black plastic bag at the bottom of a steep bank on the edge of the woods. Curious, I crawled down the ditch and looked inside. It was full of clothes! I went home to ask Mom if I could bring it home. With her consent, Julie and I retrieved the bag. Wondrously, inside were clothes that fit both of us, even though we were different sizes. There was a maroon wool maxi length coat that fit me perfectly. With my new ditch wardrobe, including groovy bell bottom hip huggers, I found new confidence as we headed to junior high.

I was sitting on the front step of the cow shit house when Dad's dirty red pick-up truck pulled into the driveway. He had sold the property in Idaho and made another trip up the dusty Alcan Highway. He was contrite, with another round of amends and promises. His arrival coincided with our 12th birthday. For gifts he gave Julie and me five dollars each. With excitement and five dollars in my pocket, I took off on my second hand banana seat bike. I loved that bike even though it only had bars for peddles causing my feet to frequently slip off, bruising the inside of my ankle. The five dollars bought a heart shaped gold locket and a candy bar. As I rode my bike back home, making my way through busy city streets and then on narrow edge-of-town roads, I pretended that Dad actually bought the necklace for me. It was a momentary comfort to imagine having a dad who picked out gifts for me, who thought I was his princess.

We moved the following month to a trailer park in east Anchorage. The oil boom on the north slope provided a surplus of cash to the state, which gave Dad many job opportunities. He worked in remote locations in Alaska, as far away as Adak, as well as local jobs in the city.

Seventh grade was a hormonal roller coaster ride as I budded into womanhood. I made new friends, learned to sew in home economics, learned to type in business class, learned to swim in PE, and took humiliating group showers at the end of gym classes with all the other equally embarrassed girls. Hoping to impress Dad, I joined the rifle team. Back then, it was perfectly fine to take a single-shot .22 rifle on the bus to school as long as it was in a case. It was fun to learn how to shoot and travel to different towns for competitions. My favorite shooting position was prone, lying down on my belly with the arm strap holding the rifle firm, and being able to control my breath before pulling the trigger. Dad even showed me how to clean the rifle, which for him was really something.

In the summer between 7th and 8th grade, Julie's friend Jenny invited her to go on a road trip with her and her family. They were going to drive all the way to Texas. Their plan was to drop Julie off in New Mexico to visit Elaine and then pick Julie up on their way back. Only Julie never came back. She stayed with Elaine and Alex. Life without her was strange and lonely and weird. Up until then we had separate groups of friends and fought like stray cats, but we had always been together. It was a relief to no longer constantly bicker, yet it felt like half of me was missing. As with so many other events, there was no explanation as why Julie had gone to live with Elaine and no acknowledgement of my grief over the loss of my twin sister. I had to choke down my feelings and move forward.

A repurposed yellow school bus began making the rounds in the trailer park that summer, looking for kids who might want to go to Sunday School at the Baptist church. I decided to get on the bus one day and with that, found my way back to Jesus. I went to church every Sunday that summer, sitting in a pew with other kids who came on the church bus. The preacher would ask us at the end of every sermon if there was anyone who wanted to be saved. Was there anyone who wanted Jesus in their heart? The choir sang endless repetitions of "Just as I am without one plea, Oh Lamb of God I come to Thee." I wanted to be saved, but there was no way in hell I would walk down that aisle in front of all those people. It was a fierce fight between the love of Jesus and fear of being noticed. I stayed in the pew.

An announcement was given at church inviting teens to go to Victory Bible Camp for a youth retreat some ninety miles north of Anchorage. It was thrilling for a kid who never went anywhere to spend several days at camp focused on fun activities, swimming, singing and Bible study. Several times a day we heard the message of salvation, with an invitation to let Jesus into our hearts, "Are you saved? Have you asked Jesus into your heart? He's waiting, knocking at the door of your heart." Finally, by myself, walking on a trail in the woods, I asked Jesus into my heart. I thought He was already there, but I also wanted to follow the rules and do it right. Having said the right words, now I was really saved.

Ruth was the first person I told about being saved. She and her husband, Bob, were youth leaders at the church. She was also the camp counselor assigned to my cabin. Ruth's sweetness to me was like milk to a starving infant. She listened to me pour out hours of chatter, of need, of adolescent longing. I crawled under her maternal wing, finding a place of acceptance and she held me. Bob and Ruth were a young army couple in their late twenties stationed on the base in Anchorage. They welcomed me into their family, giving me rides to church, including me in outings, and most importantly, nurtured in me a sense of belonging. Research tells us that one true adult connection can make all the difference in an at-risk teen's life. I am proof that it is true.

Even though I was now a born again Baptist, at thirteen I was as equally attracted to being bad as I was to being good. My friend Kathy was a bad girl. She smoked pot, wore musk perfume, and would swing her hips and move her hands in a cool way that demanded attention.

One day before school she talked me into smoking a bowl of pot with her. The pot didn't do much but being bad made me feel great. I followed her into more dangerous waters when we skipped school with high school boys who drove us to a town outside of Anchorage. We spent a few hours hanging out and went back to school before the end of the day. Of course, the matching doctor notes Kathy wrote gave us away. When the principal hauled me to his office, I saw him stare at the Bible on top of my math book. He scoffed and told me I was suspended until my mother brought me to his office for a conference.

Though it was fun and I tried, I wasn't good at being bad. What I really wanted was to be with Julie again. I cried when I received Julie's school picture and put it next to mine. The contrast was stark. Her hair was clean and she looked so pretty with her blue eyes and clear skin. I longed for the care that Julie now had. My school picture showed a girl with a large cavity in one of her front teeth, acne covered skin, and hair several days away from a shampoo. As with many young teens, I was at a crossroads trying to decide who I wanted to be.

The turning point came during a youth group outing. I was in the back of the church bus with a boy who kissed me and tried to put his hand inside my clothes. In that moment, I looked up toward the front of the bus and saw Bob. I realized that what I really wanted was to be good, to be pure, to be the kind of girl Bob would be proud of. I got out of my seat, walked to the front of the bus and sat down beside Bob. After that day I didn't look back. My friendship with Kathy and my failed attempt to be like her was over.

Now Jesus was my boyfriend. I wrote "Jesus-n-me = 4ever" everywhere, on my yellow Pee-Chee folder at school, on the margins of my Bible, on the skin of my old hands, and in the depths of my heart. My conversion was adolescent, but genuine. I attended church twice on Sunday, once on Wednesday night, and went to every youth group activity that was offered. I read the Bible, memorized scripture, and talked incessantly with and about Ruth. Adolescent rebellion is usually against parents and their norms. In my case it meant that I became one righteous girl. The more I focused on and talked about Ruth, the more inadequate Mom felt. She would respond to my monologues with, "Ya know Neanie, we all squat to pee" or "We all put our pants on one leg at a time." I had no idea what she was talking about. I was following Jesus.

One day there was a guest speaker in health class. She was a dental hygienist. In great detail she discussed the importance of dental care while moving through a slide show of rotten teeth. It was like looking at my own mouth on the screen. I felt deeply embarrassed, as well as challenged. Her presentation became a turning point in my life; I took responsibility for my teeth. After school, I called my mom at the psychiatric hospital where she worked and asked her to buy me a tooth brush, tooth paste and to make an appointment for me with a dentist. I was sick of covering my mouth when I talked or laughed. I was sick of it hurting, too. This began my life-long effort to repair the damage of decay and neglect. Unredeemable molars were pulled, cavities filled, root canals completed, and a front tooth crowned. For the first time in years, I smiled freely.

Julie came home during the summer of 9th grade. She, too, had had her own conversion experience while living with Elaine in New Mexico. It was great to have her home again, but we quickly went back to the roles established in infancy: good twin/bad twin. Family homeostasis demands compliance. We fought in dramatic fashion, like only fourteen-year-olds can do. We screamed, pushed, clawed at each other. We acted out the polarity of our roles, each feeling justified. As twins we began to separate when she was in New Mexico, and it continued into 9th grade. We had separate groups of friends and she went to a different church. We didn't know that permanent separation was just around the corner.

While church and Jesus were center stage in my life, the dance between my parents was ever present too. Dad took jobs through the local union when they were offered, but he slipped back to his old pattern of getting pissed, walking off the job, and going on a month-long binge. Mom's functional addiction served to numb the pain of so many losses and regrets that she carried. The love and longing I felt toward Mom was painful. I wanted her to be better, to be sober, to be younger, to be more like Ruth. I wanted her to dote on me the way she did with her patients. I wanted her to put me, Julie, and herself before Dad or beer. But it never happened.

Their elusive dreams and schemes began again. Mom explained the plan to Julie and me, "We're going to sell this place. You both need to find a place to stay for a month while I drive your father to Idaho. When we find a place for him to live, I'll come back to Alaska. I'll rent an apartment and live here until you graduate from high school." Just like the story line our parents created to explain why Elaine left, there was a story line for Julie and me, now. I wanted to believe what I was being told, but I couldn't. Bob and Ruth took me in without a second thought. Julie moved in with neighbors across the street. The trailer sold, the truck was packed, and our parents drove away.

I knew I was being abandoned. I fantasized about how great it would be for Julie and me to live with Mom until we finished high school, to have Dad out of the picture. Each time Ruth hugged me good-night, after she left I cried myself to sleep. I began to dream of running into the woods and falling asleep. It would be okay if I died there, I reasoned. As much as Bob and Ruth loved me, I could see the stress I brought to their family. Their small house was crowded with me and all of my baggage. Each day I sank deeper into depression. When Mom returned to Alaska with Dad in the passenger seat, I wasn't surprised. He had had a psychotic break in Seattle. Now she had to take care of him. Bob and Ruth said I could stay until my parents found a place to live.

The next Sunday when we came home from church we found a note taped to Bob and Ruth's front door. It was in my mother's handwriting, "*Jeanine, you and Julie cannot move home. Your father said he will kill you if you do. I might as well kill myself.*" My life long fears and suspicions had come true. Just as she had done with our siblings, our mother was sending us away. I was crushed, but even then felt I had to take care of her. I couldn't let her kill herself. I would tell her it was ok, that I loved her, and that Dad was the bastard. As long as I viewed Mom as a victim, she wasn't responsible for abandoning me.

Our parents bought a silver airstream trailer and rented space in a nearby trailer park. After a few months, Bob and Ruth went to see Mom and Dad. They confronted them, telling them in as respectful a manner as possible that raising me was my parents' responsibility. You cannot reason with insanity. Within a day, our parents arranged for me to move to Eagle River, a bedroom community fifteen miles north of Anchorage, to live with Jeff, and his new wife, Hope. Jeff was twenty-three. Mom and Dad informed me that I would move that weekend, saying "Who in the hell do Bob and Ruth think they are to tell us how to live? Those goddamn sonsabitches can shove their holier than thou attitude up their ass!"

I moved into Jeff and Hope's two bedroom apartment immediately. They welcomed me into their small home. It felt so good to be with family and it was a relief to not have to defend or explain my parents to them.

Jeff and Hope had met at Maranatha North, a hippie church formed from the Jesus People movement and Campus Crusade for Christ. Maranatha North made my Southern Baptist self nervous. People sat in bean bags instead of pews. Some of them lived communally in a large building called "The Big House" which had previously been a convent. Jeff and Hope were married at the Big House wearing blue jeans and in bare feet. People smoked without shame. Alcohol flowed. By southern Baptist standards they were decidedly unholy. The whole thing made me uncomfortable. I told Jeff and Hope that I didn't want to go to their church. I had lost too much to have to also leave my church and Ruth.

Julie and I celebrated our fifteenth birthday at Jeff and Hope's apartment. Our parents even came. Hope made pizza and a spice sheet cake. Everyone smiled for the birthday pictures, but grief was palpable. I longed for Mom with an ache that was physical. Julie was moving back to New Mexico to live with Elaine, they said. The one thing in my life that I could count on was constant, unpredictable change.

Going into the tenth grade at a new school is terrifying. Mom bought me new school clothes to reduce my anxiety and her guilt. I had longed for suede leather waffle stomper shoes, bell bottom pants and a puffed down coat. She bought all of these things before school started. She put it on the JC Penney credit card and told me, "Don't tell your father." Like I told Dad anything!

At night I could hear sweet laughter and giggles coming from the bedroom next door. I was happy for Jeff and Hope, but I felt like an interloper. It seemed I was a burden to people no matter where I turned. My faith in Jesus carried me far in those times of loneliness and confusion. I read scripture and prayed, searching for comfort. The old fantasy of running in the woods became a reality. Jeff and Hope's apartment was on the edge of miles of forest. I often found myself there, running until I couldn't run anymore. Eventually, sad and worn out, I would return to the apartment.

On the first day of school I was delighted to discover that I had the same math teacher, Mr. Peissig, as I had in ninth grade at my previous school. He had transferred from Anchorage to Eagle River to be closer to his home. Mr. Peissig was a kind man who took a liking to me, often telling me lame jokes. He noticed the Bible on my desk and it didn't offend him because he was a Christian, too. As had been the case with John the bus driver, Mr. Peissig's class was one of the few places I felt that I belonged.

Autumn was in its final throes with naked trees and daylight rapidly diminishing when Jeff and Hope told me, after discussing our living arrangement with the elders at Maranatha North, that if I wanted to continue to live with them I would have to stop going to the Baptist church and attend Maranatha North. They were not angry or upset with me, yet they drew an impossible line in the sand. I had to choose between my family or my church. I knew I could not leave my church.

The following Sunday at the close of the evening service, I went to the altar for prayer. A woman named Sue Anderson knelt down, put her arm around me and asked me what my prayer request was. I said, "I can't live with my brother anymore and I don't have anywhere to go." She prayed with me as people sang hymns in the background. When church was over and folks were visiting, Sue asked me to sit with her. She told me that she believed it was God's will for me to move in with her, her husband, Jack and their kids, Diane and David. Wary, I asked, "Are you sure? I'm sick of moving." She said, "Yes, but I need to talk with my husband first." Within a week I was installed in their family. Fortunately, they lived in Eagle River too, which allowed me to stay at the same high school.

The Anderson's home was modest. Jack was an elder at the church, which meant he was a lay leader who worked closely with the pastor in guiding the church. He was employed by the City of Anchorage. Sue was a stay at home mom who led Bible studies for women, which in conjunction with her status as an elder's wife also gave her congregational power. Once their oldest daughter became a teen, they were also involved in youth group activities. We knew each other from church by name, but that was about it. I already had mixed feelings about them before Sue approached me at the altar, because Jack seemed flirty and Sue seemed harsh. Despite my apprehension I accepted their offer of a home because my intuition was over-ridden by need. I told myself, as did everyone else, "They're a good Christian family."

It's awkward to move in with people you scarcely know and this was my third family in six months. I had grown more cautious with each move. I was beginning to learn that well intended people may not be ready to take in a teenager even if it is the Christian thing to do. There were so many assumptions on their part, like assuming I knew how to set a table or clean the bathroom to their liking, or knew how to ask permission for what I wanted to do. I did not know where the fork went next to a plate, or that making the chrome faucet shine was part of cleaning the bathroom, or that I had to say "May I?" instead of, "I'm gonna." I truly wanted to be good and to please the Andersons, partly because I believed it was what God wanted me to do and what the Bible commanded me to do, and partly because if this home didn't work out I didn't know what I would do. I told myself to suck it up and be grateful.

Family dynamics quickly dispensed with whatever honeymoon period we had. Diane had been visiting her grandparents in California when I moved in and felt usurped by me when she returned home. Six feet tall at age twelve, she was a lanky, awkward girl who had yet to grow into the graceful beauty she would become. At this point, she was a spoiled, mean, displaced brat. David, on the other hand, was an adorable kindergartener. He was easy to love and easy to please, and it was my job to please everyone. It became obvious that Sue put herself in a bind by claiming it was God's will for her to invite me to live with them only to discover how unhappy this arrangement made Diane. The net result was that the more resentful Diane was the colder Sue grew toward me.

There was another reason for Sue's distance. As she distanced herself from me, Jack moved in. He was a mountain of a man at six-foot four and weighed at least twice as much as me. The first night I stayed at the Andersons', Jack kissed me on the lips at bedtime. Sue saw it but said nothing. Shocked, I told him, "My dad never kissed my lips!" Jack brushed off my comment and continued his uncomfortably close behavior.

He progressed to telling me to sit on his lap, lifting my entire body up and then placing me where he wanted. Seeing my discomfort he turned it into a joke saying, "You sure have a boney butt." His large hand moved to my armpit, holding the outside of my breast in plain view of Sue. All this time she saw him and said nothing. Not satisfied with the good night kiss, Jack started looking for me many times a day, grabbing me to kiss me when no one was looking. I had no name for Jack's behavior other than to think, "Maybe he's just friendly" or I would try to dismiss it with, "He's just that way." Having already been formed in a family culture in which fathers and their desires are the only thing that really counts, and fathers are not to be defied, I felt compelled to put up with his unfatherly behavior. I told myself maybe it wasn't such a big deal because after all, he hadn't raped me. I was confused by the way I felt both comforted and used by his behavior and that Sue seemed not to care.

The weeks turned into months. I learned how to do chores properly and how to use polite speech. Conflict avoidance and passivity were strong in this good Christian family. They didn't drink, smoke, cuss, fight, or threaten to shoot each other, nor did they say "good-night" or "good-morning."

Meanwhile, my parents moved into a one-bedroom apartment because the weather got too cold for the airstream trailer. On weekends I usually made brief visits. Sometime in the early spring, Mom announced that they were moving to Missouri as soon as the snowpack was gone and the roads were clear. When I told the Andersons about this development, they requested legal custody of me if my parents moved out of state. We went to see an attorney. I sat wedged between Mom and the Andersons when the attorney recommended adoption over guardianship. He said, "Adoption is permanent, whereas guardianship can be revoked at any time." Mom began to cry. The lawyer again explained that without adoption the Andersons could send me back to my parents at any time or that my parents could take me any time. Mom agreed to the adoption. Weeks later I was adopted into a family that wanted to do the right Christian thing, where I experienced a complicated and confusing mixture of hospitality, resentment, expectation, and broken boundaries. My last name was summarily changed to Anderson and my parents moved to Missouri without looking back.

I had grown up accustomed to keeping family secrets and not airing dirty laundry. I was an expert at living with addiction and abuse but never talking about it. These skills helped me navigate the Anderson waters. I focused on Jesus, being as good as I could be, faithfully attending to morning devotions, scripture, and prayer. A great group of friends and I formed a Christian fellowship at school which we called Faith Life. We met weekly at different homes for Bible study, singing, and games. The group included young adults who had already graduated, but mostly we were a group of sincere Christian teens. Faith Life was a life raft for me. My math teacher, Mr. Peissig, had three children who were members. We met often at the Peissig's house, so it became a place where I felt I truly belonged. Meanwhile, life at the Anderson's was filled with church attendance, chores, and the dance of Sue's ice and Jack's fire. In moments of silent reflection, I knew that I was no one's priority.

I tried with all my might to be good enough to secure the stability and love for which I longed. In addition to being involved at church and Faith Life, I was also connected to many of my teachers. Their friendship and support sustained me and their respect for my intellectual abilities helped me to have increasing confidence that someday I could go to college. I was articulate in matters of faith, due to my genuine belief in and knowledge of the Bible. The folks at church, my teachers in school, and my Faith Life group provided opportunities for me to develop leadership skills.

After they gave me up permanently through adoption, I stayed in contact with my parents through letter writing and occasional phone calls. Longing for my mother was ever present, a constant tightness in my throat and chest that could not be resolved. She had abandoned me but I didn't blame her. I blamed my Dad. Abused children almost always love their parents, something that people from loving families sometimes have a hard time understanding. In my mind and heart, I often told myself that Mom was helpless in the face of Dad's addiction, that she had no choice but to give me up. But at another level, I knew that was not true. She always had a choice. Because of that knowledge, I continued to wrestle with a conflicting sense of identity, vacillating between believing Jesus loved me and at other times feeling like a no-good piece of shit.

In the summer between my junior and senior year, I went to visit my parents in Missouri. They lived in a small cottage with a detached double car garage on ten acres in the Ozarks. I stayed in the guest room in the garage. In my joy and deep longing for Mom to tell me that she loved me and wanted me to be her daughter again, I must have said, "Mom, I love you" a million times. She finally told me it was enough, that I didn't need to tell her every ten minutes. Her words were worse than a physical blow. I had brought all of my possessions with me, unconsciously hoping to never return to the Andersons. With that rebuke Mom let me know that I could not stay. I acted like it didn't matter, that I just wanted all my stuff with me. It was agonizing, but once again I had to protect my mother from the consequences of her violence toward me. I had to keep her from feeling guilty about all the ways that she abandoned me from infancy including giving me up for adoption when I was fourteen.

Even so, I decided to tell her about Jack's behavior. I told her in detail about the kissing, wandering hands, and his lap. I told her about how he would come into my bedroom after working the graveyard shift to wake me up for school, how I would hear his footsteps coming down the hall and would flip from my back to belly so he wouldn't have access to the front of me. I told her how he put his hands under my nightgown and rubbed the back of my body from head to toes. I said sometimes Sue would send me to their bedroom to wake Jack up before working a late shift and how when I did this he would pull me on top of him, caress my body over my clothes, and tell me what a good wife I was going to be someday.

Mom was horrified and said, "What the goddamn hell! I thought they were a good Christian family!" Seeing her outrage, I automatically switched to taking care of her feelings so she wouldn't feel guilty for abandoning me to them. I played it down and said, "Don't worry, he's just touching me. At least he hasn't raped me." After a few minutes, looking beaten and defeated, she said, "Yeah, that's true. At least he isn't raping you." In this way I learned that what Jack was doing was definitely bad, even to my mother, but not bad enough for her to do anything about it.

While I was still with my parents, it was decided that Julie would move from New Mexico back to Alaska. Initially she would stay with Jeff and Hope, then move into the Big House. By then Maranatha North had changed its name to Evangelical Orthodox. When Julie returned, we went to the same high school for our senior year, sharing classes and eating lunch together. In time, Julie joined Jeff and Hope's church and immersed herself in their community which through my Baptist eyes looked more and more like a cult.

Having said that, I was part of the early purity movement just beginning to emerge in evangelical circles. I only dated Christian boys and the only physical intimacy that was allowed was holding hands or prim kisses, if that. It was important to remain a virgin until married. This was a challenge as I got older and dated older boys, but my standards were clearly communicated and respected. My sexuality was tucked away, righteously repressed with a self-imposed chastity belt.

I didn't date much, but I had a long-term boyfriend most of my senior year. Hank was older, had graduated from high school and was living on his own. He had a beard, played the trumpet at church and had a great sense of humor. We enjoyed eight months together until he found another girl. We loved to listen to the group Bread on the cassette player in his truck: *"It don't matter to me if you take up with someone better than me, cause your happiness is all that I want."* But I learned that it mattered a lot to me when he actually did.

In the spring semester of my senior year, I had a dream that I had a baby and it looked just like Jack, which scared the shit out of me. It felt like a premonition. I decided to tell the pastor what Jack had been doing for the past two and a half years. The pastor listened from his side of the desk and asked: "Do you wear a bathrobe?" "Are you being modest?" I told him that I always wore a robe and was very modest. I just wanted Jack to love me as a daughter without touching me, I said. I also expressed concern that now that I told on Jack, he wouldn't be allowed to be an elder in the church anymore. The pastor assured me that Jack would remain an elder, reminding me of the Old Testament story of Abraham betraying his wife—allowing a man to sleep with her, yet still having a heart after God.

Needless to say, the pastor did nothing. Growing more desperate, I told a few of my teachers. This was before mandatory reporting laws. They listened with compassion but didn't know what to say or do. Finally, I told the assistant pastor, Tom, who had a reputation of being a contrarian and outspoken. To my great relief, Tom believed me. He told me that I could move into his home the following day. But this meant I had to tell Sue.

I sat in the living room on the couch, with Jack in one chair and Sue in another. Diane and David were safely in bed. I told them I was going to move out. Sue demanded that I tell them why, and then in detail, everything Jack had done. I recited the long list of offenses. As the words were said, Jack looked blank and was completely silent. Sue said that she had suspected it and that I should go to bed. I was so relieved that she believed me.

The following morning I awoke with Sue shaking me hard, demanding, "Get up! The pastor and assistant pastor will be here soon. Get dressed and get ready to explain yourself." Once again, I sat alone on the couch hugging my knees and feeling exposed by the glaring spotlight of four adults who having thought about it, now had a whole lot to lose. Reputations were at stake. There could be lawsuits. It could get into the paper.

The pastor, in his southern twang, opened in prayer. He began by asking how we might heal this situation. Once again, I was told to describe in detail what Jack had done. As the four of them stared at me with accusing eyes, I listed the ways Jack sexualized me with his touch, and the way Sue saw it and did nothing. Jack denied any sexual intent in his affections expressed to me. Sue said she believed Jack. The pastor suggested that I was unable to recognize appropriate touch due to my terrible upbringing. Jack would be more careful, and I would remain in the Anderson's home. There was nothing more that I could say. The adults closed in prayer and I went to my room.

I learned several important lessons that morning that I would only fully understand when I trained to become a therapist. I learned about blaming the victim even when she is a child and the offender is an adult. I learned that being believed is often tied to socio-economic status, especially if the offender has resources and the victim has none. What I learned the most, though, was that I did not matter, not to my parents, not to the Andersons, and not to my precious Baptist church.

The Anderson household went on surreally as if we had never had the dreadful meeting. Jack continued to kiss and touch. Sue continued to turn a blind eye. Nothing I said made a difference because I didn't matter. Skilled at having to find my own way in the aftermath of adult double-speak and violence, I swallowed my pain and kept moving forward. This time though it involved my church. The foundation of my faith cracked beneath the weight of this betrayal. Shortly after graduating from high school, the week I turned eighteen, I moved out of the Anderson's house. A year later, as soon as I had enough money, I hired a lawyer and changed my last name back to Heath.

My not so safe safety net was like the Alaskan tundra which looks soft but hides boulders and ankle-breaking holes, and harsh bushes that tear the skin. Self-doubt was my constant companion. Finding a place to stay was always a problem. I felt like I was living Jesus' words when he said foxes have holes and birds have nests but he had nowhere to lay his head. I briefly shared a trailer with a friend, housesat for folks from church, and couch surfed. Getting around was a challenge, too. I was completely dependent on the lousy city bus system and bumming rides from friends. Eventually, a friend taught me to drive and I got a license, but was still too poor for a car with its gasoline and insurance. In the midst of this uncertainty, I started college. Between meeting assignment deadlines, getting rides, being to work on time, and finding places to stay, I was exhausted by the end of the first semester.

It was a great relief to me when Jeff once again opened his home to me, but this time without condition of church attendance. I decided to work full time and put off college for a while, to get on my feet. Julie welcomed me into her circle of friends at the communal Big House. I began to admire this group of people whom I had previously viewed with suspicion. They were zealous in their faith, yet not preoccupied with little things my Baptist friends focused on like smoking, drinking, and cussing. Instead they were into learning correct liturgy and the lives of the saints and the teachings of the early church fathers, because in their effort to move from Protestantism to Orthodoxy they had a steep learning curve.

What appealed to me the most was that they were helpful to one another in everyday life by being kind, hospitable, and doing good works for others. Obedience to God was paramount. As a group of converts, they were all seeking the one true Christian faith. Needing to belong and to be with like-minded followers of Christ, I was drawn to this serious group of Christians who lived their faith. I let go of the Baptist church to embrace a new community.

Our psyche whispers truth to us when we are quiet enough to hear its wisdom. Even then, especially when we are young or wounded, we will negotiate with the warnings to pay-attention, to run, to leave. We tell ourselves as we see the red flags, "Oh, it isn't important," or "They'll change," or "It will be okay." Sometimes we mix religious talk with these negotiations, "It's God's will for me to do such and such . . . I need to trust and obey." All of the warning signs, and there were many, were drowned by my desire to be good enough to belong.

Now that the community was Orthodox we were to refer to the

pastor, Harold, as Bishop Harold or Father Harold. From the get go he made me nervous. He had almost absolute authority over the people in the church. There was also a group of men called elders who were Father Herald's right hand men. We were to call them Father, as well. Father Harold was very charismatic in his style and in his profanity. He smoked, drank, talked freely about sex, and made comments about women's bodies without restraint. He enjoyed shocking people, even while he wielded charm, power, and spoke of God's grace. There was a certain relief in that he didn't pretend to be righteous like my hypocritical Southern Baptist pastor. Somehow Father Herald's unapologetic behavior, as unholy as it would have been in the Baptist Church, made him seem more holy because he didn't try to hide it. I wanted Father Harold to like me, to find me good enough, yet he scared the shit out of me. I kept my head down and avoided him. I was told that to be worthy of joining the church, I had to be obedient and go through catechism.

I was a catechumen for over a year, proving my desire to follow Christ and that I believed in the traditions of the early church, and that I was good enough to belong. As an entire church community, we were in pursuit of the faith of our fathers. We were protestant evangelicals seeking Orthodoxy. As we progressed in our journey, our theology slowly transitioned from sole reliance on the Bible as the word of God, to sacramental theology, creeds, and tradition. We met as a large community every Sunday for a worship service that was still Protestant in structure, and celebrated the Eucharist in small groups. I was not allowed to participate in the Eucharist as a catechumen, and I accepted this condition even though I had been a devoted believer for many years. By the time I was good enough to be accepted into the church, I could explain the two natures of Christ, the mystery of the Trinity, the basic tenets of the Nicene Creed, and the consequential anathema of being a heretic.

I moved into the Big House in the fall of 1981, joining a group of seventeen men and women who committed to a year of prayer, devotion, and celibacy, which in that context meant not dating. I felt that I had finally found a place where every single person loved Jesus with as much enthusiasm as I did.

Each day began with matins, an early morning time of prayer and song. Most of us went to work during the day but we met at the long dining table for dinner. We laughed, played, and cherished our time of service to our church community. We learned how to give and receive grace and to hold each other accountable. Deep friendships were formed.

However, there was a growing undercurrent of social control in which people were called out, sometimes very publicly if they didn't conform. There was one young man who was reprimanded by Father Harold for being a liar and too talkative, so he was required to be silent most of the time. If he spoke he had to preface statements with, "I don't know my ass from a hole in the ground but. . ." Obedience and humility were indications of being a good Christian even if the person you obeyed was anything but humble, and he was accountable to no one.

In our zeal to be monastic as we understood it, we didn't do anything without a blessing from our priest or from Father Harold. Almost all aspects of life needed to have a blessing. For example, I wanted to go back to college to become a teacher, but I was required to go before the group of priests and Father Harold to answer a battery of questions about faith before they gave their blessing. They wanted to be sure my faith would not be polluted by the world. I would not have gone to college without their approval. What a person did for work, where they lived, and how they behaved was open to scrutiny and judgment. If a person was considered overweight, they might be put on a diet and monitored by their deacon, whether the deacon knew anything about nutrition, diets, and health or not. We did not date, we courted, and it was only with the intent to marry, and no one courted without Father Harold's explicit blessing. With these increasingly cultish demands in the guise of monastic fidelity, my desire to be good enough was in overdrive.

As the yearlong celibacy commitment drew to an end, nature took over. Single men and women started eyeing each other as potential mates. Our selection was narrowed to considering only those in our small community or in other Evangelical Orthodox communities in the lower 48 that originated from the same small circle of former

Campus Crusade for Christ leaders. Between college classes, teaching at our church school, cleaning the church on Saturdays, and attending church, I began to check out the small pool of available men. Stephen caught my eye. He worked as an aerial photographer. He came from a good family. His father was one of the original founders of our church. In fact, his dad was a leader in the original Jesus People movement, starting the Christian World Liberation Front (CWLF), evangelizing and baptizing people in the fountain at UC Berkeley. Stephen was intelligent and unassuming. His quiet, shy, outdoorsy way attracted me. He didn't appear to be a drunk or to own guns. Perhaps I was good enough for him to love me. And if he loved me I would be good enough to be in his family. My lifelong dream of belonging in a home with a family would come true.

CHAPTER NINETEEN

Expanding Horizons

AFTER LIVING IN THE BIG HOUSE for more than a year, I moved into a small 12′x24′ dry cabin located in the church community. In case you were wondering, a dry cabin has no indoor plumbing. Usually there is an outhouse, which was the case in our situation. I shared the cabin with two other single women. In time, with Fr. Harold's blessing, Stephen and I began to court. Our courtship felt transactional to me, like a friendship that was supposed to end with a marriage contract. I longed for the kind of romance I saw expressed in movies and that I heard about in songs, but I told myself that Stephen's restraint was virtuous self-control. Repressing my own wants and needs, and working hard to be good enough to be chosen as a wife, I filtered this issue and everything else through a lens of how I wanted things to be, versus how they really were.

One cold December morning, I trudged to the outhouse in my pajamas to find the roof had caved in due to heavy snow. That was it. After eight months of hauling water in and a honey bucket out, I had had enough. When I told the Peissigs, my former math teacher and his wife what happened, they invited me to stay with them, which was the best news I'd had in a long time. Moving in with the Peissigs was the beginning of a season of fun, rest, and not having to prove myself 24/7.

They gave me a sweet bedroom and the use of an old station-wagon that I called, "Snow Pig." In lieu of rent, I cooked dinner and baked homemade bread once a week. I found myself relaxed and more and more at peace as we sat around the dinner table, talking, laughing, and at ease. One evening I pulled a freshly baked loaf of bread from the oven and sliced it as Bill, Pat, and their son, Russ, watched in mouth-watering anticipation. As the slices of bread fell onto the cutting board, a worm appeared to writhe its ghastly way out of the hot bread. I had inadvertently kneaded a large rubber band into the dough. We roared with laughter as we stuffed buttery slices into our mouths.

At my church community, the priest was offended. He saw my move into the home of folks who belonged to a different, inferior church as a threat. This religious exclusivity should have been a major red flag for me, especially because I didn't know anyone more Christian than the Peissigs, but I ignored that warning and many other whispers in my heart. My longing to be loved and to be married, overruled the ancient voice of wisdom inside of me that urged me to pay attention and protect myself.

After courting for over a year, Stephen asked me to marry him. Now that we were engaged, we had our first kiss. We married three months later on a snowy December day. It was a beautiful, simple wedding. As Jeff escorted me down the aisle, I was full of hope and anticipation of a strong marriage. My life with my new husband would be nothing like the crazy relationship my parents modeled. If we were blessed with children in the future, I would devote myself to their well-being.

My students sang songs at the reception and we folk danced in celebration. Our marriage was the first of eight weddings in the community that year. We all found someone with whom to say, "I do."

Our marriage was sweet, gentle, kind, and quiet. We created a pool of safety for each other, calm waters that neither one of us disturbed. Riddled with insecurity and with perfectionistic desires to be good enough, I dove head first into the deep end of being a good wife. I didn't really know what that was, but I was determined to prove myself worthy the best that I knew how. I cleaned, cooked, did laundry, and ironed. Stephen appreciated my work ethic, as I did his. We both enjoyed hiking and cross-country skiing, and continued to be immersed with the church. I completed my bachelor's degree in secondary education, with an emphasis in social science. We bought property and a trailer in the church community. It was time to think about starting a family.

In due time we welcomed our first child, Stephanie. She was a healthy, beautiful, dark-haired baby. I was in awe of her. Bonding with my daughter awakened fierce maternal instincts and exacerbated the anxiety that I had carried throughout my life. Every human emotion was felt on an exponential level. I was deeply in love with her and equally terrified that I would not be what she needed. While nursing Stephanie one evening, I told Stephen, "I would rather cut off one of my arms than leave her with a sitter." He tried to understand my desire even though I had just received certification from the state of Alaska to work as a high school teacher. Prior to Stephanie's birth we had planned for me to work as a teacher after her first year. The income would be necessary for a growing family. With my staunch new resistance to have anyone but myself care for her, we scrapped that plan. We would adjust. I would find other ways to contribute financially to our family.

Stephanie was five months old when I found a position as nanny for two boys, Paul and Douglas, ages five and two, who came to our home for daily care. These lovable children became like brothers to Stephanie and remained a part of our family over the next eight years. Their single father, Larry, was a surgeon with a very busy medical practice. It was a blessing to care for Paul and Doug, and my nanny income helped a lot with our family's expenses.

Less than two years after Stephanie was born, we welcomed our second daughter, Elizabeth. She was an easy-going baby, with bright eyes and black hair. Stephanie couldn't pronounce her sister's name, so Elizabeth gained the nickname, Liddy or Lid. I was twenty-seven years old with four children in my care.

Paul was a serious child with a keen intellect and advanced attention span. He was deeply sensitive and kind. During our first year together, I read the entire *Chronicles of Narnia* series to him when the other children napped. Doug was the essence of sweetness and mischief all wrapped into a blonde haired, blue eyed bundle of wonder. Watching him find delight with sticks, small pebbles, and in nature was a lesson in celebration and finding the divine in all things. Stephanie was a curious preschooler, creative in her imagination and shy like her parents. Being the fourth child, Elizabeth went with the flow with patience and a good sense of humor. By the time Elizabeth was born, I had much more confidence in my maternal instincts.

This season of motherhood was precious even with its monotony of meals, messes, and management of never enough income. The trailer we lived in was getting small for our growing family. We lived paycheck to paycheck, which was what I was accustomed to growing up in poverty and because of not having had experience in money management. I longed for a real house not a cramped trailer.

A home came up for sale in the heart of the church community, at the end of Monastery Drive atop a hill. It was a two-story, cedar sided house with massive windows in every room that boasted expansive views of the forest, mountain ranges, Cook Inlet, and on clear days, even Mount Denali. With Larry's generous help, Stephen and I purchased the house, which was beyond my wildest dreams. There was abundant space for family, guests, and others who might need a place to stay. Community members gave us gently used furniture and helped us move into the new home that seemed like a palace to me.

Though my days were busy, pleasant, and filled with children I adored, I dreaded going to sleep at night. Several times a week, I had nightmares. In most of them, my adopted parents, the Andersons, were after me, chasing me down roads, in stores, through fields. In addition to night terrors, I experienced unbearable anxiety if I had to leave my children with anyone, including their own father who was the soul of trust and dependability.

The problem was within me. I was so terrified that my children might be hurt like I was as a child that I could not trust anyone. Fatigued and fearful, awakening to the fact that I needed help, I decided to try therapy. My intent was to only go to a few sessions, say as little as possible, spend as little as possible, and to get a list of recommended books that related to my issues. Partly from shame and partly for economic reasons, I determined mostly to figure it out on my own.

Our priests frowned on the use of secular psychotherapy, but Martha had been recommended by another woman in the church, so she seemed safe enough. I called her for an appointment. At the end of our first session, I told Martha that I wanted a list of books to read that would help me, and I could take it from there. In her Mississippi drawl she said, "Jeanine, you have so much trauma and abuse to work through, I think you'll need to be in therapy for at least a year." Like trauma survivors everywhere who cope through minimizing what they endured, I said, "But I wasn't abused!" She asked, "What would have had to happen for you to have been abused?" I told her, "I wasn't burned with cigarettes." Martha gently helped me understand how my severe standard of abuse helped me survive by minimizing my experience in the face of something worse, but that I needed to deal with the impact of trauma and abandonment. The relief of being believed and of Martha's clear articulation of the abuse I experienced offered immediate solace to my weary soul.

Martha's prediction was true, I was in therapy for well over a year. It was life changing, one of the best decisions I ever made. Our relationship was sacred, as Martha's therapeutic midwifery helped me to birth my authentic self. It was a painful, long, but ultimately joyful labor.

Throughout that time I read many books that catalyzed fundamental shifts in my thinking. Clarissa Pinkola Estes' explanation of women's development in *Women Who Run With the Wolves* changed my life. Jungian psychology's archetypal theory resonated with my experience. In time, I was able to understand the dynamics of being an adult child of alcoholics, the dysfunctional dance of codependency, of the holistic impact of sexual abuse, of abandonment, of neglect, of shame. As trust grew between us, Martha compassionately helped me to examine my inner narrative of shame, of being unlovable and never good enough. It took months and months for me to cry in therapy, fearing that if I started to cry, I would never stop. Martha's response when I voiced that fear was characteristic of her pragmatism and gentle humor. She said, "Jeanine, if you start crying and you cry and cry and cry, eventually you'll just go to sleep."

Ever so slowly my frozen emotions thawed. I walked through the valley of anger. I was furious with all the bullshit! I was exhausted by trying to be perfect. Being nice had worn me out. Now I was ready to kick somebody's ass. The pendulum swung from trying to be good enough to "I'm mad as hell and I'm not gonna take it anymore."

As you might imagine, this change in me was disturbing to people in our church. Mad women are often dismissed as bitches and being dismissed as a bitch makes women mad, so women are not allowed to be mad, only happy or depressed. In the church world broadly, mad women are a threat because anger is a threat and is traditionally interpreted to be a sin. The church has not done well with helping people feel and appropriately express righteous anger.

People at church began to suspect I was being seduced by a secular counselor into evil liberal thinking. Yet on the side, more and more women from the church quietly asked to go for walks with me in which they privately shared their problems and their pain. Stephen, ever patient and not wanting conflict, was careful what he said to me so he wouldn't set me off. He was bewildered by my newfound emotions.

In growing synchronicity, Elaine and I became companions in our sacred healing journeys. Through letters and phone calls we worked through the abuse and abandonment of our childhood together, and supported each other's work in naming, feeling, and moving through our trauma. We shared poetry, journal entries, and prayers, and supported each other in ways our spouses couldn't or wouldn't.

Elaine had completed her bachelor's degree and was in the middle of grad school when she called to let me know that she was very ill with Lyme Disease. As quickly as possible I caught a plane to Michigan to be with her. The days with her were spent making soup, cooking and freezing meals, listening to her teenage daughters, sitting with her through painful medical procedures, and holding Elaine like a child in a rocking chair while my niece, Kat played the entire *December* album by George Winston on the piano. I held my sister momma, wrapped in a quilt the way she had held me so long ago.

Major changes were occurring in our church at that time, as well. The scruffy group of fundamentalist zealot leaders finally made their way from evangelicalism to ancient legitimacy. All of the Evangelical Orthodox churches joined en masse with the Antiochian Orthodox Church (AOC). Formerly known as Maranatha North, our congregation was now christened St. John Orthodox Cathedral. Joining the AOC cracked open our closed community, but the church had a long way to go to get away from the abusive, cultish dynamics of its origins. All of the hierarchy transitioned in titles and roles to correspond with Eastern Orthodox dogma. Designations of church services, liturgies, music, and rituals were all aligned with the AOC. We told ourselves we were open to change, but those who left St. John's for any reason other than to transfer to another AOC community that was linked to St. John's, were considered to have left God's church.

Adult converts are already a little crazy, intoxicated with new-found right-ness and righteousness. Evangelical fundamentalism laced with a lot of sacramental desire made for a wild competition as to who was the most orthodox. Many people changed their names to ancient Orthodox saint names. Suddenly Bob, Susie, William, and Jane became Seraphim, Macrina, Athanasius, and Thekla. Wives of priests and deacons were also given titles, so a woman I had called Jenny for fifteen years was now to be addressed as Khouria, or Presbytera Mary, or whatever her new name was. It was nearly impossible to keep the new names and titles straight especially since I thought it was ridiculous and had to work at keeping a smirk off my face when I said them. I wanted to join the Orthodox church because I loved the liturgy, but the extreme way in which we were expected to embrace it was over the top. I was flat out offended when some of the women began to cover their heads when they went to church or waited forty days to come to church after birthing a child. The budding feminist within me was not pleased.

One April morning as I walked home from teaching social studies at St. John's school, my babysitter ran toward me saying, "Hurry, your sister is on the phone. She said it's an emergency." I ran home. Sobbing, Julie told me her husband, Mike, had just died from suicide. "Jeanine, Mike has killed himself—he shot himself in the den." I was stunned. I knew he suffered from depression along with other problems, but I never thought he would actually take his own life. Leaving my girls with the babysitter, I rushed to Mike and Julie's house in a state of shock.

Emergency vehicles and red lights filled the driveway. I found Julie surrounded by the police and a chaplain. Wrapped in a blanket, she fell into my arms weeping hysterically. It was surreal. Suicide had been a concept, one that the church judged as sinful and selfish. Now it was terribly real and much more complicated than I ever imagined. As Mike's body was removed from the house, I gathered up my twin sister and her three small children and brought them home with me.

The week that followed Mike's death was full of hard, new experiences processed in slow motion. Priests came to see Julie, to let her know that because Mike had killed himself, the funeral could not be held at the church and his body would not be allowed to be buried in the church cemetery. We accepted this judgment and this shame without protest, even though it was devastating to hear. Together we went to a funeral home in Anchorage to make arrangements. Neither of us had ever made funeral arrangements before. The mortician was kind and thoughtful, carefully using compassionate language, specific in his distinction between Mike and his body. The contrast between the gracious secular undertaker and the judgmental priest was obvious, but this juxtaposition would have to wait for another time to be fully examined. Each day brought a bizarre mixture of people's insensitive comments on suicide, casseroles for dinner, and emotional convulsions as the violent reality of Mike's death set in. After the funeral, Julie and her children found a new place to live.

I felt responsible for Mike's suicide. He had been depressed for a very long time. When Julie had made a decision to leave him for the second time, I supported her because I believed it was an act of courage on her part to make a change toward a better life for herself and her children. I longed for her to have freedom and peace, and a stable environment for her kids. She had called me for advice asking, "Jeanine, should I remove the gun from the den before I tell him I'm leaving? The last time I left, he threatened to shoot himself."

Quick to advise and only thinking of her and the children, I responded, "Julie, quit thinking about him! Just get out!" Wisely, Julie also contacted Mike's psychologist, expressing her concerns about the potential for suicide. It was not Julie's fault that Mike died. Blame cannot be fixed on anyone in a situation like this, including the person who dies from suicide, because there are multiple mental health issues and complex life histories. In this case there were multiple traumas in the background long before the day Mike died. I felt that it was my fault.

The guilt I felt was matched with rage. A part of me wanted to kill Mike for the suicide—the violence and trauma inflicted on my sister, his children, me, and my family. The angry part of me agreed that he shouldn't be buried in the church cemetery, it would serve him right. Yet, my compassionate self was appalled that he couldn't. Another part of me wondered how the hell I got entangled in this mess of a theological controversy in the first place.

As Easter approached, I spent a day sequestered in my bedroom for a Lenten retreat. I needed to process thoughts and feelings about Mike's death. As I moved through the day in reflection, journaling and reading scripture, I thought about Jesus' forgiveness and how his disciples abandoned him, one by one, going their own way. Peter was an emotional, exuberant man who would become the cornerstone of the church even though he denied Jesus not once but three times. In my meditation on Peter's story, in my imagination I heard the cock crowed the first time. I focused on Peter's failures. For example, how he wanted to protect Jesus, who had spoken of trials to come. Peter thought he knew better than Jesus about what needed to happen. I thought of Jesus' shocking response, "Get behind me Satan. You are a stumbling block to me; you do not have in mind the concerns of God. . ." The cock crowed again in my imagination. This was Peter, the man whose faith allowed him to walk on water and who rightly declared Jesus as the Messiah, the Son of the Living God, Peter who was afraid of a little servant girl in the courtyard, Peter who made terrible mistakes and failed the one he loved the most at the hour of greatest need. The cock crowed within me the third time.

I saw then how much I was just like emotional Peter. I, too, rushed in with protective declarations and instructions. I, too, was sure that I knew what to do. I saw how I was like Peter in his fear, with fear driving my own righteous instructions, all the while denying my own weakness. I began to weep in remorse, begging God and Mike to forgive me for my ignorance, for my quick solutions, for my arrogance.

After that I remembered that even Judas, flawed as he was, blinded as he was by money, was a disciple of Jesus. I saw how self-loathing drove him to suicide despite his faith in Jesus. For the first time I felt great compassion for Judas, Jesus' betrayer, who was a human just like the rest of us. I felt compassion and empathy for my brother-in-law whose suffering was beyond my knowing. And I felt deep grief for my sister and her children whose lives had been shattered by Mike's death. As I continued to weep my confession, I experienced Jesus' offer of forgiveness and grace to me just as he gave it to Peter after the resurrection. It would take years of training and experience before I understood the complexity of grief around suicide and the need to make peace with so many unknowns.

Death invites us to examine our lives as nothing else can do. In the aftermath of my brother-in-law's death, I began to pay closer attention to an old desire, an emerging sense of call to become a counselor. When I had been a client in therapy, I was both a participant and an observer. I found myself resonating more and more with Martha in her vocation, as well as benefitting from Martha's skill in helping me to heal. For several months I thought and prayed about becoming a therapist.

I looked for signs from God to help in this discernment, in no small part because I knew there would be resistance from church leaders who were already unhappy with my awakening feminist self. Struggling to ignore the old, accusatory inner voice which said, "Who the hell do you think you are?" I began to check into graduate level programs offered in Anchorage, how much they cost, and what was required for admission. This time, thankfully, I did not need a priest's approval because I had my husband's blessing. In the divine chain of command, for once it worked in my favor.

I decided on the University of LaVerne, California, which had a satellite campus in Anchorage on Elmendorf Air Force Base. I was elated when I received my letter of acceptance. All of my professors were both academicians and practicing clinicians and psychologists which grounded their teaching in the real world of practice. With each new class and each new subject, my heart opened wide with gratitude and wonder. I embraced my sacred vocation.

Secular study made some more conservative church members suspicious. Not only was I in graduate school studying clinical psychology with godless humanists, I withdrew my daughters from St. John's church school and put them into public school. I wanted them to be educated by trained professionals instead of well-intentioned moms with a religious agenda. I wanted my daughters to have a chance to meet people beyond our church community and to develop social awareness of our world, and to learn to live and work in a pluralist society. This decision was met with sideways glances, raised eyebrows, and condemnation. One woman asked me, "Why are you throwing your children to the wolves?" All of these changes coincided with Paul and Doug's father, Larry, remarrying and moving to Anchorage, so my nanny services were no longer needed. It was a time of change, grief, and reckoning. Most of all, it was a time of rapidly expanding horizons.

CHAPTER TWENTY

Birch Trees

LIKE A BIRCH TREE shedding its bark as it grows, I was shedding the skin of compliance. The more I lived into my worth, the less I listened to shame and the better I became at asking the right set of questions. Those questions were important for my relationships with others, but especially for my relationship with myself.

Each morning I greeted the day sitting in my living room, cup of coffee in hand, giving space for prayer and stillness. The white birch trees outside my window became icons of God's steadfastness through different seasons. I gazed upon them noticing every detail, their branches, the scars in the bark from growth, and the beauty of their leafless branches against a winter sky. They seemed dead but they were actually resting. In time new leaves would spring forth, providing oxygen and shade for the world. But for now it was time for tree sabbath.

One morning during prayer when it was still dark outside with a full moon reflecting on the snow, I noticed that by moving my head slightly, the full moon disappeared behind a single birch tree. The moon was still there, yet with a small change of perspective it seemed to be gone. If a full moon could be hidden behind a single tree, what else was I missing? What were the shifts in perspective that I might need in order to see what was hidden in plain sight? Did I have the courage that would be required to see new perspectives and expand my world? How would those changes in perspective affect my relationships?

The following summer I had the incredible opportunity to be one of three women chaperoning a group of teenagers from our church community, who traveled from Alaska to the Russian Far East city of

Khabarovsk. As an expression of gratitude for helping her through Mike's death, Julie offered to pay for my trip. I accepted her generous gift. We were hosted by a group of Russian teens and their parents. I stayed in the home of our interpreter, Irina, who lived in an apartment on the fourth floor which she shared with a married couple. In this way, I was fortunate to be able to enter into Russian life as a guest, rather than a tourist.

Over the course of two weeks we toured a few different cities, visited museums, orphanages, city squares, and picnicked along the Amur River. We were treated with generous hospitality everywhere we went. For many Russians, we were the first Americans they had ever met. At the end of the first week, we rode the Trans-Siberian train for twenty-four hours to the city of Vladivostok and then to Nakhodka where we spent several days at a children's camp on the Sea of Japan.

When we got off the bus at the entrance of the camp, we were greeted by a large crowd of children and teenagers. The camp director and other employees were there, too. Showered with cheers, clapping, bouquets of flowers and music from an accordion, we made our way through the camp streets until we came to the dormitory. We were treated like royalty. The American and Russian children played games, spent warm afternoons at the beach swimming in the ocean, danced, ate delicious food, and at night the adults would gather to share a drink, lifting a glass to friendship. It was truly a miracle for a girl who grew up thinking of Russians as enemies, to be eating fish-head stew under the stars and singing the Trisagion, an orthodox hymn, in a communist indoctrination camp for children.

Sasha, the assistant camp director, was especially kind to me. She could not speak English and I did not speak Russian. Through the interpreter I learned that she was Muslim, had a husband and children, and lived in a nearby town. Sasha had an easy laugh and was quick to smile. It was a new experience for me to have such affection for someone I didn't know and couldn't communicate with. It was a text book case of mutual projection. She doted on me, constantly anticipating my needs, and unabashedly, I drank it up. On the last day, while sailing in a yacht on the Sea of Japan, Sasha noticed I was cold from the cool ocean air and placed a sweater around my shoulders. I accepted her kindness and leaned into her shoulder, touched by her care. One of the other American women chaperones said in a critical tone, "Geeze Jeanine, you're acting like a child with Sasha." Weary of being checked by people in my church community, I snapped back, "Don't you know it is a gift to mother, as well as it is to be mothered?" I replayed this scene and dialogue over and over for the rest of the trip and beyond. In the grand scheme of things, it was a small moment, but it marked a major step forward in which I wasn't going to be shamed for accepting love that had been offered to me. I was finding my voice.

On the flight back to Anchorage, I thought about how far I had traveled, not only to Russia but in my personal journey. It was no small thing that I had been able to be away from my children for two entire weeks, separated by an ocean and a foreign country, and the whole time I was gone I knew they were okay. I was returning home with a greater sense of self respect, knowing that I could trust my perceptions. I was learning to feel safe in my own skin; that while I had been abandoned as a child, I would not abandon myself.

My new found confidence and courage were tested the following winter during a ski trip over the Resurrection Trail. We were planning on taking three days to ski 38 miles of pristine mountainous wilderness. My husband had skied this route many times, but this was the first time for me. We had a large group of thirteen church people of various ages and ability. We divided into two groups, staying at different forest service cabins. A dear friend, Jenny, was part of my group. It was in March with longer daylight, warmer temperatures, and corn-snow conditions. The morning of the second day we noticed a lot of wolf tracks and there was fresh, steaming scat along the trail. Though we never saw them, the wolf pack was just ahead of us. We followed their tracks the entire day.

I was not afraid partly because I had never ever heard of a wolf attacking a group of humans. As the day went on, the group began to separate because of differing abilities, levels of fitness, and experience, creating greater distances between each other. By the time Stephen and I reached the summit of Devil's Pass there was a group ahead of us and behind us, but we were on our own. The sun was beginning to go down but it was still daylight. In the brilliant white snow we found several areas of bright red blood, fur, and white bones. It was clear that the wolf pack had killed a moose just ahead of us and with great efficiency eaten every part of it. It was also clear that it had happened recently. The scene reminded me of a national geographic special demonstrating the dance between the predator and the prey. As I examined it, I knew we needed to move on as it would soon be dark. We still had several miles to go to reach our cabin.

Jenny and her husband were behind us. Both of them were strong and experienced back country skiers. Yet as darkness descended, I began to worry. Where were they? Hours later, long after dark, they arrived. Jenny burst into tears as she limped into the cabin. The moose kill scene had terrified her. She was certain that she would be the wolves' next meal. The scene that filled me with wonder and awe at the wolves' efficiency and lack of waste, she had only seen as the threat of death. Her fear of the wolves was in part from having injured feet which slowed them considerably. Yet they had no choice but to continue skiing on until they reached the cabin.

As I listened to Jenny's tale of fear, I remembered what she had told me in previous conversations. Her husband was an abusive bully. Being caught in the wilderness with her husband, the pack of wolves, darkness descending, the cabin miles away, and her feet screaming in pain, she felt utterly desolate. We helped her get her coat off and sit down. Once she removed her ski boots, her feet immediately began to swell showing black toe nails and bloody blisters. It was impossible for her to put her ski boots back on until her feet were healed. One of the men skied out early the next morning making arrangements for Jenny to be picked up by a small airplane that afternoon. Throughout the following day as we skied to our next cabin, I thought about Jenny's endurance in the face of so much fear and pain. She thought of herself as a weakling because she was so frightened. But what I saw in her was tremendous perseverance.

Mike's death, traveling to the Russian far east, and skiing the Resurrection with a pack of wolves expanded my perspectives on the world. Conversely, these experiences made my church community seem smaller and smaller. As a woman, literally and figuratively, I was delegated to the basement of the church. I wanted to contribute more than muffins for coffee hour. When I inquired about becoming a reader of scripture during the Divine Liturgy, I was told that I could not and that I needed to repent of the sin of pride. I was told that I should be thankful and focused on being a wife and mother, the most important calling of all. Leading worship was for the men.

As is all too common when women start to step out of line in a patriarchal structure, I was gaining a reputation in the community for being a dangerous humanist, radical and feminist. Some husbands didn't want their wives spending time with me anymore. My ideas could be contagious. I complained bitterly to my husband about how unfair and dismissive the church leadership was to me. He would listen to me vent, but did not defend me or my desire for leadership. His passive response to the priests' corrections communicated his tacit approval, making me feel even more alone and increasingly unhappy. Slowly, I was moving away from the community as well as my willingness to put up with lack of support in my marriage. What had given a sense of safety and belonging was increasingly oppressive in its demand for me to live a diminished life.

In my morning prayers with coffee and birch trees, I began to imagine leaving St. John's church and moving out of the neighborhood community. When I brought up the idea of moving or going to another church to Stephen, he would get overwhelmed by my discontent and my desire for change. He would bring up a long list of reasons why moving was too difficult, how leaving our church would hurt the children, and asking me to please try to be happy with our life. Neither one of us yet realized how desperate I was. My therapeutic journey with Martha had ended a few years prior. I was nearly finished with graduate school and I longed for a competent female spiritual advisor—not from St. John's church—to help me discern the next path I would take, professionally and spiritually.

Looking for options, I attended a retreat led by two Catholic nuns, Sr. Marguerite and Sr. Suzanne from the Mercy Center outside of San

Francisco. There I met a diverse group of women who were from various religious backgrounds, who spoke with depth about spirituality and life. Martha was also at the retreat. After our therapeutic relationship had ended, we slowly transitioned to friendship. Martha was one of my biggest cheerleaders as I moved through grad school. It was a breath of fresh air to be with a group of women who were courageous, full of laughter, and asked difficult questions. On the last day, I met with Sr. Marguerite privately. I told her about my church, the community, and how my husband was unwilling for anything about our lives to change. She listened to me with compassion and tenderness. She told me to trust the voice of God speaking to my heart and encouraged me to seek out spiritual direction. What a relief it was to not be told to repent of my pride. The two sisters taught us retreatants a prayer that would become a life-long guide for me: "*Lord, help me to show up, pay attention, speak the truth in love, and to detach from outcome.*"

It was a bold step for me when I called the Holy Spirit Retreat Center in South Anchorage to inquire about spiritual direction. I knew my orthodox priest would not approve of my seeking guidance from a Roman Catholic. I did it anyway. I was showing up to myself. Kathryn was a tall, middle-aged woman with short graying blonde hair and she wore understated, classic clothing. I thought she might be a nun. It surprised me when I learned that she was married and had two grown sons. We quickly formed a friendship recognizing that we were kindred spirits. My initial goal in spiritual direction was related to my new vocation as a therapist. I wanted to deepen my experience of God, as I identified as a wounded healer. I had worked with Martha to heal my psyche. Now I needed to work with Kathryn to heal my soul from toxic church people and institutions. It was and is extremely important to me to be a therapist who walks her talk.

It was not an easy thing to sort out what was healthy and unhealthy in my church community. There were so many incredibly devout people at St. John's who were not toxic. Having lived in the church community for over fifteen years, I had a shared history with them. Undoing decades of shaming messages in the name of religious conformity wasn't going to be quick or easy. The priests at St. John taught us that to leave orthodoxy and the local church community was apostasy, the equivalent of leaving God. Kathryn was patient as I would push against hard truths and then back away in fear of what the truth asked of me. With each new insight I became increasingly confrontational at church. Slowly and painfully, I also learned that I didn't need to correct every single wrong in the church community. I was learning to pick my battles.

The fruits of spiritual direction were bountiful. Kathryn's primary goal was to help me experience God's love on a cellular level. Through a daily practice of prayer and guided journaling, I methodically focused on sorting God's love for me as distinct from what I experienced through my religious practices. Kathryn recommended books on women's development written by both secular and Christian authors. She was well versed in identifying power-differentials within church. In therapy I worked to develop healthy boundaries, and in spiritual direction I was learning to expand those boundaries to church leadership and community.

It was amazing to me when Kathryn would say with love and enthusiasm, "Jeanine, you are so delightful!" She didn't tell me I was prideful or too much or tell me to be satisfied with making muffins for coffee hour. She did not see me as a collection of body parts meant for mothering and being a wife. She believed in me as a whole person. After more than a year of spiritual direction, Kathryn asked if I would be part a leadership team for a ministry called "Sarah's Circle." This group offered a series of ecumenical retreats throughout the year. She was giving me a place to lead because she saw that I had qualities of leadership. The team was made up of seven women which included a few Lutherans, a Baptist, some Catholics, and me, a wavering convert to Orthodoxy. As a group, we offered retreats of various lengths on relevant topics, sometimes leading the retreats ourselves, and sometimes inviting outside speakers.

My world kept expanding beyond the church as I completed my master's program, which then gave me the credentials to work as a therapist and as a school counselor. By this time Stephanie and Elizabeth were in elementary school, so I began to look for work that allowed me to be with them as much as possible. I came across a part-time position as a crisis counselor at the community mental health center. I was intrigued and called for more information. The job involved working in all the schools, K-12, with students who were in crisis, and making appropriate referrals for them. It was a job-share position, so I would work half time and it would be during the school day. This job was made for me! I was thrilled when after the interview I was offered the job.

After job shadowing my counter-part for a few weeks, I was on my own. We had our first snowfall of the season the morning of my first call. I was driving an old Nissan with summer tires. I needed to go to an elementary school to help students process the death of a classmate. My car fish-tailed but managed to stay on the slippery roads. As I drove to the school, parked the car, and walked inside, I thought, "I'm an imposter! What do I have to offer this school, the staff, the little children?" Nevertheless, I showed up. As I sat in the nurse's office, children would come to talk about their friend who died and they would talk about other losses, maybe their dog or their grandma. It was an honor to attend to hurting children, helping them to feel safe and to articulate loss. Even though I was as green and new as spring grass, I knew this work was my work, what I was always meant to do. I felt fully alive.

It's probably the most natural thing in the world to think that once you've gone to therapy or spiritual direction or confession that you're done, but really, it's just the beginning. We are always beginners in some sense, no matter how long we journey. We're continuously given opportunities to go deeper, reach higher, to see what's behind the next birch tree. And so it was, when my parents asked if Stephen and I would help move them from Missouri to Oregon when they were in their early seventies.

Jeff offered to build a one-bedroom apartment onto his home in southern Oregon, in which our parents could age in place with Jeff and his wife close by to help as needed. Our folks would pay for the materials but their home was built by their children. Ironically, they felt it was time for them to move toward their children for support as they were growing older and frail. It did not seem to occur to them that they were expecting from us the kind of protection and care they never gave to us. After Stephen and I agreed to help them move, they put their place up for sale in Missouri. A few months later we loaded their belongings into a large twenty-six-foot U-Haul truck and made our way west.

Initially, Stephen and I rode in the U-Haul while Mom drove Dad's pick-up. Wanting to do my part, I was driving the massive U-Haul when we arrived in Kansas City on a national holiday. Being an Alaskan girl, I am not afraid to hike in the wilderness. I know how to guard against bears. I was not frightened by the pack of wolves. But city traffic? That's another thing altogether. Imagine my surprise when I found myself suddenly driving in the middle of a parade with a big rig and my parents following me as if I knew where in the hell I was going while people along the parade route clapped and waved.

These were the days of folded maps and phones that were attached by cords to the kitchen wall. I drove over a few curbs, swore like our father, and was close to hyperventilating by the time I found a large parking lot. When I got out of the U-Haul I screamed, "I'm never driving that damn truck again!" At the same moment, Mom got out of the pick-up and declared, "I'm not driving the pick-up with your dad bitching at me the whole way to Oregon!" For these reasons, we traded rides, with Stephen in the U-Haul with Mom, and me driving Dad in his truck for the two thousand miles that remained.

Dad's truck had always been off limits to us kids. It was immaculate. There was no sign of anyone ever having used it. The only time I had ever ridden in his truck was the summer we spent on Heath Mountain and Mom was in Spokane. Now in my thirties, I was driving his truck with him in the passenger seat, feeling a weird mixture of childish wonder and panic.

The time we spent in the truck was the most concentrated time I ever had with Dad, before or since. He talked, smoked, and slept while I listened and drove. I don't recall all the monologues he covered in conversation, but I remember feeling more and more protective of him, which was strange in light of our history. This fierce, angry, violent man who made all our lives hell had grown old and uncertain, with shaky hands and liver spots on his olive skin. When we stopped at a café for coffee and a break, I walked him to the door of the men's room, as if it was the most normal thing in the world, which it would have been for anyone else. In the evenings we met Stephen and Mom at an agreed upon destination, and then try to find a motel. I could hardly wait to stop driving and stop listening. I wanted more than anything to go to sleep.

We were gaining elevation in Wyoming while Dad smoked and talked non-stop. We had grown up with thick clouds of smoke in our trailers, but I wasn't used to it any more. Dad's window was cracked but my eyes were tearing with mascara running into my eyes. I couldn't take it anymore. "Shit!" I yelled, and pull off the road in order to wipe my eyes and gasp some fresh air outside the truck. Dad looked bewildered, sad even, as if he thought I was crying from something he said. I immediately apologized for cussing and told him it was okay. There was so much for me to process. There was so much I didn't know about him. In fact, I hardly knew him at all. The work I had done in therapy with Martha helped me to detach from childhood fear so that I could have compassion for Dad in his weakness.

Not long after the apartment was completed Dad was diagnosed with lung cancer. He also had advanced congestive heart failure, thus he decided not to have any medical treatment. I went to see him a few weeks before he died. We sat on the back porch while he smoked. His body had wasted away, leaving him looking like a skeleton with half closed eyes. He spoke in a halting whisper, confessing, "I'm sorry I wasn't a good father. I was a drunk and an asshole." He took a drag on his cigarette. I told him I loved him. He exhaled and said, "I love you, too." In the quiet moment there was peace. I helped him stand up and walk inside, to sit in his recliner. Before heading back to Alaska, I helped Mom to set up hospice care. Dad died the following week.

CHAPTER TWENTY-ONE

Sacred Love

WE SEE IT EVERYWHERE, in nature, in families, and in history. The birth, life, death, and rebirth pattern cycles around us, through us, and within our own lives, over and over again. Within the individual psyche, the way the cycle shows up is that we find ourselves restless, chafing, in need of change. At such times most of us only gradually realize we are invited to let die whatever is no longer serving us, in order to give birth to a new, healthier way of being. I think of it as birthing yourself, not just once, but many times over a lifespan. The season usually involves labor pains that mark the before and after of what is emerging. Birthing yourself is a messy process with convoluted feelings and fears that create a rhythm of moving forward between "contractions" and retreating backward when the pain returns. Eventually new life comes forth, bringing a new normal.

Often times there is a pivotal event that starts labor. For many people, a life transition triggers labor. For example, a graduation, a new relationship, childbirth, retirement, or the death of a family member can open space within us for a new set of questions and awareness that then lead to a new season of self-birthing.

Dad died the same week that I started a new job as a school counselor at a large high school. As a crisis counselor, I had developed good relationships with many counselors, psychologists, and principals throughout the district. Now, as a school counselor, I was grateful to have the opportunity to work in one school community with students on a wide variety of issues, not just crisis response. Despite my excitement at new opportunities, starting a new job while processing Dad's death was demanding and stressful. These two events triggered the self-awakening that changed the course of my life in ways I never could have imagined.

When we sit with our grief, holding it like a newborn child, it will show us the way forward. In the months following Dad's death and my starting a new job, as I carried the stress of endings and beginnings, Stephen was kind and patient with me. These were very busy days. Our girls started school and we all settled into a routine. Living in the church community, following the church calendar, and attending vespers on Saturday followed by the Divine Liturgy on Sunday was an established way of life. This familiar regimen provided comfort and structure while integrating change. The pattern of liturgy, work, and home life offered regular touchpoints for my grief.

That fall the Sarah's Circle leadership team met to plan a three-day retreat to be held in January. Through prayer and collaboration, we discussed possible speakers and topics for the retreat. I suggested asking Elaine to lead the retreat. We were delighted when she accepted the invitation to be our guest speaker. Mom and Julie agreed to attend the retreat, too. It would be a mini family reunion, and the first and only time the four of us experienced a spiritual retreat together. I was excited to share Sarah's Circle with them and for them to experience my leadership and of this ecumenical group of women. I was also extremely proud of Elaine, eager to show her off to my friends.

About thirty-five women from various faith traditions gathered at the retreat. Elaine and I laughed when we noticed that regardless of their denominational backgrounds, a lot of the women including ourselves wore variations of the same trendy church lady outfit, a long-sleeved turtleneck under a calf-length jumper with tights and flats or boots, the picture of feminine modesty.

The retreat focused on seasons of our lives using the metaphor of an oak tree. One of our Sarah's Circle leaders who was a professional artist had painted a large image of an oak tree with its foliage divided into four seasons. This became the metaphor for the retreat as we explored the rhythmic cycles of birth, growth, death, and rebirth that make up our lives. Elaine's talks drew from the Psalms and classics in Christian spirituality.

After each of Elaine's presentations, we gathered into small reflection groups which allowed participants to risk in sharing matters of the heart. I noticed a woman, Jackie, in my group who naturally helped lead the conversation. She was energetic and engaging. Because I already had a full plate of responsibilities in leading the retreat as a whole, I appreciated Jackie's spontaneous leadership of the small group and her way of drawing out each woman in our group so that everyone participated and felt safe.

At the close of the retreat Elaine encouraged all thirty-eight participants to gather with those who were in their geographic areas and continue to meet in small groups for spiritual formation. She offered some suggestions for resources and a format for the groups. The women had come from all across Alaska, by far the largest state, with a land mass one fifth the size of the continental United States. It would be helpful for retreatants to have a group of spiritual friends when they returned to their homes across the state.

In private Elaine suggested to Jackie and me that we co-lead one of the groups in our town, Eagle River, because she saw how compatible we were in leadership, and as the three days progressed, she saw that Jackie and I had quickly become friends. The formation of the group was effortless. Within a few weeks, thirteen of us began meeting regularly. Most of the women were Roman Catholic, except for one Baptist and myself. We were all seeking depth in our lives of prayer and discernment.

As my involvement with Sarah's Circle and this prayer group expanded, my attachment to St. John's contracted. I was finding it more and more difficult to go to church. The fundamentalist, patriarchal spirituality that had formed me and had given me structure from my early teen years, was dying in direct proportion to my awakening strength as a female spiritual leader in the company of other spiritual women. The restrictive, exclusive Christianity of my youth was giving way to a more expansive, inclusive vision of God and faith. At early midlife I was reading a new set of authors including Joan Chittister and Julian of Norwich, and rubbing shoulders with women who were ordained clergy, including Elaine.

Throughout that spring in addition to our small group gatherings, Jackie and I met regularly to walk and talk. I found out that she was raised in a large Catholic family in northern Maine. Despite our radically different childhoods we discovered we had much in common. As a teenager, she seriously fell in love with Jesus, too. Whereas I had joined a very restrictive evangelical intentional community after high school which then turned to monasticism for inspiration, Jackie had entered a convent as a postulant nun which is the first step toward taking traditional monastic vows. After a year of discernment, however, she decided to leave monastic life, hoping to someday marry and have children. In time she did marry, and by the time we met twenty-five years later, Jackie and her husband had two children, one in college in Maine and the other in high school. A teacher and entrepreneur, Jackie owned and operated an academic preschool. Her faith remained of paramount importance throughout her life.

There are some relationships that feel timeless, as if we might have always known each other and when we finally meet we only need to catch up on details. It was like that for Jackie and me. We found solace in each other's company for the struggles in our lives. We both loved God with all of our being. We were devoted to our children and our husbands. We were both successful professional women. What we didn't realize for many months was that we were falling in love with each other, and for both of us this was the first time ever to truly be in love. That dawning awareness brought joy and agony in depths we did not know possible, upending our sense of identity as each of us came home to ourselves and God in ways for which society as a whole, our families of origin, and especially the church had not prepared us.

As fall moved into winter with less sunlight and plenty of snow, the routines of school, work, home, children, and church structured our busy days. Still, Jackie and I made time to walk almost every day. Arm in arm, we made our way through neighborhoods or along nearby forest trails, talking about life, our dreams, and God. Sometimes we simply walked in silence. I felt energized and nourished when I was with her, I felt more fully alive, as if I were finally becoming me without restraint. But I was unaware that it was anything more than deep spiritual friendship.

One day while walking, Jackie asked if I would pray for her. She was worried about a sick family member. Together, we sat on a large rock in the woods. I put my arm around her, holding her close while she cried and we prayed. Something new awakened in me toward her as I supported her in her pain, something beautiful, good, and confusing, so I did not name it and tried to put it out of my mind. Repression and denial helped me manage what was still beneath conscious awareness.

Jackie is a private, reserved New Englander, but with me she was increasingly exuberant when we greeted each other and our goodbye hugs became longer and longer. It all seems so obvious looking back, but at the time I did not have words or experiences to articulate what was happening, because I had never been in love in this way and my conceptual framework had no place for being in love with someone of the same gender. As people do when falling in love, I found myself thinking about her all the time. Between our daily walks I longed for the next time we would be together. We started writing to each other, stumbling toward naming what we both experienced even though we were still devoted to our families and busy with all the demands of our lives.

There was deep snow on the ground and we were in Jackie's Suburban drinking coffee when we both said, almost at the same time, "There is something I need to talk with you about." Jackie said, "I have feelings for you and I don't know what to do about it." I said, "I feel infatuated with you, I think." It was a shy and awkward conversation. It was also full of the longing and passion that I had never experienced before.

Forbidden love is a tsunami. Being profoundly religious women in very conservative traditions, married to men, and with children at home propelled the joy and agony in which we found ourselves. We prayed desperately that God would transform our love back into mere friendship, while at the same time doing everything we could to be alone together. We felt deep regret that we were unable to experience with our husbands the kind of love that bound us together.

The shadow side of our repressed sexuality, as well as our individual efforts to be perfect Christian women, all came crashing down when we finally owned the truth about ourselves, that each of us was deeply in love for the first time in our lives, with a woman. With that truth-telling so much about our previous lives finally made sense. We were women in midlife waking up to our sexuality for the first time.

Where there had been years of ambivalence, now there was clarity about many things, including the kind of church where I could be myself and find a spiritual home. As we sat at the dinner table one night, I told Stephen I would not go to St. John's any more. He was upset with this decision. He was not willing to go to another church with me, either. It was clear to him that I was unhappy, but we were experts in avoiding conflict. After years of restless discontentment, I finally had the courage to leave an oppressive, patriarchal church.

One night, Jackie's husband overheard her tell me that she loved me. When she got off the phone, he confronted her. The following day, deeply distraught she told me our relationship was over and that she would be leaving to go on retreat at a spiritual center in Biddeford, Maine. She planned to meet with Sr. Mary, a former spiritual guide and mentor, who was the mother superior. It was Jackie's intent to repent and to return to her marriage, with help from Sr. Mary.

I was devastated. I couldn't get out of bed for several days. The love I experienced with Jackie became the measuring stick for everything else in my life. What was the point of knowing such a mutual love only to have it evaporate? It all felt so cruel. A few days after she left, I called Jackie at the retreat center. She told me that God was the only love of her life. She had been meeting with Sr. Mary and had made the decision to stay married to her husband. Jackie said she hoped we could remain friends. I sobbed as I heard her words.

Stephen didn't know the whole story but he wasn't blind. He didn't ask and I didn't tell. The secret of loving a woman and the shame of having an affair kept me completely isolated. Avoidance bought me time to determine my next steps. Somehow, I went to work and got through the day and I began to wonder if I would be better off dead. As I made the forty-minute commute to and from work, I questioned whether my kids would be better off with a gay mom or a dead mom? Returning to the mom I used to be was not possible. Over and over, my mind teeter-tottered. Would I be a dead mom or gay mom? Dead mom—gay mom. I walked further down the path of suicidal thinking, imagining how I could do it. Even though I wasn't imminently suicidal, having an exit plan provided psychic space to catch up to myself.

Jackie and I spoke again before she returned to Alaska. Her resolve was wavering. She expressed her love for me and said that she wanted to do God's will but with the guidance she had been given these two things seemed mutually exclusive. Walking the rugged coast line, listening to the waves and her own heart, she begged God to show her the way through this unfathomable valley of loss. Just before hanging up the phone, Jackie told me that she had one last appointment with a priest for confession before leaving the following day. We said good-bye, not knowing when we would see each other again.

The old priest was waiting in a small room for Jackie. He, too, had to catch a plane and only had limited time. She made her confession with him face to face, not behind the usual screen. Bravely, Jackie told her story of being faithfully married for twenty-five years and falling in love for the first time in her life, with a woman. She told him that her constant prayer throughout her marriage had been that God would help her to love her husband more. Jackie explained that she did not think it was possible for her to love her husband the way she loved me, despite all those years of praying for such love for her husband.

The priest listened to her confession without judgment. He listened to her heart. When she finished pouring out her need, her deception, her sins, and her love for me, the old priest told her she was forgiven. Just before departing, he turned and asked her to consider what was the greater sin: to stay married to someone she didn't fully love, or to end a relationship with someone she did? What if her love for me was actually a gift from God, an answer to her long years of prayer to be able to love more?

The lives we lived before we knew each other were unraveling fast. The desperate attempts to stay apart, to just be friends, to pray the gay away, to fix our marriages, in general to avoid the truth, wore holes in the tattered fabric of our marriages. It was mid-summer when I told Stephen that I wanted a divorce. Regardless of what Jackie ultimately decided for herself, I knew I couldn't stay married any longer. Stephen deserved better, and so did I. Telling our children about the pending divorce was one of the most painful conversations I have ever had. We all cried and cried. It broke my heart to hear their sorrow, but it did not break my resolve.

When I look back upon my marriage to Stephen, I am grateful for the time we shared and the family we created. We had two incredible daughters together, and we helped to raise Paul and Douglas. Mostly, we were good to each other. The sweet gentleness between us was genuine but it wasn't enough as I outgrew the need for the safety and predictability that marked our relationship. I also outgrew the belief that I had to follow all the rules to be good enough to be loved. While I am not proud of breaking my vows to Stephen, I have never felt guilty for loving Jackie. I have only felt awake and alive, and became adamantly committed to living truthfully. After fifteen years of marriage and twenty years of living in the church community, I needed to be free.

Shortly after Stephen and I began to plan toward separate futures, I was sitting in my office preparing for school to open when the phone rang. It was Stephanie. She was thirteen and in an argument with an evangelical friend of hers. She asked, "Mom, Roberta said being gay is a sin. I told her it wasn't. What do you think?" I had not come out to her, so I told her that I would talk about it when I got home. That night we talked in the guest room where I was sleeping. Stephanie said, "Mom, I'll tell you why it's not a sin to be gay." "Okay," I replied, eagerly wanting to find out why I wasn't a sinner. She said, "It's never a sin to love anyone."

Her simple logic was perfect medicine for my wounded heart. I told her that I had something I wanted to tell her but I wasn't quite sure how to say it. With a bit of hinting from me, she finally asked, "Are you gay?" I said I didn't know, but I did know that I loved Jackie. Stephanie's wisdom and mercy paved the way for me to tell her younger sister. It was hard for Elizabeth, yet her love for me was constant. It would take time for everyone to adjust.

Around the same time, Jackie made the same decision to divorce. She moved into a small home with an extra bedroom for her daughter, Katy. I moved into a three-bedroom duplex. Jackie and I held onto each other as our children, our families, our friends all processed the divorce and our relationship. It was incredibly painful to experience harsh judgements, sweeping statements of morality, and to have folks turn their back on us. More than a few friends and family members stopped speaking to us. We were together, but also very much alone.

After that when I drove down Monastery Rd. in the neighborhood where I used to live, people from St. John's shunned me. Those who previously waved now literally turned their backs. One afternoon I was taking my daughters to their dad's house and a person turned their back as we drove by. I shouted one of Dad's favorite phrases, "They can kiss my ass!" Stephanie, wise as ever, said from the back seat, "Oh Mom, don't you know the energy you give is the energy you'll receive?" Her words hit me almost physically. As I spent time digesting her insight, I thought about what it means to turn the other cheek. I had a choice in how I responded to judgment, rejection, and being excommunicated.

Coming out to yourself can take a long time. Some people never do, remaining closeted because it is so hard to imagine how their families, friends, or faith community will react. I didn't call myself gay or lesbian or bisexual when I talked to others about my newly awakened self. In my innocence and inexperience, I didn't have definitive language. I said, "I'm not a lesbian, I just love Jackie." Labels, intrusive questions, scripture verses, adamant opinions and judgments were freely expressed whether I wanted them or not. I found people wanting to use a label to box me into something neat and tidy. Like Mary Oliver's poem, *The Journey*, it seemed everyone demanded that I mend their life. I simply wanted to live with the love of my life and I hoped everyone would eventually be okay. We grieved for all of the sorrow and pain our children and family were experiencing, even as we found peace through living a life congruent with our love for each other and God.

One of my closest friends even to this day, was my principal,

Dwight. His love and support buoyed me through many difficult days. When he found out about Jackie, he took my hand and gently said, "Jeanine, love knows no gender." He helped me feel safe at work when the rest of my world was falling apart. Slowly, I told other trusted co-workers about Jackie. It was such an ordeal each time I mustered the courage to come out to someone. I was filled with anxiety that they would change their opinion of me, perhaps even turn their back on me. What I found though was a steady stream of kindness, mercy, and affirmation.

About a year after leaving our husbands, we decided it was time to move in together. We rented a four-bedroom house with a rushing creek that ran through the back yard. The beauty and sound of the stream became a balm to us in the evenings as we sat by a campfire and talked about our day. It was a relief beyond words finally to be together, partly because it simplified our schedule and normalized our relationship.

Jackie closed her preschool and decided to attend a post-graduate teacher's program in special education. Katy and Stephanie were in high school and Elizabeth was in middle school. We were a house full of women. Blending our families would take years. It was extremely difficult at times dealing with so much change but to our children's credit, they were incredibly resilient with all of the loss, fears, and adjustments they endured. They could see how happy we were, but they also felt the weight of social stigma and judgment that came with having gay parents.

Jackie and I found a church family we loved at St. Mary's Episcopal Church. They were liturgical, progressive, welcoming, and supportive. The congregation was an eclectic group of folks, young, old, gay, straight, wealthy, homeless, and was racially and politically diverse. There was even a female priest on staff. Everyone was welcome at the eucharistic table. I was invited to read scripture during the service and to assist in serving communion, neither of which roles were permitted when I was at St. John. Thus St. Mary's became a healing community for me. The church held us as we navigated the path toward our next chapter.

Our priest, Bob, was a remarkable man whom we quickly grew to love and respect. He was profoundly insightful and a gentle, contemplative leader. His pastoral care personified grace. Jackie and I asked him if he would consider presiding over our union ceremony. His blue eyes twinkled as he said, "I would be thrilled! However, there are a few things that need to be done before I can give you an answer. I'll need to check with our bishop to make certain that I won't lose my retirement. I'll also need to have the vestry's blessing." Everything fell into place. He wouldn't lose his retirement because of blessing our union, and the vestry gave their approval. We were the first same sex couple to be married at St. Mary's. On May 12, 2001, Bob officiated our union and we said our vows surrounded by our daughters, our friends and church family.

The next decade was spent parenting our daughters and living more fully into the gift of our union. We bought a lake house and settled into a peaceful life. The interplay between the sky and the lake became my new icon, just as the birch trees had spoken to me for so many years. Seasons passed. Jackie worked as a middle school special education teacher and I worked in school counseling. When Elizabeth went to college, I opened a small private therapy practice in addition to being a school counselor. Our days were rich with gratitude. After all that we had gone through to be together, we did not take our love for granted.

Twelve years later after our union ceremony, on Jackie's sixty-third birthday, we were married legally. Not only had our nation moved toward accepting and legalizing same sex marriage, so did Jackie's family of origin. Our ceremony was held in Jackie's brother's yard in Scarborough, Maine. Her son, Kirk, escorted his mom to the place where I stood and her mom officiated our exchange of vows. The yard was filled with Jackie's siblings and their spouses, aunts, uncles and cousins. We celebrated with an Alaskan feast of salmon, halibut, and reindeer sausage dinner in the back yard. Everyone who came blessed us with their presence and their love.

Our kids are amazing people who make us burst with pride. In their own time, each one of them healed from the divorce and embraced our blended family. All four of them finished college and graduate school, and now work in careers that help others. Their lives are busy with families of their own, but we have strong bonds and stay closely connected. Jackie and I are known as Nana and Grandma to our ten grandchildren. Elaine says we remind her of the nursery rhyme about the old woman who lived in the shoe, only there are two of us.

Our life together has been abundant. We still laugh at each other's jokes and dance in the kitchen to our favorite love songs. Jackie still takes my breath away. Her love has changed me, healed me, called forth the best in me. When I make mistakes, she forgives me. She always believes in me. As expressed in k.d. lang's song *Barefoot*, Jackie has demonstrated to me over and over her willingness to walk barefoot through the snow for me. I waited my entire life for Jackie. She is my true love, my sacred love. And I am hers.

CHAPTER TWENTY-TWO

Warrior

SOMETIMES I BELLY LAUGH at how God surprises me. As if God were my big brother, lightly punching me in the arm, saying, "Love ya, Neanie." I am privy to these divine moments of surprise again and again. The Bible tells us about this irony in 1 Corinthians 1:27, "But God chose the foolish things of the world to shame the wise; God chose the weak things of the world to shame the strong." The shaming voices in my head want me to believe that I will never be enough or that I don't belong at the table or that I'm too broken to be whole. However, the wounded warrior within me fights with the truth of God's promise to transform my foolishness into wisdom and my weakness into strength. This paradox, this holy humor, invites me to shake off self-contempt.

I was an observant little girl. The gift of being a good listener seems to be from the way I'm wired combined with the impact of a traumatic childhood. To this point, Mom often told me the story about going to a parent teacher conference when I was in first grade. I stood waiting for her in the school hallway while she met with the teacher who said, "I'm very concerned about how withdrawn and quiet your daughter is in class. Jeanine will answer me only when I call on her but otherwise will not talk." When mom came out into the hallway, I asked her eagerly, "Did my teacher say I was the best listener in the class?" Mom said, "Just a minute, I need to tell your teacher something." She went back into the classroom to tell the teacher that what the teacher perceived as being withdrawn, I saw as being the best listener.

The truth is that I was both extremely withdrawn and a good listener. Just to be clear, my being withdrawn was from a place of hypervigilance and fear. This is distinct from being an introvert, which is a personality type characterized by internal processing. Being withdrawn was a reaction to my chaotic and violent homelife. Even then God was taking my weakness, or wound, and making it a strength.

Perhaps then, a part of me has been preparing my whole life to be a counselor, one who listens well to what is said and unsaid. Out of my weakness, my wounds, healing gifts are offered to others. In his spiritual classic, *The Wounded Healer*, Henri Nouwen writes about the absurdity of God's cosmic plan to use the very parts of ourselves we think are most broken to become the avenue of grace for ourselves and others. Nouwen states that the degree to which we are able to be with our pain is the degree to which we can be with another's pain. A wounded healer must be a warrior in facing their own pain.

As courageous warriors, we bravely go toward the thing that frightens us most. Perhaps it is confronting old stories, old lies, old assumptions. Maybe it is finally bringing a secret shame into the light. A wounded healer is a warrior in going into the consuming fire of fear but in the momentum of truth telling and emotional connection, the monster of pain dissipates.

It is incredibly helpful to know that not all pain is dangerous or death dealing. Physical pain helps infants to communicate to their parent when they are hungry or need their diaper changed or have a fever. Their pain is essential to survival. A toddler must learn to deal with emotional pain of being told "no" or to wait, which helps them become more socially appropriate with an internalized locus of control as they mature and enter school. Pain teaches us physical and emotional boundaries. Pain is also a powerful motivator for change. In fact, people rarely make changes in their life without some sort of pain helping them advance. As a wounded healer, I have learned that being with people in pain and attending to their pain is the primary road to recovery. The capacity to do that is in proportion to attending to my own pain.

When I went to therapy, I had to unpack the steamer trunks full of pain that I carried. Martha helped me take out hidden, crumpled up parts of myself that I did not want to own, or name. In Jungian psychology these suppressed parts of ourselves are called our "shadow." Many aspects of my trauma and neglect were stored intellectually or in muscle memory that would flinch at the slightest provocation. I had not truly integrated them into my own story through naming and feeling. It was safer to not need or want. In our childhood we were not able to be needy because to do so caused negative and at times violent reactions from our parents. Through processing the pain from the abuse and neglect from my childhood, I had greater capacity to live consciously as an adult. This means I became increasingly aware of the difference between pain that is "now" and reactivity to a trigger for pain that was "then."

Living consciously involves feeling pain instead of numbing ourselves to it, which demands increasing insight and personal responsibility. Elaine wrote a poem many years ago about this dynamic. In the poem, a woman had laid out all the clothing of shame she wore in childhood. One by one, she took out saddle oxford shoes, a yellow dress, and pink polka dot shorts from her bag where they had been drowning in an ocean of pain, and laid them in the sun to dry. Eventually, all of them were transformed into butterflies: a saddle oxford butterfly, a yellow butterfly, and a pink polka dot butterfly. By truly facing and feeling our pain, there is hope for resurrection, for transformation.

To be authentic wounded healers, we must walk our own path of pain, and revisit it again and again as required for wholeness. Like a prayer labyrinth, this path circles around and takes unexpected turns. We cannot ask our clients, students, patients or parishioners to travel down roads that we are unwilling to walk. To hide from or numb our pain is disingenuous and leads to dangerous potholes of deception. When a wounded healer has done their own work, descending into their own hell of pain, of shame, of abuse, a sacred space is created for others to in turn share their pain with the wounded healer bearing empathetic witness. In this way we also reduce the potential for vicarious projection of our pain and issues on to others. With humility and integrity, wounded healers must continue to walk their talk in seeking care and accountability.

As life unfolds, we are given opportunities to continue healing in ways that sometimes confound us. A few months after working with Martha, she told me, "Jeanine, you have an incredibly low expectation of men. You don't even expect much from Jesus Christ." I laughed hard, a little embarrassed. Although what she said was absolutely true, before that moment I had never named it. My early formation of men was skewed, to say the least. My general experience of men was that they had the power to hurt, but paradoxically needed to be cared for and served because they were so fragile. Women had to over-function for men which guaranteed their under-functioning. Being male was a one-way street of selfishness. It wasn't that good men didn't exist, it was that my perception was distorted by my experience. I needed to learn to view men in a more fair and reasonable way, which meant I needed to raise the bar of expectation. It would take years of intentionality to heal in my expectations.

The good and honorable men who helped to heal my expectations of men were colleagues found within the walls of Wasilla High School. Our school mascot was Warrior which holds special meaning for me for reasons already noted. Over the course of my twenty-four years as a school counselor, these colleagues became friends and brothers. They flanked me, encircled me, and honored me with their respect as I increasingly came home to myself. They taught me to raise the bar of expectation for men. Of course, they were not perfect, nor did they have super powers. But in their way of being in the world, their relationship with me, one another, and our students they taught me to trust and expect goodness from them. Because of them, I learned not to over-function for them which was a great relief for me. They were essential to my becoming a wounded healer.

In my mind's eye, I imagine the men in a sacred circle. They are peaceful warriors. The first of the four men is Dwight, who was my principal. He is a cross between Viking and Atticus Finch from *To Kill A Mocking Bird*. As a school leader he was a master at creating community, a place of belonging. Above all, Dwight wanted to make a difference in the lives of students and staff. He opened doors for me to serve others and he created safety when my world fell apart. Our friendship grew deep, with roots of trust and mutual vulnerability. Words cannot tell of the solidarity and unconditional love that marks our cherished friendship.

Dan is next in the circle. He was a young, single man when I first met him. Dan's tall, athletic stature made it easy to see why he played football in college. He taught PE and Social Studies, and eventually became an assistant principal. His jovial personality brightened our busy days. Eventually Dan married, had two sons, and grew into maturity. His heart is as big as he is, with a perpetual desire to reach new heights of growth and enlightenment. After Dan worked as an administrator within the school system for some time, he decided the stress wasn't good for his soul. He is now a lean, vegan, yoga instructor as well as a high school teacher. As Dan's boys became men, he leaned into his life with the spiritual paradox that less is more. Simply being in his presence helps me to rest.

Standing next to Dan in the sacred circle is Mark, a profoundly private man. He was always impeccably groomed with slicked back blonde hair and he wore well-made suits with fancy shirts with cuff links. Being professional in presentation was paramount to Mark, but there is much more to him than his appearance. He is a solitary man who reads more voraciously than anyone I have ever met. Words mattered to Mark. He is intentional and thoughtful with everything he utters. Over the years through many conversations and in different settings, Mark let down his guard, inviting me to know him. I think we covered every topic under the sun. Mark has a knack for reframing situations so I could see things in new ways. We wrestled with ideas, pushing back freely and enjoying the debate. Before I retired, Mark became my principal. He helped me to finish strong.

Blake is the fourth man in the circle. A hometown boy-man who taught English, we hit it off right away. With the deeper things in life we intuitively trusted each from the beginning. Blake often stopped by my office to discuss a student he was concerned about or to share "scar story" essays in which students wrote about how a painful event left a scar but helped them grow. And just as frequently, he would stop by to tell a joke, have a good laugh, and to check in with me. He was a little brother. In the course of time, Blake married and had two sons. To say he was popular seems trite, like, who cares? He was much more than that, he made an absolute life-long difference in so many of his students' lives. He and I often tag-teamed each other during crisis counseling with students. Blake courageously asked questions that led toward a more examined, authentic life. Time after time, we shared sacred warrior moments of helping students in pain find their way out of darkness.

My actual brothers, the sons of our father, are in the center of my circle of men. Being fourteen years older than me, I don't have any memory of Mike living at home. As with all of us, he was often farmed out to a neighbor or a relative. As soon as he was old enough, he joined the army where he was deployed to Viet Nam for multiple tours as a paratrooper. Mike is an incredibly handsome man, with the ruggedness of Clint Eastwood's gaze and a smile that can light up a room. He suffered more than I'll ever know from our Dad and Mom, and then from the trauma of combat. When I was nine, he married his love, Carol. Recently they celebrated their fiftieth anniversary surrounded by their children and grandchildren. I admire his consistent willingness to face another layer of pain leading to another layer of healing. He rides a Harley, hikes mountains, teaches classes that allow people to carry concealed weapons, and attends yoga classes with other vets. Sometimes I wish he could see himself through my eyes. He would see a gentle man of great faith and endurance.

Jeff stands in the center next to Mike. We have always shared a sweet connection. He has given me more nicknames than I can count and has taken me into his home on several occasions. As a man, he has taught me that conversion is truly possible, in the deepest possible sense, on the level of Jean Valjean in *Les Miserables*. After moving from the St. John's community in Alaska, Jeff and his family made their home in the Pacific Northwest. With stubborn resolve to do right and to be right, Jeff realized he was in a losing battle. It took years for him to face himself, his pain and the shame inherent in growing up with abuse, neglect, and addicted parents. He survived his childhood through avoidance which did not serve him well as an adult. After years of struggle, he came to embrace his true self, a contemplative.

He has come to trust his innate belovedness, and he is at peace. Jeff finally embraced his true self, which is wholly good as it is. Finally, he is at home with himself. I so admire his knowledge and articulation of faith, of feminism, of dream interpretation, of social justice, and that he can tie flies like a master fisherman.

These men, these peaceful warriors healed my bias, my prejudice by being real with me. Over the ebb and flow of seasons, years, decades they risked being vulnerable with me in their strength/weakness, wisdom/foolishness. They are the epitome of good men. Their belief in me raised me above my fears. Through laughter and tears, we raised each other up. My cup overflows with gratitude.

As I write this, our world is in a pandemic. We are hunkered down in our homes, trying to flatten the curve of infection which hopefully prevents overwhelming hospitals with sick and dying people. The pandemic has changed who we identify as warriors. They are the teachers, the store clerks, the hospital janitors, the emergency technicians, the nurses, the doctors, and the first responders. They are showing up to heal the wounds from an enemy we cannot see. Some of these warriors are under-employed, making minimum wage, living paycheck to paycheck. Now they are considered essential. They show up to their work.

As a school counselor and now a therapist, I show up to my work. There were the mundane tasks of managing schedules and balancing class sizes and proctoring exams. And there were countless student requests to change classes for an array of reasons. These routine conversations, though, were often the door to a sacred moment of a student reaching out for connection; a risk toward relationship. People desire to be known, to be seen, but they are afraid of being rejected. By creating a genuine meeting, a holding space for the other—even if the topic is routine or mundane—we give opportunity for another person to know it is safe to tell us what is bothering them. They can share their pain.

It was in that space that students often told me about having suicidal thoughts. Courageously, they invited me to descend into their darkness with them. Suicide is hell. Who knew that when Mike died by suicide that I would eventually become a leader in our school district and state in the area of suicide prevention? It wasn't ever something I wanted, but again, God's redeeming wisdom gave me strength and wisdom from the ashes of experience. As a crisis counselor and school counselor, I have completed hundreds of interventions with students who were on the spectrum of suicidality. Descending into the narrowing darkness of suicidal thinking and obsession is scary. It should be. It is one of the leading causes of death for teenagers.

After an unusually high rate of suicide attempts and completions in 2001, a group of community leaders asked me and another school counselor, Susan, to attend a week-long training in St. John's, Newfoundland. Collectively, Susan and I were described as the most experienced and skilled crisis counselors in our community. We were honored to be asked.

Flying from Alaska to the most eastern Canadian maritime province took a long time. En route, I decided to come out to Susan because we were sharing a motel room in St. John's and I wanted to be able to freely call Jackie during our stay. When I finally mustered the courage during one of our several lay-over stops, she replied to my big disclosure, "Is that why you've been acting so antsy? I'm happy for you and Jackie. Thanks for telling me. Now, I'm going to go back to reading my book." Susan's lack of reaction was so surprising given my assumptions about her southern upbringing and conservative faith. She taught me a great deal about respecting boundaries and letting go of stereotypes.

Newfoundland was similar to Alaska in the sense of being remote and having a low population density, but it was also a great adventure to experience the most eastern point in North America. The bits of Irish and Scottish accents from locals were delightful. After an intense week of instruction, we completed the Applied Suicide Intervention Skills Training (ASIST) program and became the first certified trainers in Alaska. The ASIST curriculum was research based and considered the gold standard for teaching everyday folks first-aid response for a suicide intervention. At that time, we used primitive technology, an overhead projector and plastic slides. It was perfect for traveling to remote Alaskan villages. We were eager to share the training with others.

In the decade that followed, Susan and I traveled throughout the state of Alaska teaching the two-day ASIST workshop. Our transportation was varied, from jets to small planes with wheels, skis, or floats depending on the weather and where we landed. We rode in ferries and taxis and pickup trucks. One time we rode in a pickup on a frozen river road, also known as the Kuskokwim Ice Road, from Bethel to a village called Akiachak. And we stayed in a variety of dwellings, from hotels to empty teacher quarters, to classroom floors. Susan was the best travel companion and we shared many adventures. From the time we traveled to Newfoundland, she made it clear that we didn't need to take care of or entertain each other when we traveled. This allowed for a serene space in which we rested in each other's presence.

Teaching others how to help a person considering suicide was an opportunity to leave a legacy of change. Susan and I were faithful to the ASIST curriculum, which we presented in a down to earth manner, drawing from our many professional experiences as counselors. There were several times when village elders would sit in on the first few hours of our training to make certain that we were culturally respectful and were offering their community useful information contextually. One time, the entire two-day training was translated for an elder from English to Athabascan. We learned to be flexible with different cultural norms regarding start times, people's movement during presentation, and with weather dictating travel.

All aspects of suicide, from prevention to intervention to postvention, is the work of bringing light into darkness. Until recently, suicide was culturally taboo, broadly. Even talking about it was considered dangerous for fear of planting ideas into a vulnerable person's mind. We need to expose this myth, to offer hope to those who suffer, and to companion those overwhelmed with grief. Truth sets us free. Science and research with accurate, nonjudgmental data can guide us toward appropriate treatment. Like all of us who in our own ways are fighting the pandemic, all of us are essential workers in preventing suicide. And when we are not able to prevent it, all of us can play a role in supporting the survivors as they grieve.

My vocation as a therapist is grounded in my faith. It is truly humbling to make the sacred pilgrimage with my clients during their own warrior journey through pain, death, and resurrection, to new life. To descend with them into what is below the surface is for me sacramental, a mini-baptism, a response to divine invitation. This is true regardless of my clients' religious commitments. The holiness of the therapeutic process transcends religion. As individuals disclose their wounds and pain, their thoughts and feelings, my vocation is to be present to them and their courageous, healing work. They long to be set free from that which binds them.

Jesus showed us in his own life that the way of life is through descent. Between the time Christ died on the cross and his resurrection, tradition tells us that he descended into Hades to set the captives free. In the Orthodox icon of the Resurrection, Jesus is pulling Adam and Eve out of the grave, symbolizing the redemption of all people. The light of Christ transforms the darkness of hell. It illumines the pathway toward life.

As a therapist, I descend into the hell of people's lives, as a guide and conduit of holy light into the darkness, journeying with them toward a new day. I do this without religious language or verbal recognition of the divine. But as the Dutch scholar and theologian, Erasmus, said hundreds of years ago, "Bidden or unbidden, God is present." In prayer, I ask the Divine for an internal compass to guide me as I show up, pay attention, speak the truth in love, and detach from outcome. I am able to do this because I am a wounded healer, a peaceful warrior.

CHAPTER TWENTY-THREE

Table of Plenty

THEY SAY CONFESSION IS GOOD FOR THE SOUL. It's true. I've witnessed tangible relief from many clients who finally articulated their story, their mistakes, their tightly gripped narrative about critical experiences. Visceral change was palpable as they continued disclosing long held conclusions about themselves and others. The topic of forgiveness is often woven into this dialogue with clients wondering how to forgive themselves and others. Some bravely ask if forgiveness is even necessary or what does it mean to forgive? Especially, to forgive a parent or guardian who has neglected, abused, or abandoned you?

When I was a Baptist, forgiveness was talked about in magical terms of forgiving and forgetting, which is religious double speak for something impossible. Healthy humans have memory. How does one intentionally forget something? In actuality, it meant to make nice and avoid conflict, white-washing big and little infractions in the name of forgiveness. Don't be fooled by magical thinking. Quick recipes for forgiveness are driven by the anxiety of trying to avoid the wound, the bloody mess of whatever needs to be forgiven. Like unattended grief, what we don't face and forgive will continue to bite our ass until we deal with it.

Forgiveness is complicated. The Lord's Prayer asks God to forgive us as we forgive our debtors. I want God to forgive me, but is it a *quid pro quo*? Does this mean that I will be forgiven to the degree that I forgive others? Lord, I hope not! I think it is meant to inspire us to forgive, to plant seeds of desire to forgive our debtors. There is an Orthodox saying that to desire to pray is prayer, and even to have the desire to have the desire to pray is prayer. Forgiveness is like that; I desire to have the desire to forgive. It is the beginning.

The long process of forgiving Mom and Dad took years of navigating a complex maze of old narratives of minimizing, excuse making, and avoidance. During therapy, I had to step off the merry-go-round of our family dynamics and speak the truth. Slowly, I named what actually happened. In a hand-written letter I confronted our parents on three overarching topics: their alcoholism, their abandonment, and their lack of protection when I told them about the sexual abuse. I sent a copy of the letter to each of my siblings. Each one of us was certain that our parents would die when they got the letter but they didn't. Dad didn't talk to me for a year and mom played the victim, but eventually we moved toward honesty. Speaking the truth of long held secrets is incredibly scary, however it is the only path toward forgiveness and freedom.

It took years. The more I exposed the injuries of my childhood and felt emotions connected to the traumatic experiences, the less sting and power they had. It wasn't magical and I didn't forget. Forgiving another doesn't mean the person is now trustworthy or that resuming relationship is safe. Forgiveness is a process of taking personal power back. The offender is evicted from psychic space, no longer able to hurt through pain or bitterness.

Personally, for me, the desire to forgive is always fostered through prayer. It's so cliché to say "pray about it," but I am not talking in church lady platitudes. My prayers are full of honest rage, swearing, and crying. It's not pretty. After a period of time, maybe even years, there is less heat in the prayer. Eventually I am able to hold the person in prayer without anger. Later still, I pray for mercy on their soul. It is there that I am free. The long forgiveness journey is purposeful. Jesus told Peter in Matthew 16:19, "And I will give unto thee the keys of the kingdom of heaven: and whatever thou shalt bind on earth shall be bound in heaven: and whatsoever thou shalt loose on earth shall be loosed in heaven." I think Jesus was telling Peter the keys to heaven involve letting go of whatever binds us and that we can do this through forgiveness. We have a choice of binding or loosening.

The years of therapy, of being loved well, and praying with birch trees and the lake sky, prepared me to receive an unexpected gift. I was a fifty year old menopausal momma, launching children into adulthood, and at the height of professional productivity when it became clear that Mom needed to move to Alaska.

I had traveled to Texas to help care for Mom after cataract surgery and to give Elaine and Randall a break. As a nurse, Mom knew that she wouldn't die from cataract surgery, but anxiety overwhelmed her reason. She was anxious and needed me to come to Texas, so I did. While there, Elaine and I went for a long walk through the neighborhood park. She expressed bone-weary exhaustion and compassion fatigue from caring for Mom the past nine years. Tending a frail geriatric parent is completely consuming and after many years, Elaine and Randall needed to hand the baton of care to me and Jackie. By the end of the walk, we decided that Mom would move to Alaska. We were anxious that she might be upset but she received it well and was eager to return to Alaska, a place that always felt like home to her.

A few months later, Elaine escorted Mom to Alaska. Jackie and I welcomed her into our home. She had several advanced chronic conditions which required frequent doctor appointments and management of several medications, as well as oxygen. Mom stayed with us for a few months until we could find an apartment for low-income seniors and set up all the needed support systems for her to live "independently." In practical terms that meant hiring a personal care attendant (PCA) for five hours a day and having meals delivered daily.

The routine of caring for Mom was straight forward. After working at the high school and seeing clients, I would stop by her apartment to check in with her before heading home. On the weekend, we would go to the grocery store and out for soft served ice-cream. On Sundays, someone from her church provided a ride to and from the morning service. Julie also cared for mom, but living fifty miles away meant it wasn't as often as it would have been if she lived closer. Mom preferred living by herself, but her "independence" was enabled only by orchestrating a variety of supports. Coordinating her care was constant work, even so it was the most appropriate as it gave her dignity and space. It also gave Jackie and me much needed privacy.

Forgiving Mom was not a concept or an intention, but an ongoing action. Especially after Dad died, Mom personally took more and more responsibility for her choices regarding Dad and choosing him over her children. On several occasions she told me, "I regret so many things, Neanie. I made many mistakes as your momma. I've prayed to the Lord for forgiveness and I hope my young'uns will someday forgive me too." But it wasn't easy or straightforward. Mom never truly tolerated the pain required in taking full responsibility for abandoning her children. She would dance up to it, but still make excuses or minimize it in some way. Even so, in time I was able to accept the degree of what she did own without requiring any more. Choosing to forgive her was not transactional. Forgiveness was not given in equal measure to her acknowledging the depth of how she injured me. With God's grace I forgave her, but I didn't ever fully trust her. I didn't allow myself to be her "little girl" seeking solace or comfort from her as daughters do with trustworthy mothers. It simply wasn't a safe emotional space for me.

Where I met mom easily was in caring for her, in being a mother to her. It had been hurtful when as a child I cared for her like a parent, but now, it was as it should be. Mom would put her hands on my shoulders and say, "Neanie, I reckon I have become your child now." After thirty-five years of living apart, after years of longing for my mom, we were given the miraculous gift of time with each other. Grace upon grace. Forgiveness paves a road toward peace, toward possible reunion.

We shared five incredible years. Mom's tenacity and spunk amazed me. An avid Democrat, she received birthday letters from President Obama and Alaskan Senator Begich. She was able to use a low-vision machine that enlarged print allowing her to read and balance the check book independently. However, Mom enjoyed being read to, so I read many books to her including C. S. Lewis' *Chronicles of Narnia* and *The Great Divorce*. We spent hours talking about what we read, laughing and appreciating each other. Mom shared holiday meals, picnics on the lake, weddings, the births of great-grandchildren, and many family celebrations.

In the midst of the gratitude was also exhaustion. Caring for Mom had a cumulative impact on me, causing me to be overly scheduled and contributing to my not sleeping well. Compassion fatigue is standard fare when caring for an elderly parent. At least once every six months Mom was taken to the hospital via an ambulance. Eventually the staff knew her well and would call out as she was wheeled into the Emergency Department on a gurney, "Hi Helen!" or "Our favorite retired nurse is here!" COPD is a chronic condition with decreasing plateaus of stability. Even with a pacemaker, Mom's heart was wearing out. In the last year of her life, there were four trips to the hospital with overnight stays. In spite of excellent medical care, we both knew that her 96th birthday would be her last.

I was at school when I got a call from Mom's PCA. She had called an ambulance because Mom couldn't catch her breath and her blood pressure was sky-rocketing. I arrived at her apartment complex when she was being loaded into the ambulance. In between panting, she said despairingly, "Just let me die." Mom had been clear that she didn't want any heroics in keeping her alive, but she allowed the doctor to drain the fluid on one of her lungs through thoracentesis. During the procedure, mom immediately felt better, being able to fully breathe again. She told the doctor and nurses about being a nurse and how she wished it were possible to work again. Mom was moved into a private room for observation before being discharged. The doctor brought her cookies from the doctor's lounge and told her it was an honor to have had the opportunity to have met her.

Mom knew she was dying. I was waking up from sleeping on a cot in a room next to her bedroom when I heard her calling to me. She wanted to sit up but needed help. I held her close to me on the side of the bed with her feet dangling toward the floor. Hospice care had started the day before, but it was clear that her time on earth was drawing to a close. I held her like she was my little girl and I was her momma. With whispered breath and happy resolve, she said, "Honey, I'm going to hokey pokey into heaven today." Mom was 96 years old and dying but still had her keen sense of humor, ready to dance with Jesus.

We kept vigil over her. Children, grandchildren, and friends came to see her. Mom was able to bless them with loving statements. Several times throughout the day she would wake up and ask, "Am I there yet? Am I dead yet?" Disappointed, she'd fall into a morphine induced sleep. Her pastors, Robert and Tori, were a clergy couple. They stopped by to pray for her. We all held hands as we sang one of mom's favorite hymns, *Blessed Assurance*. By that time, her eyes were closed and she was in the process of leaving us, she mouthed the words, *"This is my story, this is my song, praising my savior all the day long."* A few hours later she was at peace, no longer here. She was finally there.

It was during the season of Advent when she died. Her death reminded me of when I have labored hours and hours to give birth, knowing the baby was coming but not when it would actually arrive. Transitioning into this world or into heaven is sacred labor. The work of both births required contractions of letting go of what we have known to embrace what is unknown. Mom's labor into heaven was beautiful, without pain and struggle. All of that was behind her.

The church was decorated with green garland and a Christmas tree. Mom had been afraid that no one would come to her funeral, nevertheless the little country Methodist church was filled with her friends, children, and grandchildren. Kat played the piano. Several of her medical providers came, too. Collectively they were a mighty team including a social worker, personal care attendant, primary care doctor, cardiologist, and eye doctor. They all loved Mom.

During the funeral service when folks were invited to share a memory, Mom's eye doctor walked to the microphone. Dr. Evans was wearing hot pink high heeled shoes and a black dress. She talked about Mom's sense of humor and how independent she was despite being legally blind. Then Dr. Evans surprised us all by saying with a twinkle in her eye, "Helen could see peripherally and really liked it when I wore high heel shoes. I wore these high heels for Helen. She seemed to have a joke or song for every occasion. In fact, I am going to sing one of her favorites." And with that, Dr. Evans belted out singing, "It must be jelly cuz jam don't shake like that!" Surprised, everyone laughed!

Her funeral was a celebration of redemption and grace and forgiveness. After a life time of suffering and pain, there was peace. Mom had the last word at her funeral in a video singing, "This world is not my home, I'm just a passing through. Then she waved and said, "Bye-

bye, young-uns." Her funeral, like her death, could not have been more ideal and peaceful.

The grief that enveloped me was different from when I longed for Mom in childhood. After all the work of cleaning out her apartment was done, and all the support systems were closed down, I held my grief tenderly. When Mom died, there was nothing left unsaid or undone between us. There was no unfinished business. The work of forgiveness had created an embrace of her beautiful person in totality, including her weaknesses. Mom had also done the work in forgiving herself and receiving forgiveness from her children. Mom entered the kingdom of heaven unbound.

Long ago I had asked Mom, if possible, to send me some sort of sign after she died. Maybe a special breeze in the trees or a unique bird song. About ten days after she died, I received a package in the mail. Mom must have ordered it before her last ambulance ride, just a few days prior to her death. It was a trinket, a glass globe with a red cardinal in it. The wording said, "A gentle reminder that we're never far apart, my spirit will live on forever there within your heart." Her sign is a treasured heavenly token.

I often imagine mom sitting at the table of plenty. Her smile lights up the room and her eyes resonate with divine love. She is surrounded by souls who have accepted the grace offered. Like a scene from Hogwarts in Harry Potter movies, there is an abundance of food, drink, and laughter everywhere. All are invited, welcomed to this table. No one is considered unworthy or not quite good enough. This feast of love, of forgiveness is open to all. The invitation to come to the table is now, in the present. The divine is not limited by creation, by natural law, by the sun rising and setting, by human measurements of then and now. The table of resurrection always is, overflowing with abundant life, as expressed in 400 AD by John Chrysostom. His Easter homily tells us that all are welcome at the table of plenty, the first and the last, the sober and the slothful. No one needs to fear death or hell, for both have been destroyed in the resurrection. This truth is to be lived now. In answer to Mom's question, "Am I there yet?" Yes, Mom, you are, we are. Only a thin veil of time separates us.

EPILOGUE

A New Day

HERE WE ARE, THE TWO of us, living in a new day, showing up to love.

After serving as Dean a couple of years at Duke, I, Elaine took a year's sabbatical and then retired. Now I am serving as President of Neighborhood Seminary, a non-profit I founded with some friends. I continue to serve as a consultant, retreat leader, and speaker. That work frequently takes me across the nation and around the world, although during Covid-19 like everyone else, I have carried out that work remotely. I live in rural North Carolina on a beautiful piece of forested property with Randall, and our friends live next door on the small, non-profit, natural farm that all of us tend. The farm supports refugees and other immigrants who have experienced forced migration, offering a welcoming space to grow vegetables and experience healing from trauma through connection with the earth, sheep, goats, chickens, ducks, and a community of hospitable people. Our farm and a small network of neighborhood groups that in one way or other participate in welcoming immigrants, constitute our little multicultural church.

I, Jeanine, retired from my position with the school district, but continue my private practice as a therapist, which is very rewarding. Jackie (also recently retired) and I love spending time with our children and grandchildren, including having home schooled five of the grandchildren this year because of Covid-19. Elaine and I plan to lead more retreats together in the future, and we hope to do more collaborative writing projects around some of the themes in our shared story.

We wrote this book because we just couldn't keep all this healing to ourselves. As we bring this book to a close, we bow with deep gratitude for all the people and experiences that helped us to survive, to be resilient and to thrive. They helped us to love the hell out of ourselves. We hope that our story will help you to do the same.

Mom & Jeanine (1997)

Elaine & Randall's Wedding (2000)

Elaine & Randall in Manhattan (2000)

Jeff, Julie, Elaine, Jeanine, Mike, & Mom (2004)

Jeanine & Jackie (2012)

Elaine Teaching at Western North Carolina Annual Conference (2013)

Elaine & Jeanine at Lake Lucille, Wasilla, Alaska (2014)

Elaine & Randall, London, England while on a lecture tour across the U.K. (2015)

Elaine & Mom (2016)

Elaine, Mike, & Jeanine at Elaine's Instillation as Dean of Duke Divinity School (2016)

Julie, Mom, Jeanine on Mom's 96th birthday 2 months before her death (2016)

Jackie & Jeanine with their 9 grandchildren (2019)

Jackie, Jeanine, Randall, & Elaine (2019)

ABOUT THE AUTHORS

Jeanine Heath-McGlinn is a Licensed Professional Counselor in private practice and served for many years as a high school counselor. As a therapist she works with couples, adults, and older teens. She is well known for her leadership, consultation, and professional development in crisis intervention, crisis response in schools, and suicide prevention. It is a sacred honor for her to travel with people on their journey from mental health struggles, trauma, loss, and pain to a place of resilient healing and hope. She has done the hard work that she asks of her clients, having overcome an impoverished and violent childhood.

Having lived in Alaska from age seven, Jeanine resides at the base of the Chugach Mountains in Anchorage, with her wife, Jackie. They enjoy family gatherings with their four children and spouses, and ten grandchildren. Camping, walking, skiing, reading a good book, and drinking strong coffee are some of her favorite things.

Elaine Heath is an ordained elder in the United Methodist Church and has served as the McCreless Professor of Evangelism at Perkins School of Theology at Southern Methodist University, and as Dean and Professor of Missional and Pastoral Theology at Duke Divinity School, Duke University. She co-founded now serves as president of Neighborhood Seminary. She is the author of eleven books and is a sought-after speaker, retreat leader, and consultant.

Elaine lives on a small farm near Hillsborough, North Carolina, with her husband Randall. They enjoy kayaking, hiking, camping, movies, and campfires, and spending time with their daughters and friends.

Made in the USA
Columbia, SC
06 June 2021